RAF WWII OPERATIONAL

AND FLYING ACCIDENT CASUALTY FILES IN THE NATIONAL ARCHIVES

In memory of

WOB & VMB

to whom I will always owe a debt of gratitude

RAF WWII

OPERATIONAL

AND FLYING ACCIDENT CASUALTY FILES IN THE NATIONAL ARCHIVES

EXPLORING THEIR CONTENTS

MARY HUDSON

AIR WORLD

AIR WORLD

RAF WWII OPERATIONAL AND FLYING ACCIDENT CASUALTY FILES
IN THE NATIONAL ARCHIVES
Exploring their Contents

First published in Great Britain in 2020 by
Air World
An imprint of
Pen & Sword Books Ltd
Yorkshire – Philadelphia

ISBN 978 1 52678 352 3

Typeset by SJmagic DESIGN SERVICES, India.
Printed and bound in England by TJ Books Limited, Padstow, Cornwall.

Pen & Sword Books Limited incorporates the imprints of Atlas, Archaeology, Aviation, Discovery, Family History, Fiction, History, Maritime, Military, Military Classics, Politics, Select, Transport, True Crime, Air World, Frontline Publishing, Leo Cooper, Remember When, Seaforth Publishing, The Praetorian Press, Wharncliffe Local History, Wharncliffe Transport, Wharncliffe True Crime and White Owl.

For a complete list of Pen & Sword titles please contact

PEN & SWORD BOOKS LIMITED
47 Church Street, Barnsley, South Yorkshire, S70 2AS, England
E-mail: enquiries@pen-and-sword.co.uk
Website: www.pen-and-sword.co.uk

Or
PEN AND SWORD BOOKS
1950 Lawrence Rd, Havertown, PA 19083, USA
E-mail: Uspen-and-sword@casematepublishers.com
Website: www.penandswordbooks.com

Contents

CONTENTS

CONTENTS

CONTENTS

All images are Crown Copyright (Air Historical Branch) unless otherwise stated.

Acknowledgements

The release of the RAF Second World War Operational and Flying Accident Casualty Files to the National Archives, which began in 2013, prompted the writing of this book. I spent my years with the Air Historical Branch handling RAF Casualty Files on a daily basis, studying them in depth during identity investigations or to enable answers to be provided to next of kin. In this I had the unstinting support of my friends and former colleagues of the Air Historical Branch, especially Graham Day, Clive Richards, Anna Gibbs, Stuart Hadaway and the inimitable Seb Cox, who are owed my thanks for numerous things. Thanks are also due in no small measure to Lee Barton and Mike Hatch for their much appreciated assistance along the way.

I also had the pleasure of working closely with staff from the MOD Joint Casualty and Compassionate Centre (JCCC) and the Commonwealth War Graves Commission, in particular Sue Raftree of MOD's JCCC and Nic Andrews of the Commonwealth War Graves Commission who contributed so much to my casualty knowledge and who have now joined me in retirement. My gratitude is also owed to Tracey Bowers of the Commemorations Section of the JCCC for her interest in, and support she has given, to this book.

The greatest debt of gratitude of all is owed to those who have fought and died, or been wounded or injured, in the air or on the ground, while serving with the RAF and Commonwealth Air Forces.

Per Ardua Ad Astra

Glossary

Air Forces

AAF	Auxiliary Air Force (of the RAF)
AEAF	Allied Expeditionary Air Force
DAF	Desert Air Force
IAF/RIAF	Indian Air Force later Royal Indian Air Force
MAAF	Mediterranean Allied Air Forces
MAF	Metropolitan Air Force – consisted of squadrons reserved for Home Defence of UK
PAF	Polish Air Force
PMRAFNS	Princess Mary's Royal Air Force Nursing Service
RAAF	Royal Australian Air Force
RAF	Royal Air Force
RAFVR	Royal Air Force Volunteer Reserve
RCAF	Royal Canadian Air Force
RNZAF	Royal New Zealand Air Force
SAAF	South African Air Force
SRAF	Southern Rhodesian Air Force later subsumed into RAF
2TAF	2nd Tactical Air Force
WAAF	Women's Auxiliary Air Force

Miscellaneous

ADGB	Air Defence of Great Britain – the name given to the remaining element of Fighter Command after the formation of the 2nd Tactical Air Force
AFU	Advanced Flying Unit
AIB	Air Investigation Branch
AM	Air Ministry

RAF WWII OPERATIONAL

AMCS	Air Ministry Casualty Section (P4)
AMES	Air Ministry Experimental Station (name given to Radar units)
AMO	Air Ministry Order
AP	Air Publication
BAFO	British Air Forces of Occupation (Germany)
BCLC	Bomber Command Loss Cards
BGH	British General Hospital (Army)
BPO/BPSO	Base Personnel Officer/Base Personnel Staff Officer
EMS Hospital	Emergency Medical Service Hospital
FTC	Flying Training Command
ICRC	International Committee of the Red Cross based in Geneva
IWGC/	Imperial War Graves Commission post-1960 became
CWGC	Commonwealth War Graves Commission
MRS	Missing Research Section (with the Air Ministry P4 Casualty Branch)
MRES	RAF and Dominion Air Forces Missing Research and Enquiry Service
MREU	Missing Research and Enquiry Unit
MU	Maintenance Unit
OR	Other Ranks
P4(Cas)	Personnel 4 (Casualty) the wartime Air Ministry Casualty Branch
PoW	Prisoner of War
RC	Registry Clerk
SMC	Station Medical Centre

Foreword

Sebastian Cox, OBE BA MA FRHistS,
Head of the MoD Air Historical Branch

The beautifully maintained network of Commonwealth War Cemeteries spanning the globe are familiar to many. Understandably, few of the thousands of people who visit these sites and pause perhaps to reflect beside the graves of fallen airmen, whether they are relatives, old comrades or strangers, consider how the individuals named on the headstone might have been identified and reached their final resting place. The answer, in part at least, is set out in the pages of this book. Mary Hudson explains in detail the fascinating contents of the RAF's casualty files which were, and still are, the key foundation documents for those who worked and still work behind the scenes on identifying the dead. The individuals concerned were, and still are, part forensic detectives, part experts in historical analysts and part bureaucratic toilers in the archives. Without their dedication to the task of identifying the dead many more gravestones around the world would bear the sad inscription 'Unknown airman, known unto God'.

Whilst identifying the dead from the conflicts of the Twentieth Century was clearly always going to be a mammoth and difficult task the identification of the military airman is doubly so. In battles at sea those who perish are most often claimed by the ocean deep. On land, they were generally known to have died on a battlefield within a relatively small area and were usually quickly buried, often with some temporary grave marker in place. Airmen, however, ranged quite literally far and wide and often lost their lives anywhere between their base and some far distant target. Their aircraft may have descended at high velocity from several miles up in the atmosphere and buried itself and any occupants deep within the ground. As the War drew to a close the Royal Air Force established teams of searchers to comb the areas in which the RAF had operated seeking to find and identify the dead and relocate them to British war cemeteries, where the graves could be tended, and loved ones informed of a man's last resting place. Their efforts were carefully recorded in the casualty files providing the basis for an accurate picture of an often complex jigsaw to be pieced together.

The formal work was largely complete by the early 1950s, but in an era long before DNA testing, many airmen could not be formally identified and were laid to rest as unknowns – their names recorded on one of five memorials to the RAF missing around the world. Others were simply never found. As Mary Hudson shows, while formal searches ended in the early 1950s, the work continues to this day with the Air Historical Branch working alongside the Joint Casualty and Compassionate Cell in the MoD, whether seeking to identify recently uncovered human remains exposed by building work, or to re-assess cases where new evidence emerges from the contemporary records allowing comparison with the original files and hopefully an 'unknown' grave to be remarked with the man's name.

Introduction

The term 'casualty' covers death, wounding, injuries and sickness suffered by members of the armed forces (whatever the cause) and also individuals taken prisoner. There are thousands and thousands of them from the Second World War alone. At that time each of the British services had its own casualty handling department. The Royal Navy's casualty department was part of the Admiralty, the Army's was a department of the War Office and that of the Royal Air Force was part of the Air Ministry.

A photograph, taken in 1945, of the wreckage of Halifax LK75 lying in a street in Düsseldorf. The aircraft from 10 Squadron crashed on 8 April 1945. It was taking part in an attack on Hamburg. Five of the crew died and two were injured.

The Air Ministry Casualty Branch had the responsibility for handling all casualties involving members of the RAF, RAF Voluntary Reserve (RAFVR), the RAF Auxiliary Air Force (RAF Aux AF), Women's Auxiliary Air Force (WAAF), Princess Mary's Royal Air Force Nursing Service (PMRAFNS) and their Reserves, and also initial casualty handling for members of Dominion Air Forces and foreign nationals serving with the RAF including those from the remnants of Allied Air Forces such as those of Poland, Czechoslovakia, Norway, the Netherlands and the Free French. Understanding the role of the Air Ministry Casualty Branch is an important element in understanding the contents of the P Files and so I have included some background information on the Air Ministry Casualty Branch and the role and tasks of the sections within it.

The P4 (Casualty) Files, commonly referred to now as RAF Casualty Files, are the files opened for each casualty notified to the S7 (Casualty) Branch of the Air Ministry and its successor P4 (Casualty). It is important to remember that the P Files contain a collection of working documents which were intended for use by the Air Ministry Casualty Branch and the idea that they would eventually be perused by members of the public was not considered. The files were referred to by the Casualty Branch as P Files, the P standing for Personnel. The files can relate to a single individual or to a number of persons, such as the whole crew of an aircraft, or all the casualties suffered in a single incident. The contents of the P Files are often not in good condition and some documents can be difficult to read. Wartime shortages meant the quality of paper used was poor and was unable to stand up well to the frequent handling of the files. Shortage of paper itself resulted in scraps of paper being used or information being recorded on the back of previously used paper. Files which were handled the least are in the best condition and inevitably it is P Files concerning aircraft lost with several crew on board which are in the worst condition. Papers particularly badly affected are the RAF Missing Research and Enquiry Service reports.

The various sections within the Casualty Branch were the originators of a considerable amount of the contents of the Casualty Files but all correspondence received by the Casualty Branch relating to the casualty (or casualties) the file covered was placed on it. For example, letters to and from next of kin were added to the relevant P File. These letters are often very poignant but there are also cases where married men had girlfriends and the files contain letters from both wife and girlfriend. Some letters reveal other family secrets such as illegitimate children, bigamous marriages and financial hardship, or express sentiments which a person today would find distasteful. The Air Ministry Casualty Branch did its best to deal with all tactfully and sympathetically.

INTRODUCTION

A word of warning needs to be included at this point. If you are planning to research a family member using the Casualty P Files you should be aware that the information you find could well be distressing. In addition to the type of information outlined above, the contents of the P Files are, on occasion, gruesome in their detail, and anyone reading them needs to be aware of this. Unfortunately, when an aircraft crashes, the impact usually causes severe injuries to the bodies of the crew. There are many cases of crashes in occupied Europe were it was impossible for those gathering the remains and clearing the wreckage to determine how many crew members were on board. Similarly when an aircraft blew up in mid-air, especially with a bomb-load still on board, the retrieval of remains was complicated.

The RAF documents included in the files are full of abbreviations and acronyms; indeed there is a standing joke amongst service personnel that the RAF has swallowed a Scrabble board. This habit of using abbreviations can make the documents difficult for the uninitiated to understand and I have tried to make the meaning clear with explanations and 'translations'.

Not all RAF Casualty Files have been selected by the National Archives for permanent preservation in their collections. The RAF Casualty Branch P Files which have been chosen relate to the period of the Second World War. It is important to note that while all service personnel who served during the Second World War were regarded as being on active service, they were not always classed as being operational. The files selected by the National Archives cover RAF casualties suffered as the result of **operations** in the air and on the ground (such as air attacks against RAF stations), and flying accidents suffered either in training or while operational. The P Files are held in the National Archives under reference AIR81 *'P4(Cas) Files relating to casualties suffered during Air operations and aircraft accidents 1939-1945'* and can be searched by the surname of an individual, the place or location of the incident, date of the incident and type of aircraft. It is these P Files commonly called RAF Casualty Files which are the subject of this guide.

The P Files relating to casualties suffered through sickness, death from illness or natural causes, suicides, road traffic accidents (other than those occurring on operations overseas) and non-operational ground accidents, have not been selected for preservation in the National Archives. These Casualty P Files have been retained by the Ministry of Defence and requests for information from them should be sent to the Air Historical Branch (RAF). Family researchers may also wish to contact the England and Wales General Registry Office which holds a consolidated index of RAF War Deaths for all ranks from 1939 to 1948.

Part 1

Casualty Handling of the Dead, Missing, Wounded and Injured

Chapter 1

The Air Ministry Casualty Branch

Early Days

'This morning the British Ambassador in Berlin handed the German Government a final note stating that, unless we heard from them by 11 o'clock that they were prepared at once to withdraw their troops from Poland, a state of war would exist between us. I have to tell you that no such undertaking has been received, and that consequently this country is at war with Germany.'

With these words, at 11.15 am on 3 September 1939 the Prime Minister, Neville Chamberlain, announced to the British people, via BBC radio, the start of the Second World War. The Royal Air Force was immediately involved and less than one hour later a Blenheim aircraft took off from RAF Wyton near Huntingdon to reconnoitre the German Naval bases on their North Sea coast. The Blenheim pilot spotted German capital ships in the Schillig Roads and, in the late afternoon, twenty-seven aircraft from Bomber Command took off to attack them. Daylight was fading; the weather deteriorated and despite lengthy searching the aircraft failed to find the ships. All returned safely to base, the last landed close to midnight.

The next morning, 4 September 1939, a further reconnaissance flight confirmed the German ships were still in Wilhelmshaven and a second attempt to attack them was made. A force of fifteen Blenheims was involved, while fourteen Wellington aircraft were sent to attack shipping at Brunsbüttel. Seven out of these aircraft were lost; five Blenheims and two Wellingtons together with their crews; only two men survived to become prisoners of war. The Royal Air Force had suffered its first casualties of the war; the twenty-four young air crew who lost their lives were the first of the 70,253 officers, Non Commissioned Officers (NCOs) and airmen killed or missing on operations between 3 September 1939 and 14 August 1945.[1]

---

1. Casualty figures given on page 393 of *The Royal Air Force 1949 to 1945* Vol 3 The Fight is Won HMSO.

Of those who were lost, the oldest were in their fifties and the youngest was 16-year-old Flight Sergeant E.J. Wight, an Air Gunner who had lied about his age to join the Royal Canadian Air Force (RCAF). He was killed on a training flight with 428 Squadron RCAF on 30 April 1945, only a week before the end of the War in Europe. Many other air crew were killed or injured in flying accidents.

In addition to the losses suffered during air operations, other RAF fatal casualties were suffered on the ground. These resulted from enemy action, ground accidents at airfields, road traffic accidents, losses at sea during transit to overseas stations, and some personnel – often ground crew who contracted pneumonia when servicing aircraft in the open in all weathers – died from natural causes. In addition to these there were non-fatal casualties: the prisoners of war, the sick, the injured or the wounded who added many thousands more to the total casualty figures for the Second World War, but it was clear from early on that the Royal Air Force needed a robust casualty organisation capable of dealing with such enormous numbers.

The Royal Air Force's first experience of casualty handling had come during the First World War, with the RAF's formation on 1 April 1918. A few months later Air Ministry Order Number 63 dated 27 September 1918 created a department designated P2(Cas), within the Directorate of Air Personnel Services to be 'responsible for all questions relating to casualties to officers and ranks'.

The interwar years saw various reorganisations of the Air Ministry; the Secretarial Division (which was responsible to the Air Member for Personnel[2]) was given the task of casualty handling for the Royal Air Force. The part of the Division which was given the job was known as S7(Cas) and it was to them that the news of the losses suffered on 4 September 1939 was sent. All the information that the staff of S7(Cas) had from the squadrons who had taken part was that seven aircraft were overdue and their crews missing. Frustratingly S7 had no other sources of information about the fate of the lost crews other than that provided by the BBC which listened to German broadcasts and other media. Three of the aircrew who had been captured were interviewed on German radio. The Germans had also broadcast information about the burial of Sergeant D.E. Jarvis, killed during the raid against Brunsbüttel. This broadcast was picked up by the BBC and through them the Air Ministry learnt that Sergeant Jarvis had been

2. The Air Council controlled the Air Ministry and RAF until 1964. Amongst its members were very senior RAF officers responsible for various departments within the Air Ministry. They were known as Air Members and identified by their area of responsibility, for example Air Member for Supply and Organisation.

buried at Cuxhaven Naval Cemetery. 'One company of German sailors and a naval band paid honours at the funeral. The Commander of Wilhelmshaven sent a wreath, and was represented at the funeral.'[3] Three weeks later the families of two survivors from the Wellington attack on Brunsbüttel passed on details of what had occurred to the Air Ministry. They were able to do so because the Germans had permitted the two captured airmen, who were in hospital, to communicate with their relatives, and the two prisoners had been able to send their families details of what had happened.

It was clear that relying on information being supplied through unofficial sources was a highly unsatisfactory situation and immediate action was taken to improve the matter. The S7 branch contacted the International Committee of the Red Cross (ICRC) in Geneva for advice. With the help of the ICRC a system which allowed the passage of official information from Germany about the fate of Royal Air Force and Dominion aircrew was established. The Germans provided *Totenlisten* (Death Lists) to the ICRC which acted as an intermediary in accordance with the 1929 Geneva Conventions. The information received from the Germans was then passed from the ICRC to the British authorities. The first German list of RAF injured and dead was passed to the Air Ministry by the ICRC in October 1939 and published in Missing Memorandum No 8 issued by S7 Cas on 14 October 1939. Below are examples of the information received from the German authorities in the first List:[4]

Sergeant Prince – Brought down by enemy on 3/9/39 – Broken neck and both thighs – Died in Marine Hospital Wesermünde – Buried Geestemünde Cemetery – soldiers' section

F L G Slattery, Sirvy – Born on 1/5/1914 at ANNACARTY, CO.TIPPERARY.

(F.K.) Multiple injuries sustained in aircraft accident on 4/9/39, include broken lower jaw, concussion, wounds on neck and left cheek, tip of nose torn off. Admitted to Marine Hospital, Wesermünde, on 4/9/39. No 2.D

---

3. The National Archives AIR2/6474 *Air Ministry Report on RAF & Dominion Air Forces Missing Research and Enquiry Service Report 1944-1949 by Gp Capt E Hawkins Air Headquarters BAFO dated March 1949 Appendix B to Part 1 Air Ministry Missing Memorandum No 1 concerning Sergeant Oswald Edward Jarvis.*
4. Ibid Appendix E *Missing Memorandum No 8 dated 14 October 1939.*

The ICRC also passed any information which they received from other sources through to the British authorities. The new system for receiving information was put into place swiftly; the first Totenliste came through on 14 October 1939.[5] However, Totenliste information was not always accurate, as can be seen from the example below.

The Totenliste extract for the crew of Lancaster W4828 of 103 Squadron which crashed near Le Mans France on the night of 13/14 April 1943.

Squadron Leader Sinkinson of the Missing Research Section (MRS) of the Casualty Branch gave some interesting examples of inaccuracies found in *Totenliste* information. One was that the Germans had reported the death of a sergeant but provided the name and service number of a WAAF! The Casualty Branch's careful checks established that the sergeant had in fact exchanged identity discs with his girlfriend. It was circumstances such as this that led to stories that WAAFs had been smuggled onto aircraft by bomber crews and had been killed on operations. No evidence has ever been found to support this. In another instance the Germans sent information that an airman called Llude Sing Cuccu had been shot down and killed over France in January 1944. In fact the words were from an Elizabethan song which had been parodied in Tee Emm, a monthly magazine produced by RAF Training Command. Checks

---

5. Ibid *page 3.*

Flight Lieutenant 'Paddy' Finucane together with other pilots of 452 Squadron RAAF at RAF Kenley in 1941. All are wearing their 'Mae West' life jackets. The pilot 2nd from left has his name on his life jacket; another has used a cartoon saint to identify his Mae West while a third pilot has used the sign for the Ace of Spades.

by the Casualty Branch established that Pilot Officer James Bassett, lost on 10 January 1944, had painted the words 'Llude Sing Cuccu' on his Mae West (life jacket).[6] The Germans had assumed that these words were his name as it was common for Mae Wests to be marked with some indication of their owner's identity.

Before D-Day the main source of official information was the Totenliste and the answers to British enquiries sent by the German authorities via the ICRC in Geneva. However, there were various other sources of information about the fate of aircraft and their crews. The national Red Cross organizations of France, Norway, Belgium and the Netherlands passed information to Britain with the permission of the German authorities, and in addition there were other organizations that passed information to the Air Ministry both before and after the Liberation. These included the French *Anciens Combattants* (Veterans), the *Aero Club de France*, and (primarily in the early stages of the war) the German Aero Club also forwarded information on losses in Germany to the Royal Aero Club in the UK.[7] Members of resistance groups

---

6. The National Archives AIR2/6330/33a *Missing Research Section P4. (Casualty Branch)*
7. Ibid.

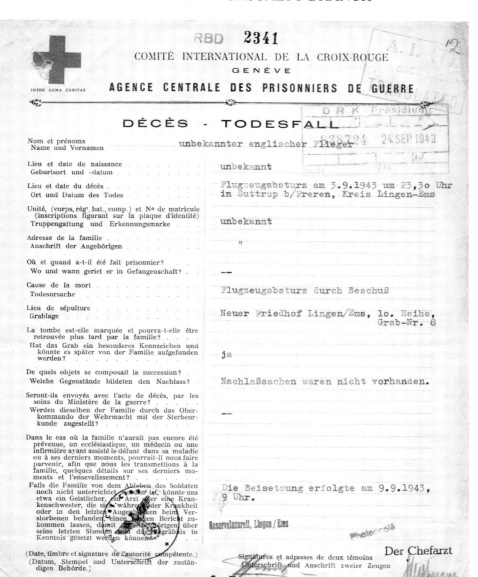

RBD **2341**

COMITÉ INTERNATIONAL DE LA CROIX-ROUGE

GENÈVE

AGENCE CENTRALE DES PRISONNIERS DE GUERRE

INTER ARMA CARITAS

DÉCÈS - TODESFALL

Nom et prénoms / Name und Vornamen	unbekannter englischer Flieger
Lieu et date de naissance / Geburtsort und -datum	unbekannt
Lieu et date du décès / Ort und Datum des Todes	Flugzeugabsturz am 3.9.1943 um 23,3o Uhr in Suttrup b/Freren, Kreis Lingen-Ems
Unité, (corps, régt, bat., comp.) et Nº de matricule (inscriptions figurant sur la plaque d'identité) / Truppengattung und Erkennungsmarke	unbekannt
Adresse de la famille / Anschrift der Angehörigen	"
Où et quand a-t-il été fait prisonnier? / Wo und wann geriet er in Gefangenschaft?	--
Cause de la mort / Todesursache	Flugzeugabsturz durch Beschuß
Lieu de sépulture / Grablage	Neuer Friedhof Lingen/Ems, lo. Reihe, Grab-Nr. 8
La tombe est-elle marquée et pourra-t-elle être retrouvée plus tard par la famille? / Hat das Grab ein besonderes Kennzeichen und könnte es später von der Familie aufgefunden werden?	ja
De quels objets se composait la succession? / Welche Gegenstände bildeten den Nachlass?	Nachlaßsachen waren nicht vorhanden.
Seront-ils envoyés avec l'acte de décès, par les soins du Ministère de la guerre? / Werden dieselben der Familie durch das Oberkommando der Wehrmacht mit der Sterbeurkunde zugestellt?	--
Dans le cas où la famille n'aurait pas encore été prévenue, un ecclésiastique, un médecin ou une infirmière ayant assisté le défunt dans sa maladie ou à ses derniers moments, pourrait-il nous faire parvenir, afin que nous les transmettions à la famille, quelques détails sur ses derniers moments et l'ensevelissement? / Falls die Familie von dem Ableben des Soldaten noch nicht unterrichtet worden ist, könnte uns etwa ein Geistlicher, ein Arzt oder eine Krankenschwester, die sich während der Krankheit oder in den letzten Augenblicken beim Verstorbenen befanden, einen kurzen Bericht zukommen lassen, damit wir die Angehörigen über seine letzten Stunden und das Begräbnis in Kenntnis gesetzt werden können?	Die Beisetzung erfolgte am 9.9.1943, 9 Uhr.

Reservelazarett, Lingen / Ems

(Date, timbre et signature de l'autorité compétente.) (Datum, Stempel und Unterschrift der zuständigen Behörde.)

Signatures et adresses de deux témoins Unterschrift und Anschrift zweier Zeugen

Der Chefarzt

San.-Hauptfeldwebel

Oberfeldarzt

An ICRC Death Notice completed by the German Authorities providing information about an Unknown English airman killed when his aircraft crashed on 3 September 1943 and buried on 9 September. The aircraft crashed at Suttrup near Frerens, District of Lingen-Ems. The Unknown was a member of the crew of Lancaster ED410 which was lost on an operation against Berlin. Postwar the crew's remains were moved from Neuer Friedhof Cemetery to Reichswald Forest War Cemetery.

and secret agents operating in occupied countries also provided information on missing air crew and crashed aircraft. RAF Air Attachés in neutral countries such as Sweden also forwarded information which had been passed to them. Inevitably information from such sources contained inaccuracies and everything had to be carefully checked by the RAF Casualty Branch.

In October 1939 it was announced that a new branch within the Air Ministry's Directorate of Personnel Services would be responsible for casualty handling. The new branch was designated P4 (Casualty), usually shortened to Cas. The P indicated that it was a Personnel Branch. The new branch was headed by Wing Commander Roger Burges (a former Royal Navy Commander) and the main element was housed in London. Initially the new P4(Cas) was responsible for handling all casualties involving officers of the Royal Air Force, the Auxiliary Air Force (AAF), the RAF Voluntary Reserve, the Women's' Auxiliary Air Force (WAAF), the Princes Mary's Royal Air Force Nursing Service (PMRAFNS) and their Reserves and also initial casualty handling for non-commissioned ranks of the RAF and members of Dominion Air Forces and foreign nationals serving with the RAF. By May 1941 the wartime Casualty Handling Procedures had been formalized in Air Publication 1922 Notes on Casualty Procedure in War, which provided guidance on casualty handling and was issued to all RAF units. A second edition was issued in 1943.

In April 1943 the aspects of casualty procedures involving non-commissioned ranks, (often referred to as 'Other Ranks'), which had been handled by an section of the old S7 based in the Royal Air Force Record Office in Gloucester, were taken over by P4(Cas). Casualty handling for both officers and other ranks was thus brought together under P4(Cas) in new offices at 73/77 Oxford Street, London.

The newly amalgamated P4(Cas) was split into various departments staffed by a mixture of RAF, WAAF and civil servants. The departments were:

1. *TELEGRAMS*	The staff of this department was responsible for sending the initial telegram to the next of kin, and other persons nominated by the casualty, informing them of what had occurred.
2. *AIR COUNCIL LETTER*	This department sent the Air Council letter of condolence to next of kin and handled the subsequent enquiries from them. The letter was referred to within P4(Cas) as the AC Letter
3. *MOVEMENTS*	The department supervising movement of bodies.

4. *PRESUMPTIONS*	The department which was responsible for casework concerning presumption of death.
5. *CERTIFICATION OF DEATH*	The department responsible for certification of death casework.
6. *ACCIDENTS*	Casualties resulting from accidents were handled by this department.
7. *PRISONERS OF WAR*	The staff in this department was responsible for handling casualties who became Prisoners of War and related matters.
8. *PERSONAL EFFECTS*	This department, in conjunction with the RAF Central Depository and the Accounts Branch, dealt with the personal effects of casualties.
9. *MISSING RESEARCH SECTION*	When aircrew went missing, whether on operations or otherwise, the Casualty Branch was responsible for establishing their fate but it was not until early 1942 that a dedicated Missing Research Section of P4 (Cas) was introduced. The initially small section was responsible for investigating any report concerning missing personnel. Post D-Day it was the reporting point within P4 (Cas) for the MRES teams in the field.
10. *VISITOR HANDLING*	P4(Cas) operated an 'open door system' which permitted next of kin, relatives and friends to call at the Oxford Street offices to make enquiries in person. This department was responsible for meeting and assisting the enquirers.
11. *SICK & INJURED*	The department which handled cases of sickness and injuries.
12. *GENERAL MATTERS*	This department dealt with general correspondence sent to P4(Cas) and any related matters.

Far East Casualties

Following the Japanese attacks in December 1941 a special Section was established to handle the Far East casualties; this was co-located with P4(Cas). With Japan's entry into the war the P4(Cas) Branch began to be notified of losses in the Far East but information was sketchy. The Japanese were by no means as punctilious as the Germans in notifying the Allies about killed and captured personnel, nor did they provide information about the hundreds of Allied prisoners who died in captivity.

In addition to the Japanese stance on the provision of information, the conditions in which the fighting was taking place made definite information other than that a person was missing difficult to obtain. As well as those killed and captured in late 1941 and early 1942 many other Air Force personnel were lost in the fight back. RAF and Dominion aircraft and crews were lost in Malaya, Burma, Thailand, French Indo-China (now Vietnam) and the Dutch East Indies (now Indonesia). The prevailing conditions associated with flying in the Far East all too often meant that all that next of kin could be told was that the aircraft failed to return to base.

Although Casualty information was scarce any that did arrive was meticulously filed by the Far East casualty staff. The Section had to wait until the end of the War in the Far East before they received the majority of the information filed on the Far East Casualty P Files.

Post-War

Post-war reorganizations took place within the Air Ministry and the Casualty Branch left the control of the Director Personnel Services and returned to the Secretarial Department. On 19 August 1946 P4(Cas) was once again designated S7(Cas) and a civil servant replaced Group Captain Burges as head. With a further organizational change in 1947 the Casualty Branch became S14(Cas). The physical location of the Branch also changed when it moved to RAF Stanmore in north London. After a number of further organisational changes, single service casualty handling ended in 2005 when the casualty handling departments of the Royal Navy, Army and Royal Air Force were amalgamated to become the Joint Casualty and Compassionate Centre.

Chapter 2

The Air Ministry Casualty Branch P Files (RAF Casualty Files)

All the deaths, injuries or wounds of Air Force personnel which resulted from operational duty were reported to the Air Ministry Casualty Branch. Deaths from accidents and suicides were reported. The Casualty Branch was also informed of injuries from accidents (and self-inflicted injuries) which resulted in an absence from duty of more than forty-eight hours. All cases where the casualty was classed as *Dangerously Ill* or *Seriously Ill* by the doctors were reported. The official definitions of these were:

Dangerously Ill – The patient was very ill and there was reason for 'immediate anxiety'.

Seriously Ill – The patient was very ill, but there was no reason for 'immediate anxiety'.

Information about casualties was sent to the Air Ministry Casualty Branch by the parent unit in a signal message, a form of military telegram. Units were instructed that the message was to be sent in the appropriate format which was laid down in AP1922 *Notes on Casualty Procedure in War*.

Message A format was to be used for all flying casualties and crashed aircraft
Message B format was used for all non-flying battle casualties
Message C was the format for all cases of natural deaths or illness
Message D was the format for all cases of accidental or self-inflicted injuries.

These messages to the Air Ministry were allocated a priority from amongst the designated military classifications of IMMEDIATE, PRIORITY, IMPORTANT and ROUTINE. In the UK, when the reporting unit had informed the next of kin about the casualty, the signal to the Casualty Branch was given an IMPORTANT classification. When next of kin had *not* been informed the signal was given the higher classification of IMMEDIATE. Message signals from overseas units were all classified IMPORTANT.

Telegram messages to the next of kin were classified as PRIORITY with the added letter C for casualty and A, B or C according to the degree of urgency for delivery by the Post Office. For example, PRIORITY CA on the message to be sent by telegram to the next of kin meant the casualty was classed as 'Seriously' or 'Dangerously' ill, injured or wounded and the Post Office was required to deliver the telegram at the first opportunity whether it was day or night.[1] Telegrams sent to next of kin of persons known to be dead began *Deeply regret to inform you* whilst those sent to next of kin of the missing began *Regret to inform you* as there was a chance the person was still alive.

When the casualty notification message from the reporting unit arrived with the Air Ministry Casualty Branch they opened a Casualty P (denoting Personnel) File. These files were opened for all known casualties or possible casualties (i.e. personnel later reported safe) including individuals listed as Missing on operations or in training accidents and those later declared Prisoners of War. The first document to be included in the newly opened P File was the casualty notification message. All subsequent documents connected to the same casualty or casualties were placed on the same P File. The first document placed on the P File can be found at the back of the file, subsequent additions to the P File were placed on top of this in the order they were received; the last entry on the P File will be the one at the front. P Files therefore need to be read from back to front.

There are instances of casualties from more than one aircraft being included on one Casualty P File. Examples of this are two 1939 P files; only one P File is used for the five Blenheim crews lost on 4 September 1939 in the attack on Wilhelmshaven; similarly the five Hampdens lost on 30 September 1939 are combined on one P File. These Casualty P Files are from the early days of the war time Casualty Branch. Better practices evolved as the Casualty Branch grew in experience and separate P Files were opened for each aircraft and its crew reported as lost. However, there are the occasional later instances of more than one aircraft on a single P File, although these are uncommon and usually involve collisions between two aircraft.

As a Casualty File was opened for each notification there are a number of individuals who have more than one P File. For instance a pilot might

---

1. AP1922 Notes on Casualty Procedure in War 1st Edition 1941 & 2nd Edition 1943.

have been listed as missing during the Battle of France who was later found to be safe and well. The P File opened when he was reported missing was closed when he was listed as safe. The same pilot was then wounded during the Battle of Britain and another Casualty File would be opened when the Casualty Branch was notified of this and closed when the pilot recovered and returned to his squadron. The same pilot was then posted to Malta where he was killed and another Casualty File would be opened when the news was received by the Casualty Branch. This one individual would thus have three separate Casualty Files, all of which would be selected to go to the National Archives.

The Air Ministry Casualty Branch opened P Files for deaths from natural causes, deaths and injuries resulting from enemy action while the individual was on leave (e.g. killed at home in a bombing raid), deaths and injuries in road traffic accidents which happened in non-operational circumstances, self-inflicted injuries and deaths, and instances of illnesses required to be reported to the Casualty Branch. These Casualty Files are not going to be sent to the National Archives but have been retained by the Ministry of Defence. Information from these files may be available to members of the public but please note that the information they contain is limited. Requests for information from these files should be sent to the Air Historical Branch (RAF).[2]

The P File Reference System

With the number of Casualty Files which had to be opened, a reference system which allowed each file to be easily traced was required. Files were held by the Casualty Branch Registry, the element of the Casualty Branch which received incoming mail for distribution through the branch and outgoing mail for posting out. It was also the repository for all files held within the branch. The registry was responsible for opening new files which originated in the Casualty Branch and allocated identifying reference numbers and subject matter to them to facilitate storage and retrieval by the Casualty Branch Registry. The registry also recorded the movements of all files both within the branch and when a branch file was sent to another part of the Air Ministry. The person to whom the file was sent was recorded in the registry and also appeared on the file cover.

---

2. Contact details for the Air Historical Branch (RAF) are given in Appendix J.

File covers

No special file covers were used to denote Casualty files; all the Casualty P Files have standard Air Ministry brown file covers. The front of the file cover is divided into sections. The top section has designated spaces for the file reference number, the date the file was opened, and a subject. The bottom half of the front cover has a table of columns. These columns allowed the file's whereabouts to be tracked. The files were held in the Casualty Branch Registry and, when required to be worked on, they were sent to the appropriate person or section by the Registry. The destination of the file was noted in the column by the registry clerk sending out the file together with the date it was sent. The letters RC frequently appear in the columns and stand for Registry Clerk, an indication that the file had been returned to the registry.

Reference Number

Thousands of Casualty P Files were created by the Air Ministry Casualty Branch during the Second World War. For storage and retrieval purposes the Casualty Branch gave each P File an identifying reference number, for example P404272, together with the year abbreviated to two numerals (P404272/43). These were entered on the brown front cover of the P File when the file was opened and were quoted on all papers and correspondence relating to the casualty or casualties to which the P File referred.[3]

Subject

P Files concerning operational aircraft losses and flying accidents were referenced by the allocated P File reference number and given then given a 'subject'. The subject included the aircraft type, the date of the loss, and often a crew list. P Files relating to individual personnel killed or wounded through enemy action rather than an aircraft crew, were given a P reference number and the subject was either the individual name (or names), Service Number or Numbers and date of death or injury. Sometimes lists of crews or individuals are annotated 'killed' or 'injured' next to a name. A unit name or designation was often included, for example. Casualty File P359146/41 (now AIR81/6476) covers multiple casualties suffered at RAF Bircham Newton, Norfolk on 16 May 1941.

In cases of non-flying casualties the subject was normally the name or names of the casualties. However, a unit name or designation was often included.

---

3. On entry to the National Archives collection RAF casualty P Files are given a new reference number in the AIR81 series but can still be searched for in this collection under the original Air Ministry reference.

For example, Casualty File P359146/41 (now AIR81/6476) covers multiple casualties suffered at RAF Bircham Newton, Norfolk, on 16 May 1941.

Causal Prefix

Most casualty file covers also have a two-letter annotation. These are taken from the two-letter prefix which was given by the unit in their notifying Casualty or 'Crash Signal' sent by the reporting unit to the Casualty Branch. Guidance on which prefix to use was provided to units in AP1922 (*Notes on Casualty Procedure in War)* which was issued by the Air Ministry. There was a single prefix for all non-flying battle casualties of **BC (Battle Casualty)**. P Files for flying casualties were given a classification according to the reason for the aircraft loss and/or casualty. These prefixes were:[4]

FB   **Flying Battle** which was to be used for:

     a. Operational flying casualties or accidents whether due directly to enemy action or not. An operational flight was considered to start with the beginning of the aircraft's run for take-off and ended when the aircraft finished its run on landing.[5] All ferrying flights over land or sea from a theatre of war or a war zone were classified as operational flights. In this case a theatre of war or a war zone was defined as any place where 'interference with aircraft in flight may reasonably be considered to be due to enemy action from the air, ground or sea'.[6]

     b. Non-operational flying casualties or accidents directly due to enemy action. The notifying casualty signal was to state that the loss was caused by enemy action.

FA   **Flying Accident** – This prefix was used when casualties or accidents happened during non-operational flights and were not directly caused by enemy action. Casualties to personnel on local ferrying practice or training flights were also classed as **FA**. Casualties from ground accidents involving aircraft taxying or stationary, such as propeller accidents or collisions during taxying, were not to be given the **FA** prefix in the notifying signal. Such casualties were notified to the Casualty Branch by the unit using the unprefixed Message D given in AP1922.

---

4. AP 1922 Edition 1 of May 1941 and AP 1922 Edition 2 of October 1943 Appendix A.
5. Air Ministry Order A.479/43.
6. ibid.

FC   **Flying Casualty** – This classification was used when it was not known whether the casualty should be classified as **FB** or **FA**.

EA   **Enemy Action** – This prefix was to be used when aircraft were damaged on the ground by enemy action unless the crew of the aircraft suffered casualties. In these cases the **FB** prefix was to be used. The **EA** was sometimes incorrectly used by units reporting ground casualties; the correct prefix for these was **BC** (**Battle Casualty**).

Examples of Casualty File Covers for Flying Losses

Below is an example of the front cover of a Casualty Branch P File opened after the loss of Mosquito VI168 and her crew which was due to a Flying Accident.

1. *The FA next to the aircraft type and serial number indicates that the crash was due to a Flying Accident.*

2. *The cover is also stamped 'MR Section' for the Missing Research Section of P4(Cas) and has a handwritten MR Section reference of 211701 in addition to the main Casualty Branch P File reference of P428708/45.*

3. *The reference BPO/Cas/1670 19/2/45 which can be seen on this file cover is the reference given the loss by the Base Personnel Office of the Air Headquarters or Group to which the original notification of the loss was sent and the date their file was opened. The Air HQ would then forward the information to the Air Ministry Casualty Branch in London.*

4. *On the top right is the information which tells us that the aircraft came down in North East Kolar (a district in Karnataka State, India), on Sunday 18 February 1945. (The crew are buried in the Madras War Cemetery, Chennai.)*

5. *The 'Referred to' column reads thus: P4 Cas opened the file on 19 Feb (P4 Cas 19/2). The file then went to A3 (Accident Department in P4Cas to person designated A3). We are unable to decipher the next entry other than date, 18/12/50. A3 has it again on 26/4/51 (probably for review before storage). We are unable to decipher RAB, and then the file goes to the Registry Clerk on 26/6/51.*

   The modern barcode reference at the bottom is an archive reference relating to Ministry of Defence storage arrangements.

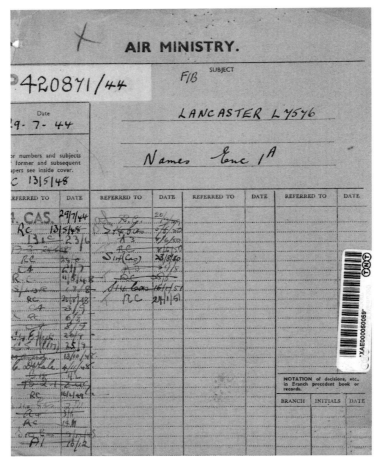

This example relates to an Operational aircraft loss (Flying Battle).

1. The Casualty Branch Reference Number for this file is P420871/44
2. The prefix FB (Flying Battle) can be seen near the word SUBJECT at the top of the file cover.
3. Subject is Lancaster L7576.
4. The names of the crew in this case have not been added to the file cover but a note states that they are given on Enclosure 1A.

   The modern barcode relates to Ministry of Defence storage arrangements.

   Lancaster L7576 belonged to 662 Squadron and was lost on a mission to attack Stuttgart on 29 July 1944. The aircraft crashed in France and the crew of five were killed; one member was 18 years old.

Chapter 3

Casualty Files for Non-Flying 'Battle Casualties'

The Casualty P Files relating to non-flying casualties, whether deaths, wounding or injury, classed as being a 'Battle Casualty' (which means the incident occurred in *operational* circumstances), have been selected for preservation in the National Archives. Non-flying Battle Casualty P Files include those relating to ground personnel taken prisoner. Covers of pre-1941 Casualty P Files concerning personnel killed or injured on the ground during air attacks have the P File Reference Number and the letters **EA** for *Enemy Action*; post that date the correct prefix was **BC** for *Battle Casualty*. The date of the incident is given and a subject which can include the type and place of the incident, for example 'Air Attack, RAF Driffield'. The subject sometimes includes names of those killed or injured.

Signal Message B

Non-flying Battle Casualties were reported to the Air Ministry Casualty Branch by units using the Signal Message B format from AP1922 *Notes on Casualty Procedures in War*. They began with the originating unit's reference number and date and had the prefix **BC**. The signal was then split into alphabetically marked sections each of which required stipulated information as follows:

A. The place, date and time of casualty
B. Details of each person involved by service number, rank, initials, surname, nationality (if not British) and parent unit. The signal was to state whether the rank held was substantive or acting, paid or unpaid (in the Air Force rank system a person could hold one rank (usually acting) but be paid the rate of a lower rank. This is called 'unpaid' rank). In this section the reporting unit also stated whether the casualty was killed, wounded or injured. The nature of the wound or injury was to

be given and whether the casualty was 'Dangerously' or 'Seriously' or 'Slightly' wounded or injured.

C. This section required the nature and cause of the casualty to be given. Whether the person was on or off duty had to be clearly stated. If the casualty was a fatal one caused by enemy air attack, exactly where death took place had to be included. This information was required for applications for award of a war pension.

D. The current location of the casualty was to be given whether the individual was dead or alive. In the case of a death the unit would state where the body was being held. In cases of wounds or injury, units were required to provide the name of the hospital or other medical unit to which the casualty had been sent and admitted.

E. In this section the unit was required to state whether or not the next of kin had been informed. This was usually given as KINFORMED or KINNOT.

Ground Operational Casualties

There are a number of P Files for deaths and injuries amongst non-flying personnel which occurred during action on the ground. The first of these Casualty Files were opened when the Branch was notified of casualties from incidents during the Battle of Belgium and the Battle of France in 1940 and the resultant evacuations. Amongst these are Casualty P Files relating to incidents such as the bombing of a troop train and the station at Rennes[1] on 17 June 1940 (during which members of No 4 Base Ammunition Depot were killed and injured), injuries suffered by a dispatch rider on duty in France, personnel reported missing from 57 Wing while on evacuation convoy duty but later reported safe, and a road traffic accident. All have been selected for preservation. There are also some Casualty Files recording non-flying casualties suffered during the Invasion of Crete and during the advances and retreats in North Africa.

This type of Casualty P File is referenced by number, date and unit designation and/or individual names. For example P File Reference No P353283/40[2] has as a subject a unit designation which is '2 Squadron'. The file covers the ground personnel from 2 Squadron who were listed as missing after the evacuation from Boulogne on 20 May 1940. On the other

---

1. National Archives references AIR81/967 and AIR81/2317.
2. Now National Archive Reference AIR81/1103.

RAF ground personnel crowd the decks of a steam packet at Brest during Operation Ariel, June 1940, the evacuation through ports in western France.

hand the Casualty File Reference No P352823/40[3] has as its subject a list of the names of missing personnel from 615 Squadron and no mention of the unit. Information concerning 1940 casualties in Belgium and France held in the P Files is very thin owing to the chaotic conditions prevailing during the evacuations at Dunkirk (Operation Dynamo), and the later one, which involved a lot of RAF ground personnel, from ports in the west of France (Operation Ariel). In the chaos many unit records were lost.

After June 1940 Air Force operational non-flying casualties in the UK resulted primarily from enemy attacks on RAF stations and establishments and some losses which occurred during bomb disposal work and other operational non-flying duties. Where the casualties were fatal, information in these files tends to be limited to the date and place of the incident, funeral arrangements and the place of burial or commemoration. Where injuries occurred and personnel were hospitalized there can be information about this on the Casualty P File. Usually this will be an indication of the nature of the injuries together with any updates received by the Casualty Branch regarding the casualty's state of health. Information about which RAF

---

3. Now National Archive Reference AIR81/855.

Station Medical Centre or military or civilian hospital the casualty has been admitted to and information on which next of kin was informed about the casualty and, sometimes, whether they visited the casualty (if hospitalized in the UK) is included in P Files.

Non-Flying Air Force Losses at Sea

Amongst the non-flying Casualty P Files are those relating to Air Force personnel lost at sea. These files include personnel lost in transit on troopships, during evacuations, in landing craft during amphibious landings, as well as Air Force air and ground crews serving on Navy aircraft carriers. For example the 1940 Casualty Files included RAF casualties from the coastal steamer SS *Abukir* which was lost evacuating soldiers, airmen and

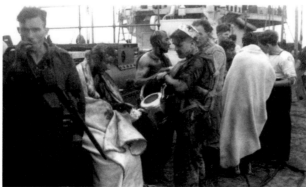

Above: *Passengers cover the hull of HMT* Lancastria *as she sinks, and* Left: *Survivors from HMS* Lancastria *aboard HMS* Highlander.

civilians from Belgium, RAF casualties from the carrier HMS *Glorious* lost in the ill-fated Norway Campaign of 1940, and from the troopship HMT *Lancastria* lost during Operation Ariel (the evacuation of western France). The latter resulted in the worst case of loss of life at sea. Nobody knows how many were aboard the *Lancastria* when she was hit and sank off St Nazaire, no passenger manifest was kept. The captain had been told to pack her with as many service personnel as he possibly could and the *Lancastria* was also carrying some civilian evacuees. Although the full death toll is not known, it appears to be over 2,000. What is known is that in the disaster 73 and 98 Squadrons lost their ground crews who were amongst about 239 Air Force personnel who died. Other RAF formations and units who lost personnel in the sinking were the Headquarters, British Air Forces in France (BAFF), No 2 Air Mission, No 67 Wing and ground units such as No 2 Heavy Mobile Wireless Telegraphy Unit. Air Force casualties also occurred during the sea ferrying of ground support personnel post D-Day.

The front covers of Casualty P Files relating to marine incidents have a P File Reference Number and the date of the incident but the subject given can vary from the name or designation of the vessel to the name of the unit to which the casualties belonged or individual names or a list of individual names. In the case of losses resulting from the sinking of HMS *Glorious* the P File reference number P352817/40[4] for it has a subject 'Personnel lost due to the sinking of HMS Glorious off Norway 8 June 1940', but there are also a series of individual Casualty P Files for officers[5] and one for two sergeants.[6] Officer casualties were always only handled by P4(Cas), but before the 1943 amalgamation of all casualty handling at P4(Cas), element of other ranks' casualty handling were undertaken by S7's RAF Records Office at Gloucester although P4(Cas) retained the major responsibility.

When casualties resulted from the sinking of a passenger or troop ship the Casualty Branch either used the names of individuals and/or their unit and usually the name or designation of the ship as the subject. An example is P250337/39[7] relating to Squadron Leader Thripp dated 17 October 1939; he was lost when the SS *Yorkshire* was torpedoed on her way from Rangoon to Liverpool. When multiple casualties occurred they were usually all placed on the same file, for example when the landing craft LST420 hit a mine and sank on 7 Nov 1944 while carrying the RAF's No 1 Base Signals and Radar

---

4. Now National Archives Reference AIR81/853.
5. National Archives References AIR81/912-928.
6. National Archives Reference AIR81/929.
7. National Archive reference AIR81/31.

Unit to Ostend. The unit lost 207 personnel who are covered by a single file reference. This type of P File contains very little information about the actual sinking other than when and where it occurred. It will usually include relevant correspondence with next of kin and a record of the place of commemoration.

In addition to RAF, RAFVR, WAAF and PMRAFNS personnel lost at sea while passengers on troopships, the RAF also suffered casualties amongst those serving in its own RAF Marine Section.

The RAF Marine Craft Section

It is often forgotten that the RAF had a Marine Craft Section which manned a variety of vessels from small boats such as pinnaces and Seaplane Tenders (used, as the name implies, for ferrying crews, ammunition, depth charges etc out to seaplanes), to the larger High Speed Launches and Long Distance Rescue Launches. By the end of the war the Marine Craft Section had some three hundred High Speed Launches and over a thousand other craft. The main role of the Marine Craft Section Launches was Air Sea Rescue (ASR) duties. These craft operated wherever the RAF was flying over water, from the cold North Sea to the Indian Ocean. The Marine Craft Section crews suffered their own fair share of casualties while plucking air crew and others from the sea as these rescues often took place in hazardous circumstances caused by bad weather or enemy attacks. At that time a surprising number of service personnel were unable to swim.

Other Marine Branch casualties occurred in support of operations; some Seaplane Tenders and ASR Launches were amongst the Little Ships which took part in the evacuation of Dunkirk. These RAF craft rescued 500 soldiers but one of the tenders was lost. Some RAF Launches took part in clandestine landing operations in occupied Europe and the western Mediterranean. Fourteen RAF Launches were involved in the Dieppe raid in August 1942 (three were lost together with two officers and nine crewmen), and on D-Day ninety-three RAF Launches were supporting the invasion.

Casualties were also suffered amongst the crews of small craft which the RAF Marine Craft Section operated from sixty-seven locations[8]

---

8. The Operation Record Books of Marine Section Units are held in the National Archives in the AIR29 class.

RAF Marine Section Seaplane Tender 879 and High Speed Launch 139.

A locally constructed RAF Rescue boat on the River Nile.

around the coast of the British Isles, in the waters around Malta, off the coasts of the Middle East, and in the Far East waters around Sri Lanka (Ceylon), and the coasts of India, Burma, Malaya and the various island bases the RAF set up. Some of these casualties were due to enemy action but others were the result of Marine Section crews being involved in accidents.

Casualty P File covers relating to RAF Marine Craft Section losses are normally listed by the vessel's designation (eg HSL 2586) and the names of the crews killed or injured together with the date of the incident.

Casualties caused by Enemy Action (EA) on land

The RAF Regiment
The RAF Regiment was formed in 1942 to provide a ground defence force for the protection of RAF airfields, and the protection needed to operate aircraft and the essential ground units such as AMES (radar) units from airstrips and positions in forward areas. Made up of Light Anti-Aircraft Squadrons (with Bofors and Hispano guns), Field Squadrons (with a variety of infantry weapons including mortars) and Armoured Car Units, the RAF Regiment used offensive tactics in their approach to airfield defence, carrying the fight to the enemy, as well as a more static defensive stance

The crew of a Humber Light Reconnaissance Car belonging to No 2777 Field Squadron RAF Regiment guard the airfield B89 at Mill, Holland in February 1945.

RAF Regiment gunners of 1307 Wing clean their Hispano light anti-aircraft gun at Meiktila airfield in February 1945.

more static defensive stance. RAF Regiment units were deployed in Europe, the Balkans,[9] North Africa, and the Middle and the Far East. The regiment was sometimes used to supplement the army and fought offensive actions in North Africa, and in the Far East campaigns to recapture Burma and Malaya.

In their various actions the regiment took numerous casualties, killed and wounded. In March 1945, 270 men of the RAF Regiment together with men from an Indian army brigade defended the airstrip during the struggle for Meiktila in Burma. For two weeks they withstood day and night attacks by crack Japanese forces determined to recapture the strip. Fourteen RAF Regiment personnel were killed including the commanding officer, twenty-five were seriously wounded and fifty others evacuated by air with slight wounds or sickness. The regiment also played a vital role defending the airfield during the Battle of Imphal.

All RAF Regiment casualties have Casualty P Files; some are individual files, others are collective. The P Files are referenced by file number, name and date of casualty.

---

9. National Archives AIR23/6722 RAF Regiment in North Africa, Sicily and Italy – Wing Commander E.M. Downes 1944.

Below is the cover of the Casualty P File relating to the death of Leading Aircraftman Thomas Tabram of 2762 Squadron of the RAF Regiment, killed in a ground accident on 24 May 1944. His service number and name form the subject. The casualty notification was made on Message Form D format which required no prefix so the word Accident has been added. LAC Tabram is buried in St Patrick's Roman Catholic Cemetery, Leytonstone, having been returned to his next of kin for a private family burial. (The modern barcode relates to MOD storage arrangements).

Ground Personnel

Attention tends to be focussed on the air crew losses suffered during the Second World War but, in addition to the personnel of the RAF Regiment and the RAF Marine Section, the many ground trades also suffered considerable casualties. Some personnel were killed or injured in attacks on airfields and other RAF installations (see casualties due to Enemy Action) but significant numbers of casualties were caused by accidents on duty. There were also many instances of sickness amongst ground personnel caused by their working conditions. The RAF found that many of the new types of bombers such as the Lancaster were too large to get into pre-war hangars and the personnel who serviced these and other large aircraft were forced to do so in the open in all weathers. A considerable number of ground crew died from the pneumonia they suffered as a result.

Overseas, servicing personnel and other ground trades were not only subject to attacks by the enemy but also suffered from diseases prevalent in the countries in which they were stationed. There were many cases of malaria and other unpleasant illnesses. All personnel off sick for more than forty-eight hours were reported to the Casualty Branch and P Files were raised. However, only P Files relating to non-flying operational deaths and injuries have been selected for preservation in the National Archives. Information from RAF Casualty files retained by the Ministry of Defence can be applied for by writing to the Air Historical Branch who will release such information as they are able to, although little is liable to be held.

The conditions in which ground crews had to work were often harsh, many suffered illnesses and some died as a result.

Escapers, Evaders and Internees

Escapers and evaders were personnel of the RAF and Dominion Air Forces of all branches and trades who either escaped from or evaded Axis captivity. Internees were military personnel who found themselves in a neutral country. During the Second World War these were Sweden, Spain, Portugal, Ireland, Andorra, the Vatican City, Switzerland and Turkey.

Neutral countries were required by the Hague Convention of 1907 to place any military personnel, whether of the Allied Forces or the Axis Powers, who arrived in their territory in camps or other suitable holding places for the duration of the war to prevent them returning to fight further.[10] Air Force personnel who evaded capture were interned by the neutral countries they reached if they declared themselves or were identified. Although personnel who were interned were supposed to be held until the end of hostilities some were later repatriated before the war ended. Escaped prisoners of war who made their way safely to a neutral country were not required to be interned.[11]

The Casualty Files record the safe return of successful escapers, evaders and internees. Often included in the record are reports made by the escaper or evader of their experiences. The Casualty P Files also record the deaths or woundings suffered by Air Force personnel during escape attempts or while evading. The deaths of the fifty air crew shot after their recapture following the mass escape from Stalag Luft III known as the 'Great Escape' are recorded in the Casualty Files.

The Casualty Files also include instances where Air Force evaders have been killed or wounded while on the run. In one instance an airman was killed while fighting with the French Maquis when the Germans attacked their camp. In another case a young flight sergeant was shot as a 'terrorist' by the Germans when he was captured wearing civilian clothes in a house belonging to a member of the Dutch resistance. There is some indication on his Casualty File that this action by the Germans might constitute a war crime but the position of military personnel caught wearing civilian clothing is ambiguous. During both the First and Second World Wars armed military personnel captured in civilian clothing were often executed on the spot as they were not considered to be combatants but outlaws or 'terrorists'. Certainly the failure of combatants to distinguish themselves from civilians, who are protected under the Geneva Conventions, is regarded as a breach of the law of war.

---

10. The Hague Convention of 1907 relating to the Rights and Duties of Neutral Powers Article 11.
11. Ibid Article 13.

Chapter 4

Casualty Files for Flying Casualties

Most of the Casualty Branch P Files held in the National Archives concern casualties suffered while on flying duty, either operational flights[1] or during flying training. Flying was a dangerous business in the 1940s, even before the hazards of operational flying were added, and accidents occurred in training and on operations. Training accidents took a heavy toll of air crew both at home and at the various overseas training schools which had emerged to cope with demand. RAF and Dominion personnel were sent for training in America, Canada, South Africa and Rhodesia under various schemes. The large numbers being trained inevitably led to a considerable increase in casualties from aircraft accidents.

Until autumn 1942 crews near the end of their training, flying with instructors as aircraft captains, took part in operations alongside fully operational squadrons. Aircraft from Operational Conversion Units took part in eight major attacks and 128 of their aircraft were lost. After September 1942 this practice stopped, although aircraft from Operational Training Units continued to be lost on anti-submarine patrols or on Operation Nickel sorties (leaflet dropping missions). However, by far the greatest losses suffered by Bomber Command Operational Training Units were during training flights: some 2,300 aircraft were lost[2] this way. Many aircraft were also lost from Coastal and Fighter Command training units.

---

1. An operational flight lasted from the moment an aircraft completed its take-off run until the moment the aircraft completed its run on landing. Ferry flights (flights delivering aircraft between units) over land or sea to or from a theatre of war or a war zone were classified as operational flights.
2. *RAF Bomber Command Losses Vol 7 Operational Training Units 1940-1947* by W.R. Chorley p.361.

When an aircraft accident occurred and the reason was not known an investigation was held to try to establish the cause so that steps could be taken to prevent a reoccurrence. Sometimes, but not always, the investigation took the form of a Court of Inquiry. The written record produced by a Court of Inquiry is known as 'The Proceedings'; occasionally copies of these were placed on the P File (see page 70). Courts of Inquiry were not held for aircraft lost as a result of enemy action on operations.

The Courts of Inquiry Proceedings belong to a class of documents which were not made available for disclosure to the public at the time[3] and elements of modern Service Inquiries (the equivalent of a Court of Inquiry) remain closed today. Where Casualty P Files contain copies of the Proceedings these papers are not on open access in the National Archives. However the vast majority of wartime Court of Inquiry Proceedings have not survived.

Flying Casualty P Files are the ones which contain the most information, including details about the aircraft and the tasking the aircraft was on. P Files concerning operational losses hold information on equipment carried, bomb load, engine numbers, date and time of loss, area of loss and the circumstances surrounding the loss of aircraft where they were known. The P File will contain information on a single individual when a single seat aircraft, for example a Hurricane, was lost, or information on a number of people when the aircraft carried several crew. Multi-crewed aircraft included Sunderland Flying Boats which carried crews of up to fourteen, heavy bombers with crews of up to eight, and transport aircraft with crews of three or four. In large Bomber Command raids air crew losses could be very heavy; in one night alone, during an attack on Nuremberg on 30/31 March 1944, 745 air crew were killed or wounded (over 550 lost their lives), and another 159 were captured, some of whom were seriously wounded. This was the highest loss for any single air operation during the war.

Multi-crew Casualty P Files are usually, but not always, subdivided using folded card, often green in colour, to give each crew member an individual section within the main file. Some of these folded cards have been reused with the previous name crossed out in keeping with the wartime need to economise on paper usage. The individual crew sections normally begin in the file after the entries which are common to all the crew.

Where the aircraft lost was carrying supernumerary crew or passengers some information about them will usually be on the P File. Personnel

---

3. Air Ministry Order A1086/ 1943 Courts of Inquiry – Disclosure of Proceedings.

classified as Supernumerary Crew were individuals who were carrying out duties while aboard the aircraft but were not air crew and not part of a normal crew. Some of the people included in this category were:

- RAF Film Production Unit personnel. The RAFFPU produced films of the RAF in action in the air and on the ground; cameramen from this unit flew on bombers engaged on sorties over Europe.
- War correspondents (members of the press who were not in the armed forces but were accredited to them and wore a uniform with a War Correspondent flash on the shoulder were also carried on operations). For example, two war correspondents, an Australian, Mr Norman Stockton of the *Sydney Sun*, and Nordahl Grieg, a Norwegian war correspondent, were killed while flying in Bomber Command aircraft on an operation against Berlin on the night of 2/3 December 1943. Mr Lowell Bennett, an American of the International News Services, was captured when the aircraft he was flying in was shot down on the same operation. The famous American reporter Ed Murrow was also taken on the same operation but survived to make a famous broadcast about it the next day (3 December 1943).
- Operators of special equipment not carried in the aircraft on a regular basis.

Casualty handling information for any passengers who were RAF, Dominion Air Force and Polish, Czech (or other nationals) serving with the RAF, is included in the P File, but while mention was made of any Royal Navy or Army passengers or crew, the casualty handling for them was done by their own service.

All the information received by the Casualty Branch concerning the crew of a lost aircraft was placed on the relevant Casualty P File. The P File contains basic information from RAF records on the crew members themselves, together with details of their next of kin. Information received from the German authorities through the ICRC about any crew or individual was placed on the appropriate P File, as was information received from any other sources. Post-war captured German documents relating to an aircraft's loss and the fate of the crew were added to the relevant Casualty P File. This information was used by the RAF Missing Research and Enquiry Service (MRES) to assist their investigations into the fate of air crew missing overseas. The information gathered by the MRES during their searches, and the investigative reports they submitted to the Casualty Branch, were also placed on the P Files.

Flying Casualty Reporting – Signal Message A – The Crash Signal

All flying casualties, whether operational or from accidents, were reported to the Air Ministry Casualty Branch by the reporting unit using the specified signal format known as Message A or, more colloquially, the 'Crash Signal'. A signal was a military message similar to a telegram. A Crash Signal was required for all incidents involving damage to aircraft or injury to personnel. The Crash Signal format was quite detailed and followed a prescribed format as laid down in Air Publication 1922. Receipt of a Crash Signal by the Casualty Branch was the trigger to open a Casualty P File and was the first document to be placed on it. The Crash Signal can be found at the back of the file (Casualty P Files are read from back to front).

When an aircraft was lost on operations or in an accident it was the responsibility of the commanding officer of the unit from which the aircraft came to notify various Air Ministry departments of the loss. The appropriate addressees were selected from those given in AP1922 and included:

- Air Ministry (Accidents) Gloucester when it was a flying accident
- Air Ministry (P4 Cas) Kingsway
- Ministry of Aircraft Production (DRM) if an aircraft was destroyed or damaged on the ground by Enemy Action
- The Record Office Gloucester when an airman or airwomen was the casualty until officers and other ranks casualty handling was amalgamated in 1943.
- The Parent Command and Group Headquarters of the aircraft and crew (if known)
- The Parent Unit (if known) when another unit reported the crash
- HQRAF Northern Ireland when a crash happened in Northern Ireland
- HQ 43 Group (Salvage) Oxford
- RAF Station Jurby when a crash occurred on the Isle of Man.

The example Crash Signal for Lancaster W (given at the end of this chapter) gives the following addressees:

Air Ministry Kingsway rptd [repeated] Air Ministry Accidents Kingsway.

HQBC [Headquarters Bomber Command]

HQ 5 Group [Headquarters 5 Group, the Group to which 207 Squadron belonged]

Air Group Oxford

No 58 MU Newark [58 Maintenance Unit at Newark, some of the RAF Maintenance Units were designated as being responsible for salvage of aircraft].

Records Glos [RAF Record Office at Gloucester]

RAF Bottesford [207 Squadron had moved from RAF Bottesford to RAF Langer in November 1942]

Following the list of addressees was the sending unit's reference number and name and then the date and time of the despatch of the signal. These were followed by one of the prefixes **FB, FA, FC,** or **EA** *(see chapter 2).* These indicated the nature of the cause of the loss. The prefix **FB** was used for operational casualties even if they were not directly due to enemy action. As an operational flight was held to start from the run to take-off and finish at the end of the landing run an aircraft which crashed on landing should correctly be classified as **FB,** but sometimes the unit incorrectly gave the prefix **FA** on the Crash Signal.

Ground accidents involving aircraft which happened when an aircraft was stationary or was taxying (eg injuries and deaths caused by propeller accidents) were reported in a different type of casualty signal which had no prefix.

The main body of the Crash Signal was split into a series of sections each of which was designated by a letter from A to N. Units were required to give specified information in each of these lettered sections as follows:

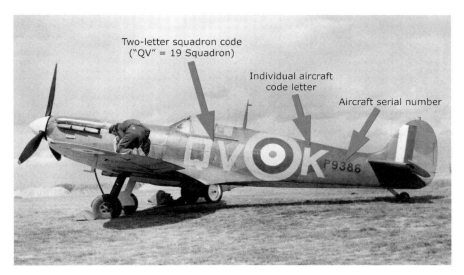

A Spitfire of No19 Squadron showing the squadron markings and aircraft serial number.

A. The type and number or identification letters of the aircraft and the number and type of engine and their serial numbers.

On entering RAF service all aircraft were given an individual, unique serial number by which they were identified and recorded. This number was displayed on the aircraft fuselage and sometimes the tail. Units also applied their own Unit Identifying Code letters which they had been allocated. During the war these letters replaced the squadron badges and numbers which the aircraft had previously borne. The normal position for the allocated letters identifying the unit was to one side of the RAF roundel on the fuselage with the individual letter the unit gave the aircraft on the other side. In April 1939, before the outbreak of war, the Air Ministry published a list which gave the allocated code letters for all existing and planned units and also all unused squadron numbers.[4] With the outbreak of war the code letters were changed when SD110 was issued in September 1939.

To complicate matters somewhat, some fighter aircraft flown by senior officers, such as Station Commanders and Wing Leaders, were marked with their initials in place of squadron code letters. When he was wing leader at RAF Tangmere, Douglas Bader had DB on his aircraft instead of a unit code. Another famous fighter pilot, Wing Commander Alan Deere, known as Al, had AL on his aircraft. Below is a picture of the personal Spitfire of Wing Commander I.R. Gleed DFC, DSO, a Battle of Britain pilot. At the time this picture was taken, Ian Gleed was the wing leader of 244 Wing and his aircraft is shown in company with two Spitfires of 601 Squadron (showing their UF squadron code) off the Tunisian coast after escorting light bombers on sortie to Mareth on 23 March 1943. Ian Gleed was shot down and killed flying this aircraft over Cap Bon on 16 April 1943. He was 26. His aircraft was found near the sea in sand dunes on the western coastline of Cap Bon. His body was not with the aircraft but he was found and buried by the Germans on 17 April 1943 at Kef Rorab, Cap Bon. He was later reburied in the British Military Cemetery Enfidaville, Tunisia

Section **A** also required information on the engines mounted in the aircraft to be provided. This was because the damage to a crashed aircraft was often so great that the serial number could not be read but engine numbers were on occasion still decipherable. The Crash Signal concerning the loss of Lancaster Mark 1 serial number W4938 of

---

4. Air Ministry Order (AMO) A154/39 dated 27 April 1939.

Wing Commander Ian Gleed leads a 244 Wing formation of Spitfires off the coast of Tunisia 23 March 1943. His initials IR G are used as markings instead of squadron markings. Below the cockpit his command pennant can be seen.

207 Squadron gives the engine numbers Port Outer 124375/394187, Port Inner 128427/396213, Starboard Inner 125273/392636 and Starboard Outer 101773/39368. It does not give the type of engine, seemingly taking for granted that everyone would know that Lancaster Mark 1 aircraft were fitted with Rolls Royce Merlin engines. Having records of the engine numbers proved to be a great help when trying to identify crashed aircraft.

B. The unit to which the aircraft belonged.
Normally this would be a squadron, but there were other flying units which took part in operations. For instance Tempest Mark V, serial number EJ531, was lost on a Diver Patrol on 5 July 1944. The loss signal shows the aircraft as belonging to FIU (Fighter Interception Unit). This Unit was part of the

Air Defence of Great Britain (ADGB) and specialized in air interception. In 1944 a detachment equipped with Tempest Mark V aircraft was sent to RAF Newchurch, Kent, to intercept V1 flying bombs. Such operations were known as Diver patrols.

If the aircraft was being transferred (or ferried) between units the name of the unit from which it was sent and that of the destination unit were entered on the Crash Signal. Ferry flights going to and from theatres of war or war zones were classified as operational and a loss was reported using the **FB** prefix. However, details concerning ferry aircraft can be confusing. For example the aircraft can be shown as belonging to one unit and the crew to another. This is particularly the case with aircraft being ferried out to the Middle East and North Africa. These aircraft often left from RAF Portreath in Cornwall and via Gibraltar to their destination sometimes via Takoradi in West Africa or Malta. The crews were often drawn from newly graduated air crew who were going to postings in areas the aircraft were being sent to, for example Hudson aircraft being sent from America to the UK were sometimes brought over by crews returning from flying training in the US and Canada.

C. The location of aircraft, date and time of crash, conditions of light (to be given where known), and a brief mention of target and operation.

The information required to be given in section **C** was to enable the Air Ministry (P4Cas) and the records offices to answer enquiries from relatives about personnel who were missing. Crash Signals involving aircraft accidents in the UK should give a map reference or place name; the minimum requirement was for a county and map reference.

It was very different for aircraft lost on operations. It was hoped that the last known general location of a missing aircraft or crew members could be given but units were reminded that they needed to say whether the position they gave was a known location or unconfirmed. Sometimes the last known position of the aircraft is given. The location of many Bomber Command operational losses could only be given as 'presumed over target' or a similar vague location. The same was true of many aircraft lost in the Far East. With fighter aircraft, which usually flew in daylight and in company, there is sometimes information given about the location of a crash or a 'baling out' provided by other pilots, but this could be incorrect.

The time of the operational loss could also be rather inaccurate. The time of take-off was easy to establish as it was recorded by station operations personnel and also included in the Operations Record Books[5] kept by squadrons. The time of the loss was usually much harder to establish, and this was recognised; 'Failed to return' was an accepted submission which had clear parameters. In these circumstances the Crash Signal was sent when an aircraft was overdue i.e. it was deemed to be beyond the flying time permitted by the fuel load carried and no news of it landing at another airfield was received. One hour overdue was the normal time allowance made before the Casualty Branch was notified. Instructions for the reporting of overdue aircraft were given in King's Regulations for the Royal Air Force paragraph 733 and in Air Ministry Orders.

Some Crash Signals concerning the loss of an aircraft on an operational flight give the aircraft's home airfield as the location. In this case the aircraft will usually either have crashed on take-off or on the return landing or been brought down by a German intruder aircraft. These intruder aircraft loitered at night near the UK bases to intercept returning bombers and attacked them when the bomber crews' guard was dropped with their home station in sight.

Many Crash Signals for operational losses just give a date and, in the case of Bomber Command aircraft, it is often impossible to tell whether they were lost on the way to the target, over the target or on the way back. Where there were survivors, their accounts about what happened to their aircraft were often not received until, in the case of PoWs, they were liberated or, in the case of those who escaped or evaded capture, they returned to England.

Section **C** also required units to provide the conditions of light at the time of the loss. Specific words[6] were to be used in the message:

- *DAY* was used when the loss occurred during normal daylight hours.
- *DUSK* denoted that the loss occurred in the half-light of evening.
- *DARK* indicated the loss occurred when it was fully dark.
- *MOON* was used when the loss occurred at a time when, but for the moon, it would have been completely dark. If heavy cloud obscured the moon making it a dark night rather than moonlit night, *DARK* was used.
- *DAWN* was used when the loss happened in the half-light of early morning.

---

5. Operations Record Books of all Second World War RAF units and formations are held by the National Archives at Kew and are open to the public. Those of operational flying squadrons can be viewed online.
6. AP1922 dated May 1941 APPENDIX A, Note vi

D. The particulars of the crew.

In this section units provided information about the crew on board the aircraft when casualties had occurred. Crew details were not required when the loss was incurred without casualties and units were instructed to state 'No Casualties'. Units were required to give service number, rank (substantive and acting 'paid' or 'unpaid' were supposed to be included but in many cases were not), initials, surname, and nationality if not British. When the casualty was a member of a British Empire Air Force the initials of that Air Force were given, e.g. RAAF, RCAF, RNZAF, IAF (Indian Air Force) later RIAF.

Service Number. The service number is the personal identifying number given to all members of the British and Dominion armed forces regardless of rank. It precedes the rank and name of an individual. It forms part of the only information a prisoner of war is obliged to disclose to his captors, i.e. Name, Rank and Number. The service numbers of RCAF personnel were prefixed by a letter. This was usually J for officers or R for other ranks although sometimes other letters appear, for example the letter C was retained for officers who had joined the RCAF before the outbreak of war. Canadian other ranks going overseas also had CAN added (see Crash Signal example 4 below). RAAF service numbers had no letter prefix and were issued in blocks for each state. Their air crew numbers ran from 400001 to 459999, ground crews from 1 to 2999999. Usually AUS appears in front of their number on Crash Signals.

Other Dominion Air Force service numbers were usually preceded by national identifiers; RNZAF for Royal New Zealand Air Force personnel, SA or SAAF for the South African Air Force, or IAF for Indian Air Force.

Ranks. In the loss signal, ranks are given as abbreviations. Before May 1940 the ranks included aircraftsmen of classes I and II who flew as gunners in aircraft such as the Battle, Blenheim and Defiant. After this date all air crew were ranked sergeant and above.

The ranks of air crew engaged on flying duties were:

Commissioned Ranks

- *Gp Capt* or *GC* for Group Captain (this would normally be the Station Commander flying on an operation although sometimes staff officers from Groups or Commands also flew).

- *Wg Cdr* or *W/C* for Wing Commander (usually the Squadron Commander in Bomber Command, or the Wing Leader for Fighter Command and fighter units overseas).
- *Sqn Ldr* or *S/L* for Squadron Leader (usually a Flight Commander in Bomber Command or a Squadron Commander in Fighter Command/2TAF/ADGB).
- *Flt Lt* or *F/L* for Flight Lieutenant
- *Fg Off* or *F/O* for Flying Officer
- *Plt Off* or *P/O* for Pilot Officer

Acting rank was denoted by A/ e.g. A/PO for Acting Pilot Officer

  Non Commissioned Ranks (NCO)

- *WO I* for Warrant Officer One
- *WO II* for Warrant Officer Two
- *Flt Sgt* or *FS* for Flight Sergeant
- *Sgt* for Sergeant

Promotion for NCO ranks was on a time-served basis but this was not automatic. Before early 1943 six months was the amount of service required between the ranks of sergeant and flight sergeant. Early in 1943 this was changed and there was normally one year between promotions to the next rank for qualified air crew, with the proviso that the unit commander must recommend, and the Air Officer Commanding (AOC) the relevant Group must approve, the promotion. Time promotion continued for prisoners of war; a man might have been captured as a sergeant but was liberated as a warrant officer. It should also be noted that it was the practice of the RCAF to promote by one rank those of their number who were killed; for example a sergeant who was killed would posthumously be promoted to flight sergeant, similarly a flying officer would posthumously be promoted to flight lieutenant. The RAF did not follow this practice.

Name. The name of the casualty follows his service number and rank. The surname is given first followed by initials. Some air crew flew under assumed names, e.g. Sergeant Hans Heinz Schwarz, a German refugee who was killed on 13 August 1944 while flying under the name of Henry Blake as the specialist equipment operator on Lancaster PB258 of 101 Squadron. There were a variety of reasons why individuals chose to join the RAF or to fly under assumed names: sometimes it was for personal security reasons; or, as in the case of D.C.G. Verbraek, a Belgian who flew under the name Pilot Officer J. Robinson, to protect family still living in German-occupied Europe. On occasion it was because the individual was underage; there are also instances of deserters re-joining under different names. The Air Ministry was not always aware that a name was assumed and units could only supply the name they held on record locally.

Crew Roles

The information provided by the unit on the crew can include their role in the aircraft. The number of crew varied between one and fourteen depending on the type of aircraft and equipment carried. Air crew roles were:

- *Pilot/Captain* – The pilot was the captain of the aircraft even if he was outranked by another member of the crew. Some units just give Captain in their signals.
- *2nd Pilot* – On Coastal Command Sunderland aircraft two pilots were carried because of the length of the flights but on Bomber Command aircraft the 2nd pilot was usually an inexperienced or newly qualified pilot gaining operational experience.
- *Observer* given as Obs (later became *Navigator* shown as Nav)
- *Wireless Operator/Air Gunner* given as WOp/AG (later the Air Gunner element was dropped and only WOp was given).
- *Signaller* given as Sig
- *Air Bomber or Bomb Aimer* given as AB
- *Flight Engineer* given as Flt Eng or FE. In Bomber Command this role came in with the arrival of the heavy bombers such as the Lancaster and Stirling.
- *Air Gunner* given as AG. Some units, but not all, included the position e.g. 'Mid Upper Gunner' or 'Rear Gunner'.
- *Special Duties Operators* given as SDO. A rare inclusion on the Bomber Command loss signals, they were German speaking volunteers selected from existing air crew who operated the jamming device known as Airborne Cigar (ABC) and flew on the special 101 Squadron Lancasters.

Condition of the casualties – Where this was known it was required to be included in this section. The reporting unit was to state whether crew had been killed, wounded or injured and (if either of the latter) whether 'dangerously' (DI), 'seriously' (SI) or 'slightly' or 'not injured'. The nature of the wounds was also to be given where they were known (e.g. gunshot wounds to right arm or broken left femur). If the casualty was reported as 'Missing' qualifying information was to be added; either 'believed killed', 'believed interned', 'believed prisoner of war' or 'particulars unknown'. Most often units would either say 'Not Known' (N/K) or 'Missing believed killed'. If an aircraft crashed but there were no casualties, just the name of the pilot was given in this section. The entry would be for example '**D** No Casualty. Pilot 508299 Sqn Ldr I.P. Sibbald'.

Next of Kin – Details of next of kin were also supplied by the unit who usually held the most up-to-date record of whom the casualty had nominated as his/her next of kin and who they wished to be informed. The unit provided the names and addresses they held to the Casualty Branch on the loss signal. The next of kin would normally be parents or spouse; fiancées **did not** count as next of kin but would usually be included by the individual as a person to be informed, as were siblings and other relatives.

Similar information to the above was to be reported when there were casualties, (both Service and civilian) who were not in the aircraft but whose death or injuries resulted from the incident. For example, when Stirling EH880 crashed into a farmhouse at Togston, Northumberland, whilst trying to land at RAF Acklington 5 children were killed and their mother and father seriously injured. Information about these casualties was required to be included in the Section D of the Crash Signal. Information about damage to civilian property caused by aircraft crashes was also to be reported (e.g. three houses damaged). If there were civilian casualties but no damage to property the words 'Damage to civilian property NIL' were used.

E. The present location of the crew.
Whether they were alive or dead information about the whereabouts of the crew was required. For operational losses, unless the aircraft had crashed within the UK or in Allied-held territory in other theatres, units were usually only able to report 'Not Known'. In the case of aircraft accidents in the UK more information was available. Units were required to report whether or not all bodies had been recovered from the aircraft. Usually when an aircraft crashed away from an RAF airfield the local civilian police were first on the scene. The police were responsible for immediately informing the nearest RAF authorities.

It was the responsibility of the RAF to remove bodies from the aircraft crash site, but if the RAF did not reach the crash site within two hours the civilian police could remove any bodies outside a twenty yard radius of the wreckage and take them to the local mortuary. The RAF was then responsible for recovering any other bodies from the wreckage. Bodies removed from aircraft crashes in the UK were usually taken to RAF Station Medical Centres. The loss signal from the unit would then state which Station Medical Centre had been used, for example '*RAF Waddington SMC*'. On occasion the name of a civilian mortuary appears when civilian police had removed bodies from the crash site.

The whereabouts of any injured personnel were also to be given. For casualties occurring in the UK this is usually the name of the medical facility to which they had been taken. This could be a civilian or military hospital or an RAF Station Medical Centre (SMC). In overseas theatres, casualties were admitted to RAF or Army General Hospitals; which one would be reported in this section of the casualty signal. These hospitals are often only referred to by their identifying numbers, such as 5RAFGH (No 5 RAF General Hospital), 9BGH (Number 9 British General Hospital). Army hospitals were designated as British General Hospitals; a list of the locations of these during the Second World War is held by the National Archives at Kew under reference WO222/1568.

F. Details of ordnance carried and any special equipment on board.
RAF aircraft carried a variety of ordnance ranging from ammunition rounds, listed as AR, to the deep penetration 22,000lb Grand Slam bomb. Both Bomber Command and Coastal Command aircraft could carry mines, and Coastal Command aircraft also carried depth charges for anti-submarine use. The loss signal instructions initially stated that the signal was to report whether bombs and any special equipment was carried. Later in the war units were expected to state the type of bombs etc carried. However, sometimes the unit did not supply this information. When Tempest EJ531 was lost the unit only reported that she was 'operationally equipped'. Below is some of the ordnance which would be listed in section **F** of the loss signal:

- **Ammunition Rounds.** The three primary ammunition rounds used by the RAF in the Second World War were the .303 calibre used in Browning machine guns, the 20mm Hispano cannon round and the .50 in the Browning Heavy Machine Gun. The loss signal sometimes states how many rounds were carried, e.g. the loss signal for Lancaster W4938 states it was carrying AR 1508 and AR15035.

- **Ground attack rockets RP-3** carried by aircraft such as the Beaufighter and Typhoon for attacks on shipping and ground targets such as trains and armour.

Rockets being loaded on a Typhoon aircraft after D-Day.

- **Torpedoes** carried by Coastal Command Beauforts.
- **Sea mines** were carried in mining operations by both Coastal and Bomber Command aircraft.
- **Depth Charges** were carried by Coastal Command aircraft such as the Sunderland and Whitley.
- **Bombs.** A wide range of bombs were used by the RAF. When war broke out the RAF was mostly using General Purpose (GP) bombs. The smallest of these was 40lb and the largest 4,000lb. The others were 250lb, 500lb, 1,000lb, and 1,900lb. Post-1941 the GP bombs were largely replaced by the Medium Capacity (MC) bombs (of 500, 1,000 and 4,000lbs) and the High Capacity (HC) bombs (2,000, 4,000 (nicknamed Cookie), 8,000 and 12,000lb). The largest bomb was the Grand Slam at 22,000lbs, known as an 'earthquake' bomb. Small bombs were grouped together in Small Bomb Carriers (SBC). Most medium and heavy bombers carried a mixed load of incendiaries and high explosive (HE) bombs. A typical bomb load was that carried by Lancaster W4938 lost on 13 May 1943 on a raid against Duisburg. She was reported as carrying:

  1 x 4000lb bomb (Cookie)
  12 x SBC (12 Small Bomb Carriers)
  3 x 30lb incendiaries.

Bomber Command had a number of standardised bomb loads which were given code names. When such a load was carried on a lost aircraft, units sometimes used just the code word in the loss signal. The main ones were:

Abnormal = 14 x 1,000lb General Purpose (GP) High Explosive (HE) bombs.

Usual = 1 x 4,000lb High Capacity (HC) bomb known as a Cookie and 12 x Small Bomb Carriers (SBC) holding incendiaries.

Pierce = 6 x 2,000lb armour piercing bombs and GP/HE bombs.

Gardening = 6 x 1,850lb parachute mines (for mining of ports, rivers, canals).

Plumduff = 1 x 4,000lb HC bomb, 3 x 1,000lb GP/HE bombs and up to 6 SBC loaded with incendiaries.

Plumduff Plus = 1 x 8,000lb bomb and up to 6 x 500lb GP/HE bombs.

Arson = 14 x SBC holding 236 x 4lb incendiary and explosive incendiary bomblets.

Armourers with bombs marked with bomb weight in pounds.

The 'usual' bomb load on a Lancaster of 57 Squadron at RAF Scampton comprising a 4,000lb Cookie and twelve Small Bomb Carriers (SBC) containing 236 x 4lb incendiaries.

There was also a requirement to report any special equipment carried. Examples of these were jamming equipment of which each type had a code name such as *Tinsel* or *Mandrel*, or navigational aids such as *Gee*, *H2S*, *Fishpond*, and *Oboe*. Sometimes units also listed the camera (an F8) which was used to take the raid photograph over the target. Without such a 'raid' photograph the crew were unable to count the mission towards their required operational tour total.

G. Cause of Loss, Accident or otherwise.
All aircraft missing on operational flights were assumed to have been lost due to enemy action and were not reported as accidents. If information later became available which showed that enemy action was not the cause and

the aircraft had crashed due to an accident the loss was reclassified. When it was known that the casualty was due to enemy action units were instructed to include Enemy Action or initials EA at **G**. When the cause of a loss on an operational flight was unknown the unit reported this.

Where the aircraft was lost or damaged as the result of a flying accident the Air Ministry required a Form 765(c) *'Report of Flying Accident'* to be submitted. When it was not known whether this form would be appropriate, units were instructed to put 'No F765(c)' and to send a second signal in confirmation when it was definitely known that a F765(c) was not required. Some units added the information that Air Investigation Branch (AIB), action and Group investigation were not required (see Crash Signal 3 below).

H. Category of Damage sustained by the aircraft

In section H a brief description of the damage sustained by the aircraft was to be given together with the category into which the level of damage was placed. The unit entry made in this section for many aircraft which went missing was simply 'Unknown' or N/A (for not applicable). There are unit reports for operational aircraft where the aircraft returned to base damaged by enemy action.

Most of the category information found on Crash Signals concern aircraft involved in flying accidents. The official categories[7] of damage were:

- **Cat A** The aircraft was repairable on site by unit engineers.
- **Cat AC** The aircraft was repairable on site but not by unit engineers and a specialist working party was needed (which usually came from a Maintenance Unit). If the aircraft was causing an obstruction or needed moving for repair the Crash Signal included 'Salvage Yes'.
- **Cat B** The aircraft was repairable but not on site. The aircraft would then be moved to a Maintenance Unit for repair or sent back to the contractor who had built it for specialised repair.
- **Cat E** The aircraft was damaged beyond repair. If the aircraft had been damaged by fire the word 'Burnt' was added.

The units were to report instances where the aircraft had been hit by cannon fire, machine gun bullets or flak.

---

7. These were varied slightly later in the war.

J. Salvage

The identity of the Maintenance Unit (Salvage Centre) which had been notified by the unit was to be given at **J**.

K. Informing Next of Kin

Units were to report whether or not the next of kin of the casualties had been informed by the unit. KINNOT on the signal indicated that the next of kin had not been informed, KINFORMED meant that they had. Whether the next of kin had been informed or not dictated the priority given to the Crash Signal by those transmitting it. In cases where the next of kin had not been told, the crash signal was given the high priority of IMMEDIATE. Where the next of kin had been informed a lesser priority of IMPORTANT was given.

L. Airfield Crash

If an aircraft crashed at an airfield the unit was to inform the Air Ministry whether or not there had been any damage to property belonging to a third party. This was to be given by stating Yes, No or Not Applicable.

M. Passengers

Particulars of any passengers were to be given, whether Air Force, Army, Navy, or civilian. These were to be taken from RAF Form 1256 (RAF Air Freight Manifest) completed prior to flight.

N. Cargo

Particulars of all cargo listed on Form 1256 as being carried were to be given.

M and **N** were normally only used when ferrying or transport aircraft were lost.

The Crash Signal ends with the time of origin given in the form of a date time group; 131145 May 1943 means that the Crash Signal was sent at 1145 on 13 May 1943.

At the bottom of the Crash Signal comes 'Circulation' which lists the number of copies of the signal passed to various departments by the recipient. The P File copy lists the copies circulated in the P4(Cas) area. The example below concerning Lancaster W4938 records two copies being sent to the Canadian Casualty officer as the crew included a member of the RCAF. The Canadian Casualty department was co-located with P4(Cas).

Examples of Crash Signals

1. *Flying Accident Crash Signal for Spitfire AR403. The reporting unit, 65 Squadron, has not provided much information and the signal has typing errors*

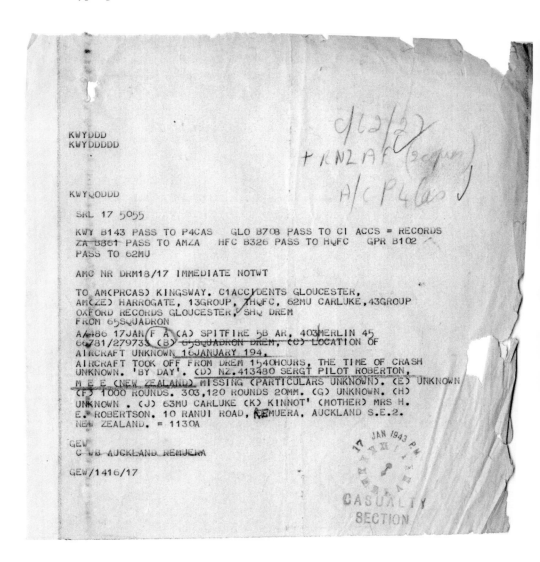

2. A Flying Battle Crash Signal for Spitfire MJ789 shot down on patrol over the Normandy beaches 11 June 1944.

IK/A   TELEGRAM EN CLAIR   114/12.

FROM: BASO AEAF

TO: AIR MINISTRY KINGSWAY   HQ AEAF   HQ 43
        GROUP

(RECEIVED A.M.C.S. (K'Y) JUNE 12)

CAS/468   JUNE 12.   (FOR P4 CAS) (F.B.

(A) (1) SPITFIRE LF IX LR MJ789
       (11) MERLIN N66 161531/447576

(B) 453 SQUADRON 125 WING.
(C) AIRCRAFT MISSING 11 JUNE 1944 2005 HRS DAY
      BEACHHEAD COVER
(D) MISSING BELIEVED KILLED AUS 411539 F/LT H.L.
      SMITH (AUSTRALIAN) PILOT
(E) UNKNOWN
(F) FULLY OPERATIONAL

(G) APPARENTLY HIT BY FLAK AIB NO 765 C NO.

(H) AIRCRAFT MISSING
(J) 405 R AND SU
(K) WIFE KINFORMED FATHER (ADDITIONAL NOTIFICATION)
      KINNOT – RICHARD LACY SMITH 1 AUSTRAL STREET
      KOGARAM NEW SOUTH WALES AUSTRALIA
(L) N/A

        TIME OF ORIGIN: 122100 B HRS.

CRASH CIRCULATION (P4 CAS 4 COPIES)
OHQ RAAF (2 COPIES)

RECEIVED

CASUALTY SECTION

Translated, this signal says

From: Base Personnel Staff Officer, Allied Expeditionary Air Force

To: Air Ministry Kingsway, Headquarters Allied Expeditionary Air Force, Headquarters 43 Group

(Received Air Ministry Communications Section (Kingsway) 12 June)

CAS/468 12 June (for P4 Cas) FB
[CAS/468 is the sender's reference, 12 June is the date the signal was sent, FB the Flying Battle prefix]

A. The aircraft was a Spitfire Mark IX serial number MJ789 fitted with a Merlin engine. The engine part numbers are N66 161531 447576
B. The aircraft was from 453 Squadron, part of 125 Wing
C. It went missing on 11 June at 2005 hrs [8.05 pm] in daylight while providing beachhead cover for the Normandy invasion beaches.
D. The pilot was missing believed killed. He had a service number of AUS411539 which indicates he was a member of the Royal Australian Air Force. His rank was flight lieutenant; his name is given as H.L. Smith and his nationality as Australian. His crew position was pilot.
E. His present location is not known.
F. Fully operational indicates that the aircraft was armed for operations.
G. The cause of the loss is given as apparently hit by anti-aircraft fire (Flak).
   AIB No means the Air Investigations Branch do not need to be informed.
   765C No means that Form 765c (used for aircraft accidents) is not required either.
H. The category of damage cannot be given as the aircraft is missing.
J. 405 Repair and Salvage Unit has been informed.
K. The immediate next of kin, his wife, has been informed but Flt Lt Smith has added his father as an additional person to be notified. His father has not been notified and his details are provided so that the RAF/RAAF can do so.
L. The aircraft did not crash at an airfield so L is not applicable.

The time of origin of the signal message is given as 12 June at 2100 (9.00pm) Bravo Hours. Bravo means European Local Time.

3. *Crash Signal for Tempest EJ531 belonging to a 150 Wing Fighter Interception Unit based at RAF Wittering. This aircraft was lost on an operational flight so the Crash Signal has an FB prefix. Later it was found that the aircraft suffered engine failure, so the cause of the loss was an accident. FIU is Fighter Interception Unit. The formations notified of the loss by 150 Wing were HQ Allied Expeditionary Air Force, and the HQs of 85, 11 and 12 Groups. The priority given the signal was IMMEDIATE and it was not to be sent by Wireless Telegraphy (NOTWT).*

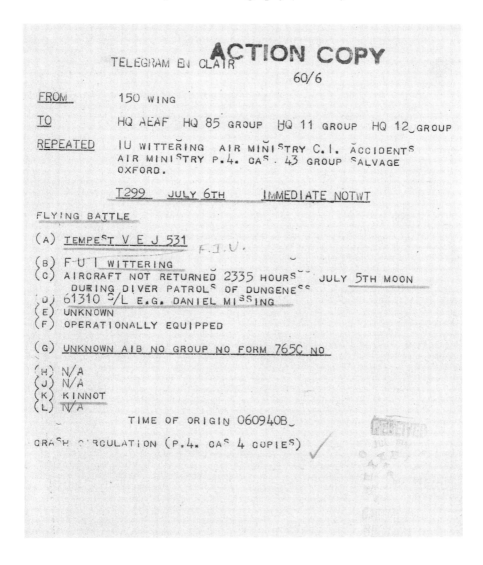

RAF WWII OPERATIONAL

4. Crash signal for an Operational Flying Battle Loss – Lancaster W4938

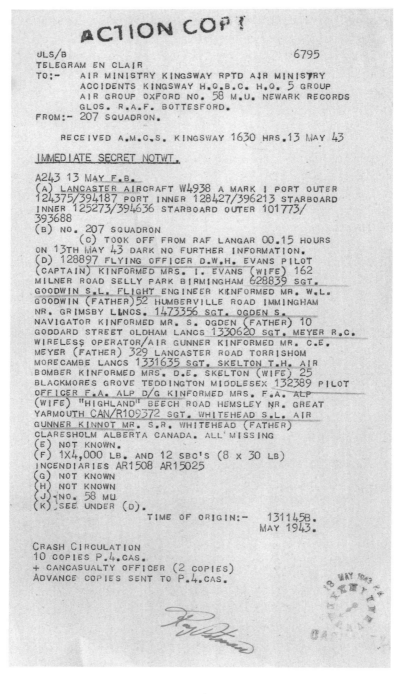

ACTION COPY

JLS/B   6795
TELEGRAM EN CLAIR
TO:-   AIR MINISTRY KINGSWAY RPTD AIR MINISTRY
        ACCIDENTS KINGSWAY H.Q.B.C. H.Q. 5 GROUP
        AIR GROUP OXFORD NO. 58 M.U. NEWARK RECORDS
        GLOS. R.A.F. BOTTESFORD.
FROM:- 207 SQUADRON.

     RECEIVED A.M.C.S. KINGSWAY 1630 HRS.13 MAY 43

IMMEDIATE SECRET NOTWT.

A243 13 MAY F.B.
(A) LANCASTER AIRCRAFT W4938 A MARK I PORT OUTER
124375/394187 PORT INNER 128427/396213 STARBOARD
INNER 125273/394636 STARBOARD OUTER 101773/
393688
(B) NO. 207 SQUADRON
        (C) TOOK OFF FROM RAF LANGAR 00.15 HOURS
ON 13TH MAY 43 DARK NO FURTHER INFORMATION.
(D) 128897 FLYING OFFICER D.W.H. EVANS PILOT
(CAPTAIN) KINFORMED MRS. I. EVANS (WIFE) 162
MILNER ROAD SELLY PARK BIRMINGHAM 628839 SGT.
GOODWIN S.L. FLIGHT ENGINEER KINFORMED MR. W.L.
GOODWIN (FATHER)52 HUMBERVILLE ROAD IMMINGHAM
NR. GRIMSBY LINCS. 1473356 SGT. OGDEN S.
NAVIGATOR KINFORMED MR. S. OGDEN (FATHER) 10
GODDARD STREET OLDHAM LANCS 1330620 SGT. MEYER R.C.
WIRELESS OPERATOR/AIR GUNNER KINFORMED MR. C.E.
MEYER (FATHER) 329 LANCASTER ROAD TORRISHOM
MORECAMBE LANCS 1331635 SGT. SKELTON T.H. AIR
BOMBER KINFORMED MRS. D.E. SKELTON (WIFE) 25
BLACKMORES GROVE TEDDINGTON MIDDLESEX 132389 PILOT
OFFICER F.A. ALP D/G KINFORMED MRS. F.A. ALP
(WIFE) "HIGHLAND" BEECH ROAD HEMSLEY NR. GREAT
YARMOUTH CAN/R109372 SGT. WHITEHEAD S.L. AIR
GUNNER KINNOT MR. S.R. WHITEHEAD (FATHER)
CLARESHOLM ALBERTA CANADA. ALL MISSING
(E) NOT KNOWN.
(F) 1X4,000 LB. AND 12 SBC'S (8 x 30 LB)
INCENDIARIES AR1508 AR15025
(G) NOT KNOWN
(H) NOT KNOWN
(J) NO. 58 MU
(K) SEE UNDER (D).
                TIME OF ORIGIN:-   131145B.
                                    MAY 1943.

CRASH CIRCULATION
10 COPIES P.4.CAS.
+ CANCASUALTY OFFICER (2 COPIES)
ADVANCE COPIES SENT TO P.4.CAS.

Chapter 5

Circumstantial Reports and Accident Forms 765(C) and 551

The Crash Signal was followed by a written report which all flying units, operational or not, were expected to submit as soon as possible and no later than forty-eight hours after the event. The written reports took two forms: firstly a 'Circumstantial Report', written in what the services termed a Formal letter format, and secondly the RAF Form 765(c) '*Report on Flying Accident*'. A Circumstantial Report was to be sent by the unit commander when the casualties on an operational flight, or from an accident, were directly caused by enemy action. Casualties resulting from accidents not due to enemy action were reported using RAF Form 765(c). Aircraft missing on operational flights where the cause of their loss was unknown were assumed to be casualties due to enemy action and a Circumstantial Report was submitted. However, if further information came to light which showed that enemy action was not the cause of the loss the unit were required to raise a F765(c).

The Circumstantial Reports and Forms 765(c) are both included in the Casualty P Files. They usually are found shortly after the original Crash Signal in the Casualty File.

Circumstantial Reports

Written Circumstantial Reports were required by the Casualty Branch to be sent by unit commanders when the casualties suffered were known be as a direct result of enemy action, a Report was not required if the crew were known to have survived uninjured. The Circumstantial Report was to be submitted in the form of a formal letter addressed to the Air Ministry.

The Circumstantial Report was required to give a reference to link it to the Crash Signal already sent by the unit. The report was then to give a brief account of the incident and state what kind of duty the aircraft and crew were on at the time. The Circumstantial Reports usually start with the aircraft details followed with date and the time and place of take-off; for example 'Lancaster Mk III, DV164 took off from RAF Wickenby at 2316 hours on 9 July 1943.' This information was followed by what duty the aircraft was on. When reporting this, Circumstantial Reports involving fighter aircraft often use code words such as 'Diver Patrol' (interception of V1 flying bombs), Rhubarb (fighter aircraft searching for targets of opportunity over France), or Rodeo (fighter sweeps over occupied territory). Reports concerning bombers sometimes refer to Gardening (mine laying), Circus (short range daylight attacks with fighter escort) or Nickel (leaflet dropping) operations but much more often simply say 'to take part in an attack on' and then give the name of the target (Berlin, Düsseldorf, Cologne etc). Some bomber squadron commanders include the planned route the aircraft took to the target and back in the form of positional references.[1]

The Circumstantial Report also confirmed details of the casualties, giving their names, ranks, service numbers, and Air Force if not RAF. Often, but not always, each individual's role in the crew was given. This information can, on occasion, differ from that provided in the Squadron's Operation Record Book.[2] The Circumstantial Report will have been written and submitted within forty-eight hours of the incident; the Operations Record Book was written over a minimum period of four weeks and submitted monthly.

Also included in the Circumstantial Report was any information given by witnesses to the incident. These are largely supplied to fighter aircraft flying in daylight with other aircraft and give information such as 'seen to go down into the sea with engine on fire, no parachute seen' or 'last seen dropping out of formation over Caen area'. There is very little similar information given for bomber aircraft which were flying together in large numbers at night. Bomber Command crews saw aircraft going down, hit by flak or damaged by night fighters, but were rarely able to identify which aircraft it was. Sadly, many of the Circumstantial Reports submitted by bomber squadron commanders only say that the aircraft took off at specified time and date and nothing further was heard from it. There was no further information available to the squadron about the fate of the aircraft and crew.[3]

---

1. Information on individual Bomber Command operations can be found in the Bomber Command Night Reports and the Bomber Command Day Reports held in the National Archives, Kew, under reference AIR14.
2. Operations Record Books for Second World War squadrons are held in the National Archives, Kew, under AIR27. Those of operational squadrons can be viewed online.
3. Bomber Command Loss Cards held by the RAF Museum at Hendon give a brief summary of what was known about the loss of a bomber and crew.

Accidents and forced landings directly caused by enemy action also required a Circumstantial Report to be submitted. However, units were warned, 'it must not be assumed that an accident is due to enemy action just because it occurred on an operational flight.'[4]

The Circumstantial Reports are sometimes signed by the squadron commander personally; others are signed on his behalf by another officer such as the squadron adjutant. Two copies of the Circumstantial Report were sent to P4(Cas) at the Air Ministry and one to the appropriate Group Headquarters. One of the copies sent to P4(Cas) was placed on the relevant P File. The Circumstantial Reports should not be confused with the letters that were required to be sent to next of kin by commanding officers. These letters are not often found on P Files unless a copy of the letter was sent to P4(Cas); this was only a requirement when a unit was overseas.

In cases involving missing air crew, a small P4(Cas) in-house form called *'Analysis From Circumstantial Report'* is often included on the P File. These forms were used to provide a brief synopsis for the Presumption of Death process.

Example of an 'Analysis from Circumstantial Report' by P4(Cas) used in the presumption of death process and often found on P Files. IJC is probably the initials of the person completing the form.

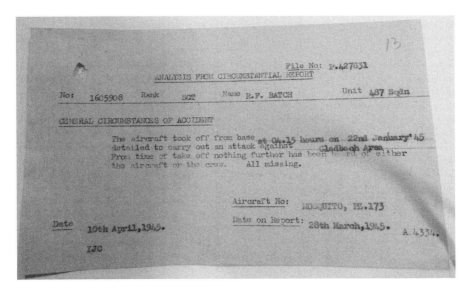

----

4. AP1922 *Notes on Casualty Procedure in War* 2nd Edition October 1943 Section VIII para 228 b.

Examples of Circumstantial Reports

Circumstantial Report submitted by Wing Commander Tait, Officer Commanding 617 Squadron, concerning the loss of Lancaster NG180 during a daylight attack on the Kembs Dam 7 October 1944.

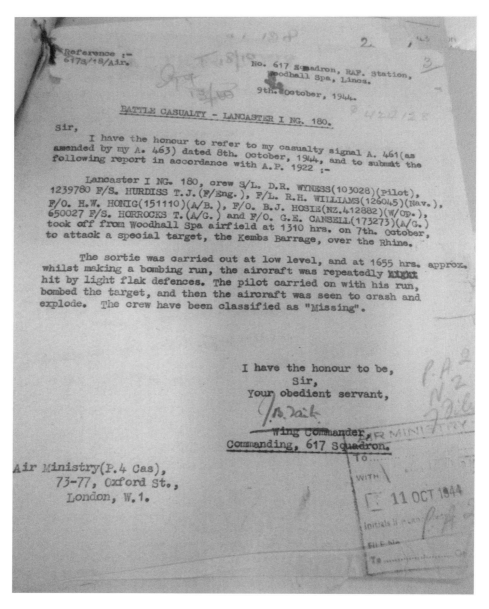

Reference :-
617S/18/Air.

No. 617 Squadron, RAF. Station,
Woodhall Spa, Lincs.

9th. October, 1944.

BATTLE CASUALTY - LANCASTER I NG. 180.

Sir,

    I have the honour to refer to my casualty signal A. 461(as amended by my A. 463) dated 8th. October, 1944, and to submit the following report in accordance with A.P. 1922 :-

    Lancaster I NG. 180, crew S/L. D.R. WYNESS(103028)(Pilot), 1239780 F/S. HURDISS T.J.(F/Eng.), F/L. R.H. WILLIAMS(126045)(Nav.), F/O. H.W. HONIG(151110)(A/B.), F/O. B.J. HOSIE(NZ.412882)(W/Op.), 650027 F/S. HORROCKS T.(A/G.) and F/O. G.E. CANSELL(173273)(A/G.) took off from Woodhall Spa airfield at 1310 hrs. on 7th. October, to attack a special target, the Kembs Barrage, over the Rhine.

    The sortie was carried out at low level, and at 1655 hrs. approx. whilst making a bombing run, the aircraft was repeatedly being hit by light flak defences. The pilot carried on with his run, bombed the target, and then the aircraft was seen to crash and explode. The crew have been classified as "Missing".

                              I have the honour to be,
                                   Sir,
                        Your obedient servant,

                             Wing Commander,
                 Commanding, 617 Squadron.

Air Ministry(P.4 Cas),
   73-77, Oxford St.,
     London, W.1.

11 OCT 1944

CIRCUMSTANTIAL REPORTS AND ACCIDENT FORMS 765(C)

A Circumstantial Report submitted by 622 Squadron which gives no information other than about the crew. The handwritten P420871 in the right hand corner indicates the P File index number.

No. 622 Squadron,
Royal Air Force,
Mildenhall,
Suffolk.

29th July, 1944.

<u>LANCASTER MK.I L.7576 'K'</u>

Sir,

     I have the honour to refer to this Units signal A.393 dated 29th July, 1944, herewith report in accordance with A.P.1301, appendix 3 Part 1 in duplicate.

2.   The above aircraft with the following on board J.22396 F/O Peabody, H.S. - Pilot, J.29847 F/O Doe, J.H. - Nav., 1547697 Sgt Payton, A. - W/Op.(Air), J.29707 F/O Fiddick, R.L. - B/A, R.220221 F/S Proulx, R. - A/G, 1813417 Sgt. Buckley, P.W. - A/G, 52167 A/F/Lt. (F/O) Wishart, G.J. - F/Eng, took off from Mildenhall at 21.59 hours on the 28th July, 1944 to bomb a target in enemy territory. (Stuttgart.)

3.   Nothing has been heard of the aircraft or crew since time of take off.

        I have the honour to be,
          Sir,
        Your obedient servant,

          Wing Commander, Commanding,
          No. 622 Squadron, R.A.F.

The Under Secretary of State,
Dept. P.4. Cas. Air Ministry,
73-77 Oxford St, London. W.1.

Copy to :- Headquarters No. 3 Group.
        No. 32 Base Mildenhall.

A Circumstantial Report submitted by 182 Squadron concerning the loss of a Typhoon piloted by Flying Officer Snowdon. P4(Cas) has had to chase 182 Squadron for the report. Note that unlike the previous examples, this letter is not signed by the Squadron Commander but by a Flying Officer on his behalf. Again, the pencilled note P404014 on the top right-hand corner gives the P File index number.

P403014

182 Squadron,
No.124 Airfield,
R. A. F.
Lasham, Hants.

Ref:-182S/C.410/P2.   20th May,1943.

117515 F/O. SNOWDON. N. Missing 16th April,1943.

Sir,
   I have the honour to refer to your letter A.H.5./43/P.4. Cas.R.1 A.4. dated 7th May,1943, and append the following report.

Flying Officer Snowdon was flying Blue 3. with Flying Officer Cotton as Blue 4. They were airborne from Tangmere at 17.25 hours on the 16th April and flying line abreast, reached the French coast at Trouville at approximately 11,500 feet.
The Target was Tricqueville airodrome, and going into line astern, approached from the S.W. to attack.

Flying Officer Snowdon was approximately 100 yds in front of his number 2, Flying Officer Cotton who saw him release his bombs, but instead of pulling out of his dive straight ahead with leaders, he pulled out violently in a steep right bank.
When next observed he was flying West towards River Seine and his aircraft was emitting white smoke, and it then turned onto its back. The aircraft was last seen smoking badly and diving vertically at 3000 feet. No flak bursts were seen near Flying Officer Snowdon during his dive, but No. 197 Squadron reported aircraft had dived into river Seine.

I have the honour to be,
Sir,
Your obedient servant,

K.C.PEARSON.
Flying Officer,
for Squadron Leader,Commanding,
No.182 Squadron,
Royal Air Force.

The Under Secretary of State,
Air Ministry, Dept. Q.J.
73 - 77 Oxford Street,
London, W.1.

Reporting Aircraft Accidents Using Standard Forms

1. RAF Form 765(c) – *'Report of Flying Accident or Forced Landing not Attributable to Enemy Action'*

Units were required to submit a Form 765(c) when aircraft were involved in operational and non-operational flying accidents. The term 'Flying Accident' applied to all accidents which involved damage to aircraft or injury to personnel other than those directly due to enemy action or which could reasonably be assumed to be so. It covered a wide variety of accidents on the ground as well as in flight (e.g. propeller accidents) and would more appropriately have been called 'Report on Aircraft Accidents'. Detailed instructions on what incidents Form 765(c) was to be used for and guidance on the entries required were provided at unit level in the cover of the file which was provided to hold the unit copies of the form, and also in AP1922, and various Air Ministry Orders.

Units both at home and overseas were required to raise a Form 765(c) when deaths or injuries occurred (which resulted in an absence from duty of more than forty-eight hours) which could not be attributed to enemy action. The RAF Form 551 *'Report on Accidental or Self Inflicted Injuries or Immediate Death therefrom'* was to accompany the Form 765(c). When casualties occurred in flying accidents, copies of both of these forms were sent to P4(Cas) and placed on the relevant Casualty P File.

Other instances when the F765(c) was required was when an aircraft was damaged so badly the unit's own maintenance personnel could not repair it within forty-eight hours or if the damage resulted in the replacement of a major element of the aircraft such as an engine, wing or part of the under carriage. It was the responsibility of the commanding officer of the unit to which the aircraft belonged to raise a Form 765(c) and submit it within four days of the incident. Collisions between two or more aircraft required the units to raise a F765(c) for each aircraft, but if an aircraft hit another aircraft which had already crashed only one F765(c) was required.

Accidents could occur on operational flights and these had to be reported using the F765(c). Some examples of such incidents were given to units in AP1922.[5] These were:

- Damage resulting from a bird strike particularly during low level flights
- Damage resulting from being hit by incendiaries or bombs dropped by another aircraft in the attacking stream

---

5. AP1922 *Notes on Casualty Procedure in War* 2nd Edition October 1943 Para 228.

- Damage resulting from violent evasive action to avoid attacks by enemy aircraft or flak or from hitting obstructions such as trees or wires when low flying to take evasive action
- Mid-air collisions between aircraft in the same attacking force.

Copies of Forms 765(c) reporting these operational incidents were only sent to P4(Cas) if casualties resulted.

At the top of the front page of the F765(c) the unit sending the form was instructed to state whether or not a Crash Signal had been sent and, if one had, to provide the reference for it with the date and prefix (**FB** or **FA**). The F765(c) began by requiring details of the unit to which the aircraft belonged, the time, the date and the location of the accident. Information on the flight came next: whether it was operational or not, the type of flight the aircraft was on, whether it was day or night, the time of take-off, the number of pilots, and what the aircraft was doing at the time of the accident. This was followed by information on the aircraft type, mark and serial number together with information on the engines fitted. The unit was also required to say whether or not the aircraft had caught fire and if so where the fire occurred and whether extinguishers had been used.

Special information was required on the F765(c) regarding some of the equipment carried or action undertaken. Examples of these are oxygen failures, glider towing and accidental dinghy release. One of the most common references found on F765(c) in P Files is to Beam Approach equipment. Beam approach was a homing system developed early in the war to assist landing in poor visibility; accidents frequently occurred during Beam Approach Beacon System (BABS) training.

When there were casualties (killed, injured or missing) their names ranks and service numbers were to be provided. Information was included about the pilot's flying experience. Civilian deaths were to be reported on the F765(c) when they were caused by an RAF aircraft. There are examples of these on some F765(c)s found on P Files; in one instance there is a list of civilians killed when an RAF aircraft crashed on a row of houses, in another instance civilian occupants of a car were killed when an aircraft crashed on it while coming into land.

The F765(c) included short reports by engineering officers, the best description available about what happened, and comments by the Unit Commander and the Station Commander.

F765(c) for Oxford W6624 of No 6 (Pilot) Advanced Flying Training Unit flown by Sergeant S.V. Crossley which crashed on 30 November 1942 night flying.

10. SUMMARY OF PILOT'S REPORT (or a description of circumstances which terminated in the accident if the pilot's report is not available). In cases of engine failure information should be given as to the behaviour of the engine and manipulation of the engine controls immediately before failure.

Duration of flight since last take off : Hours....... Minutes.....5.. If engine failure occurred during take off quote height....

Pilot took off for N/F solo after having done four dual circuits and landings, rose to approximately 500 feet, levelled out and began to lose height and turn to port. He then appeared to dive with engines roaring on full throttle and crashed into trees about 1½ miles from the aerodrome.

11. REPORT BY APPROPRIATE SPECIALIST OFFICERS (A. E. Nav., &c.) :—(i) If technical failure is involved information as to the nature and cause of the failure is required ; precise information as to the extent of the damage arising as a result of this failure is not required. (ii) If the non-embodiment of an authorised modification is considered to have contributed to the accident, the serial number of the modification and reason for non-embodiment should be stated.

The aircraft was completely wrecked with all controls and instruments smashed or torn out, petrol tanks and systems wrecked etc. The port engine had struck a tree with very considerable force and was almost completely wrecked. There was no apparent sign of seizure and the pistons showed that the ignition system had been functioning. The wrecked condition precluded any other examination. There was no apparent technical defect in the aircraft to cause the accident.

Is Form 1022 or 1023 being rendered? If "Yes" state which   No   Signature............ W/Cdr.

12. REMARKS BY UNIT COMMANDER (to be given under three separate headings) :—   CTO
   Part A. Remarks as to circumstances of the incident. (If it occurred at night on or near an aerodrome the nature of the lighting system in use at the time is to be noted in Part A.)
   Part B. Diagnosis of all contributory factors. The manner in which any particular factor contributed to the incident is to be clearly indicated.
   Part C. General remarks (including any recommendation with regard to personnel, training, airframes, engines, accessories, etc., and notes of any action taken as a result of this incident).

A. Accident occurred at night at Windrush satellite landing ground, a double electric flare path was in use, there was a bright half moon and the visibility was very good with no clouds. The pilot had been given four circuits and one overshoot dual with P/O. Rossington midnight instructor.

The pilot had flown one circuit solo on the previous night.

The aircraft, after being inspected at the taxying post, took off and climbed normally, but then unaccountably went into a left hand turning dive with considerable throttle, striking trees left wing about 30° down at about 25° of dive and 200 mph approximately.

B. The Windrush beacon was almost straight ahead of the line of take off, a good aid to keeping straight.

C. This pilot's instrument flying was good and he was assessed above average in A training. I do not know why this accident occurred, failure of port engine possible.

Signature............   Commanding............   Date 3.2/42

13. REMARKS BY STATION COMMANDER (and notes of any action taken as a result of this incident) :—
   (i) Was any assistance rendered in rescue work after the accident, which is considered worthy of recommendation ? Yes or No............ If any such assistance was rendered, the recommendation is to be forwarded separately.
   (ii) Remarks. No

Subject of an Investigation.

Signature............   Commanding............   Date............

This RAF F765(c) is for Tempest EJ531 lost on an operational flight when the aircraft engine failed.

REPORT ON FLYING ACCIDENT

R.A.F
Revi

(To be retained in, and checked against F764 until completion)

ENCL.

A/C

DISTRIBUTION:—
(i) Two copies to Air Ministry (P.A.2).
(ii) One copy to Ministry of Aircraft Production (R.M.1).
(iii) Two copies to Group Headquarters.
(iv) One copy to the Air Ministry P.4.Cas. when pilot is member of R.C.A.F.
(v) One copy to the O.T.U. or H.C.U. where pilot or crew was trained—for all accidents occurring in squadrons.
(vi) One copy to the parent unit of the aircraft if accident occurs to aircraft whilst temporarily attached to another unit.

P. 419763

Additional copies to Air Ministry P.4.Cas. :—
(a) One copy if there is a casualty to Officer or Airman.
(b) One copy for each Allied Authority if casualty to Dominion or Allied personnel.

If this incident has been reported to the Air Ministry by signal quote Ref. No. and date.
150 Wing T299 d/d 6. 7. 44.

1. UNIT Fighter Interception. | Group No. 12 | Command A.D.G.B. | Serial No. of Form 13/44

2. (i) UNIT STATIONED AT
(ii) Aircraft stationed at

3. DETAILS OF ACCIDENT
(i) Date 5.7.44. (ii) Time 2935 (iii) Moonlight. | Light, Put:—Day, Dark, Moon, Dusk or Dawn.

4. WHERE DID CRASH TAKE PLACE?
(i) Airfield
(ii) Whether "on" or "near" this Airfield
(iii) Place (see Note 1) In sea
(iv) Height above sea level (approx.)
(v) County South of Dungeness
Note 1.—Reference to be to places marked on 1 in. map.

5. DETAILS OF FLIGHT:—
(i) Operational or Non-Operational Operational
(ii) Day, Night, Day-Night or Night-Day Night
(iii) Type of operation or exercise or purpose of flight Diver Patrol.
(iv) Dual, Solo or two Pilots
(v) Time of take-off
(vi) What was aircraft doing when it crashed? In flight
Put:—Landing (i.e., on airfield), Taxying, Take-off, Circuit, Flight, Forced Land (not on A/F), Ditching (forced land on water), Picketed or moored, Starting up, Towed or Manhandled, Stationary.

6. DETAILS OF AIRCRAFT. AIRFRAME

Type/Mark	R.A.F. No.	Total Hours Flown if technical failure	Damage: E, B, AC, A, AR, U.
Tempest V Mk.11	E.J. 531		E

ENGINES

	Single or Port Outer	Port or Port Inner	Starboard or Starboard Inner	Starboard Outer
Type/Mark	Sabre 11A			
Damage † E, B, AC, A, U.	E			
R.A.F. and Maker's No.		Data below required if there has been technical failure.		
Total Hours Run				
Date Eng. last Installed				
Time of failure				

† E = Write off. U = Undamaged. | B = For repair at contractor's works or R.A.F. Depot. A = Unit repair. | AC = Contractor's repair at station. AR = Unit repair by replacing component or engine in under 48 hours.

7. DID FIRE OCCUR?
Not known
Put:—Total aircraft, airframe, engine fire only, suspected fire, No fire.
Note.—If possible state source, e.g., port inner, bomb bay, etc.

8. WHEN DID FIRE OCCUR?
Put:—In air, after crash, starting up, etc.

9. WAS GRAVINER SYSTEM OPERATED?
(i) Put:—Yes by inertia switch, Yes by hand, No, Not fitted, Not known.
(ii) Did Extinguisher Bottles Discharge?
Note.—(i) and (ii) to be filled in for all accidents whether fire occurred or not.

10. CHIEF TECHNICAL OFFICER'S REPORT.
Report in sequence, failure, cause, details. In all cases of real or suspected TECHNICAL failure, this report should be a summary of the reports of the relevant specialist officers, e.g., Signals, Armament, Electrical, etc. If the non-embodiment of an authorised modification is believed to have contributed to the accident, the serial number of the modification and the reason for non-embodiment should be stated. Precise details of damage are not required.

Aircraft serviceable before flight.

Apparently engine failure occurred with little or no warning during flight.

1022 action taken No
1023 action taken No
State number of previous similar defects :—
(a) Causing accidents
(b) Not causing accidents

Signature Sgd: G.H. Williams, P/O for
Servicing Wing, 150 Wing.

11. REPORTS OF SPECIALIST OFFICERS. (Report in sequence, failure, cause, details. Where the accident is due or partly due to failure in procedure, the report of the appropriate specialist officer should be given, e.g., Navigation Officer, Flying Control Officer, Signals Officer, Meteorological Officer, Armament Officer, etc.)

RAF WWII OPERATIONAL

<table>
<tr><td colspan="4">the crash, then the names of all other occupants. For dual
direction put instructor first.
egree of injury to be classified as :—Missing, Killed, Injured
dmitted to Sick Quarters or Hospital), Slightly Injured (not
dmitted to Sick Quarters or Hospital), Uninjured. (Quote as
d, K, I, I(s) or U as appropriate.)</td><td colspan="2">For all Accidents
¢ Total solo
(Day and Night)</td><td colspan="2">For
Night Accidents
Night Solo</td><td colspan="2">For Acc
involving
Instrument
Flying</td></tr>
<tr><td></td><td>Name and Initials
(Nationality if not British)</td><td>Rank</td><td>Number</td><td>Degree
of
Injury</td><td>On
this
¢ Type</td><td>On
all
Types</td><td>On
this
Type</td><td>On
all
Types</td><td>Hrs. on
Instru-
ments</td><td>Hrs.
on
Link</td></tr>
<tr><td>t</td><td>E.G. Daniel</td><td>S/Ldr</td><td>61310</td><td>M</td><td>17</td><td>1150</td><td>17</td><td></td><td></td><td></td></tr>
</table>

¢ N.B.
If the log book is not available estimate as close as possible and put " estimated " underneath the figure.
Total solo should include any flying done before entering R.A.F.
The word " Type " includes all marks of the type.

R.A.F. personnel killed or injured not occupants of aircraft.

13. Were any other persons killed or injured ? If so, give numbers.

Killed............Injured...........

14. PILOT'S REPORT. (This space must not be left blank or filled in " not available." If the Pilot's report is not available the best description of the circumstances possible must be inserted. If the aircraft is missing the last information concerning its whereabouts, direction of flight, intentions, probable area of crash must be given, together with notes on the weather, petrol duration, etc.)

150 Wing, Newchurch had a radio message from the pilot at 23.35 hours to say his engine had cut and he was about to bale out over the sea South of Dungeness.

No trace of pilot or machine has since been found.

Sgd: G.H. Williams, P/O.
150 Wing.

(i) All up weight............lbs.   # (ii) C.G. position.............
To be calculated at time of accident.

15. CONCLUSIONS OF UNIT COMMANDER. (This section should be a complete summary.)
Part A.   What happened and under what circumstances ?
Part B.   What errors were made or what went wrong ?
Part C.   What action is intended or has been taken ?

A.   S/Ldr. Daniel was airborne on anti diver patrol in Tempest aircraft No. E.J. 531. He was heard to call on R.T. by RAF Newchurch and also by F/Lt. Berry who was airborne at the time, that his engine had cut and that he was about to bale out. His position was fixed as five miles south of Dungeness and his height was approximately 3000 feet when the engine cut.

B.   Not applicable.

C.   No evidence is available to show whether S/Ldr. Daniel succeeded in abandoning the aircraft.

Signature ....Sgd: W.H. MAGUIRE S/Ldr.
Name (Typed or in Block Caps.)
Commanding .......F.I.U.
Date ......22. 7. 44.

16. REMARKS OF STATION COMMANDER. (Notes of any further action taken or recommended.)

It is understood that all available search facilities were employed.
I recommend that the hood jettison equipment of the Tempest aircraft be tested by the pilots themselves when the aircraft are on periodical inspections.

CIRCUMSTANTIAL REPORTS AND ACCIDENT FORMS 765(C)

The Form 765(c) for Halifax JP137 which crashed on take-off for a ferry flight on 21 March 1944. 'No 3 OADU' shows the aircraft was from No 3 Overseas Aircraft Despatch Unit, RAF Hurn and the purpose of the flight is given as 'ferrying overseas'. This edition of the F765(c) includes a reminder in red about the need to submit the form within four days. The flight was classed as operational because it was a ferry flight taking an aircraft to a war zone.

1st Page

REPORT ON FLYING ACCIDENT OR FORCED LANDING NOT ATTRIBUTABLE TO ENEMY ACTION.

Form 765 (C).
(Revised Feb. 1943)

In every case copies of this form are to be rendered as follows :—

(i) One copy direct to Air Ministry, C.I. (Accidents).

(ii) Two copies direct to Air Ministry, S.4. (Statistics)

(iii) One copy direct to Ministry of Aircraft Production (R.M.I.).

(iv) One copy through usual channels to Command Headquarters.
[*In addition*, and *only* if casualties to officers or airmen are involved.]

(v) One copy to Air Ministry, P.4 (Cas.).

Indicate here by an X to whom this copy is addressed

If this incident has been reported to the Air Ministry by signa., quote Reference No. and date.

A.O. 472 - 21st March, 1944.

Extra copies required for Dominion and Allied casualties; one for each authority concerned. When no casualties occur, one copy only if Canadians are pilots.

1. UNIT No. 3 O.A.D.U.	Group No. 4	Command Transport	Serial No. of Form 33

2. DATE OF INCIDENT 21st March, 1944.

TIME 00.31 hrs.

SITE OF INCIDENT

(a) Name of airfield or landing ground ....

(b) Place (if (a) not applicable) Roe No. No. Moordown, Bournemouth.

(c) County Hampshire.

Part (a) to be completed if the incident occurred on, or whilst taking off from or approaching to land on an airfield or landing ground.

3. NATURE OF AND PURPOSE FOR WHICH FLIGHT AUTHORISED :—

Nature { (i) Operational or Non-operational? Operational
(ii) Day or Night flying ? Night
(iii) Purpose Ferrying Overseas

This flight is being included in this Unit's flying hour summary on { Form 765A
Form 765B No (Delete as necessary)

23 MAR 19..

4. TYPE OF AIRFRAME AND ENGINE and extent of damage (*see* footnotes to this section).

Details of Airframe and Engine.	Airframe.	Engine.			
		Single or Port.	Starboard.	Centre Port.	Centre Starboard.
Type	Halifax	Merlin XXII	Merlin XXII		
Mark or series	II				
R.A.F. No. (and makers' No. for engines)	JP 137	a Liner	a Liner	a	a
		b 13576/7707	b 337576/8788	b	b
Total hours run					
Date last installed in Airframe		b	b	b	b
c Extent of damage	2 Burnt.				

a To be quoted whenever an engine is damaged or fails.
b To be quoted only for incidents involving defect or failure of airframe or engines
c To be indicated as :—
E = Missing, unrepairable, reduction to scrap or instructional. AC = For repair by contractor's working party.
B = For repair at contractor's works or R.A.F. Depot. A = For repair by nearest R.A.F. unit. U = No damage.

67

# RAF WWII OPERATIONAL

2nd Page

Duty	Name and Initials (Nationality to be quoted if not British)	Rank	No.	Degree of Injury	Part A. Type Quoted in Part 4	Part A. All Types	Part B Type Quoted in Part 4	Part B All Types	Part C Instruments	Part C Link Trainer
Pilot	Evans. D.R.	Sgt.	1323338	K	✓	No flying hours record available				
Nav.	Roberts. R.W.	Sgt.	1585160	K	✓	available at date of rendering				
B/A	Appleton. S.A.	P/O	152127	K	✓	S. 765 0				
W/A	Alexander. G.A.	Sgt.	1099966	K	✓					
A/G	McGregor. R.R.	Sgt.	Can.R/167600	K	✓					
A/G	Green. K.	Sgt.	1674977	K	✓					
F/Eng.	Gent. S.W.	Sgt.	1333177	K	✓					

The ranks of the crew indicate that they were newly qualified. The aircraft was being delivered to the RAF element with the Mediterranean Allied Air Force and the crew would be joining an RAF squadron serving in this command.

Two civilians, Mr P. Chislett and Mrs D. Bennett, were also killed when the aircraft came down on houses in Moordown, Bournemouth. Their details should have appeared on the F765(c).

68

3rd Page

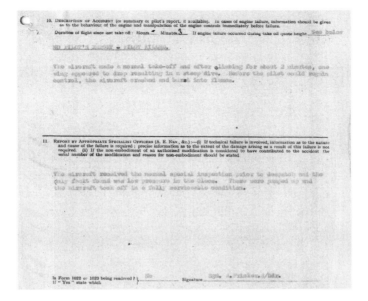

4th Page

The remarks of the unit commander show that a court of inquiry was held into the loss.

2. Form 412 *'Proceedings of Court of Inquiry or Investigation'*

After an accident, if the cause was not known, an investigation was undertaken to try to find the reason and prevent a reoccurrence. Sometimes the investigation was conducted by a specialist officer, usually an engineering officer, but if there was evidence of negligence or fault or when the circumstances of the accident were doubtful the RAF held a court of inquiry. Such investigations were also held into non-natural deaths not caused by enemy action. A Court of Inquiry record or an Investigation record is known as the Proceedings and was submitted using RAF Form 412. Courts of inquiry could apportion blame and make findings which could affect pensions payable to dependents of deceased air crew.

The Proceedings of Courts of Inquiry and Investigation reports by Investigating Officers were regarded as being 'privileged' as they belonged to a class of document which was not available for general disclosure. This rule was based on the principle that witnesses should be able to give their evidence in the knowledge that it would remain confidential. The court members and any investigating officer also had to be confident that any statements they might make and any opinion expressed would not be made common knowledge. Only those persons who required to have access for specific purposes were permitted to see Proceedings of Courts of Inquiry. The rules did allow information obtained from the proceedings to be given to the next of kin provided no mention was made that the source was the Proceedings.[6] Today, some elements, but not the entire proceedings, of modern service inquiries (which no longer apportion blame) are released.

In some instances, copies of Form 412 Proceedings of Courts of Inquiry or Investigation have found their way onto Casualty P Files for flying accidents. Where this has occurred, the decision has been made that the papers forming the Proceedings of the Court of Inquiry will be closed to the public. However, a short note giving the findings of the Courts of Inquiry are often included on Aircraft Accident Cards (Air Ministry Form 1180), copies of which are available from the RAF Museum at Hendon, London.

3. Form 551 *'Report on Accidental or Self-Inflicted Injuries or Immediate Death therefrom'*

The Form 551 report covered a very wide variety of incidents, from sports injuries to training accidents to suicides. Forms 551 were to be sent by units to P4(Cas) when any injury effected an individual's ability to perform their

---

6. Air Ministry Order A1086/43 *Courts of Inquiry – Disclosure of Proceedings.*

duties or when a death occurred. The F551 was then placed on the relevant Casualty P File; the Forms 551 in the Casualty Files held by the National Archives relate to deaths and/or injuries resulting from flying accidents or deaths and injuries which happened on operational flights but were not caused by enemy action. An example of the latter would be casualties occurring as a result of a crash on take-off. Each casualty had a separate F551.

For both flying accident and operational casualties the unit submitting the F551 was to give details of the incident and nature of the casualties. The unit was also to state whether or not a Court of Inquiry had been held or whether the incident was subject to an investigation by an investigating officer. If there was no inquiry or investigation into the incident a full account of what had happened was required to be given in the F551. In the example below an investigation was held and an extract from the Investigating Officer's Report is included at paragraph 4d. The F551 also required that a medical officer provide information on the cause of death or nature of the injuries.

A Form 551 sent to the Casualty Branch for a Sergeant Crossley killed in an aircraft accident.

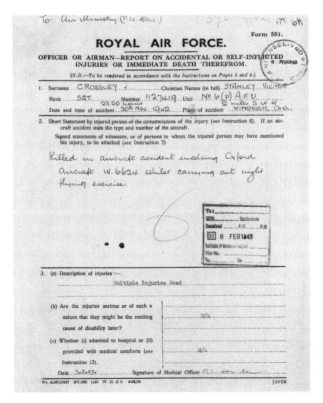

RAF WWII OPERATIONAL

2

4. Commanding Officer's statement :—
   (a) Was the injury sustained
       (i) In the performance of air force duty?..,............ *Yes*
           (*See* Instruction 9)
       (ii) In gliding, a game or other form of physical recreation definitely organised by or with the approval of the proper air force authority? ....*No*
       (iii) On leave?..........*No*
   N.B.—*See* Instruction 8 before completing the following section.

   (b) If the answer to (a) (ii) is in the affirmative state
       (i) By whom was the game, etc., organised and under whose authority?......................
       (ii) The nature of the game, etc., (*e.g.*, football)......................
       (iii) Was the officer or airman detailed to take part in it (a) as a member of an air force team, or (b) to compete as an individual? ....(a)............(b)............
           NOTE.—Questions (iv) to (vi) to be answered in addition only if the injury was sustained at practice. *N/A*
       (iv.) For what service event was the practice held? ....
       (v) Was the officer or airman a selected representative of an Air Force unit practising under authority?......................
       (vi) If so, under what authority and supervision? ....
       (vii) If the injury was sustained in gliding was the injured person participating in the gliding as a member of a Service gliding club under the supervision of an officer or fully qualified airman pilot ? ....

   (c) If sustained in a game, etc., but not in an organised game, state if there are any special circumstances which should be taken into account if and when the question of attributability comes to be decided (K.R. 3612(2))......................

   (d) Was the injury due to his own fault, i.e., did it arise from negligence or misconduct or any blameworthy cause within his own control? *Extract from Investigating Officers Remarks:*
       If so, state in what way..*"The cause of the accident was failure to maintain*
   (e) Was anyone else to blame? If so, give name and particulars *equilibrium by instruments"*

   (f) Is the accident being investigated by
       (i) Court of Inquiry? If so, state date and place ......*No*
       (ii) An investigating officer?............*Yes*
           (see para. 1325 (3) (a) (ii) of K.R. as to endorsement required in certain circumstances)

   (g) In the case of an airman, if the answer to question (d) is in the affirmative, state whether hospital charges have been or will be recovered (*see* Instruction 12) ......*No*

Date.. *5th February* ....1943 Signature.......... *F/L*
                              for G/C
                              Commanding *No 6 (P) A.F.U.*

72

Chapter 6

Kinforming

The Air Ministry was responsible for ensuring the nominated next of kin of casualties were informed of the death, wounding, injury or sickness of their relative. This was either done at unit level or by the Casualty Branch. However, which next of kin were to be informed was the choice of the individual serviceman or woman. Everyone joining the armed forces was required to nominate a next of kin to be notified in case they became a casualty, and provide the appropriate contact details. There were legal parameters as to who could be officially counted as a next of kin;[1] the nominated next of kin was usually a spouse or parent but some personnel with elderly parents chose to have a sibling informed rather than their parents directly. Personnel could change their nominated next of kin at any time if they so wished. This usually happened on marriage when a wife was nominated in place of a parent or when the nominated next of kin died.

In addition to nominating next of kin, personnel could also nominate 'a person to be notified of casualty'. As fiancées did not have next of kin status they were often given as a person to be notified. Similarly, a parent could be included in this category when a spouse was the nominated next of kin. Siblings were sometimes nominated, especially if they were also serving in the armed forces and/or posted overseas in the expectation that the Air Ministry could get the news to them faster than a member of the family.

In the RAF, copies of next of kin information was held centrally (it was included on the individual's Record of Service, kept at the RAF Record Office) and also locally by the individual's unit. In an attempt to ensure that the next of kin details were current, both King's Regulations and Air Council Instruction paragraph 2132 clause 9 stated that personnel were required to check their nominated next of kin particulars on 30 June each year. Any changes to next of kin details were to be notified to the appropriate departments.

---

1. The legally recognised next of kin in order of preference is given in Appendix E.

The casualty's unit included the details they held about nominated next of kin in the Crash Signal sent to the Casualty Branch. The RAF Record Office also supplied the information they held to P4(Cas). The Casualty Branch used an 'in house' form to collate personal information about the casualty (name, rank, number, date of birth and religion) and nominated next of kin details. These forms are sometimes found on the Casualty P Files.

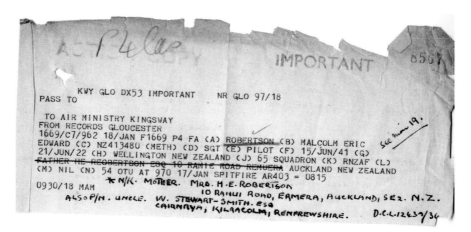

A signal providing information about the casualty and their next of kin was sent by the RAF Records Office, Gloucester, to P4 (Casualty). In addition to his name rank and number, his religion is shown as Methodist (METH), his date and place of birth is given (21/Jun/22 Wellington New Zealand), he was serving with 65 Squadron and was a member of the Royal New Zealand Air Force (RNZAF). The handwritten additions were made by P4(Cas) staff. The annotation DCL indicates that the name of the pilot has appeared on a Declared Casualty List. When a casualty was confirmed casualty the name appeared on a Confirmed Casualty List (which was given as 'CCL'). The annotation 'ALSO P/N UNCLE' shows that Sergeant Robertson had nominated his uncle (who lived in the UK) as a 'Person to be notified'. As Sergeant Robertson belonged to the RNZAF their Casualty Section would have been informed by P4(Cas) and the RNZAF would have informed his mother in Auckland.

Whenever possible the commanding officers of units within the UK were expected to notify the nominated next of kin (provided they lived in the UK) of the death of or injury to their relative by telegram. They were to use a standardised form of words which would read, for example, when a person was known to have been killed:

'Deeply regret to inform you that your son (or husband/brother/etc) Pilot Officer David Greville NAIRN lost his life on 24 FEBRUARY 1942 on air

operations (or in an aircraft accident/enemy action (air raid etc) or other cause). Letter follows. Please accept my profound sympathy.'

Copies of the telegrams sent by units to next of kin are rarely found on Casualty P Files, however copies of telegrams sent by P4(Cas) to next of kin are included. These are normally in the form of a carbon copy of the handwritten message sent by the Telegrams Section of P4(Cas) for despatch by the communications centre. The Casualty Branch sent notifying telegrams to next of kin when the unit's Crash Signal stated that the next of kin had *not* been informed by them or when casualties occurred abroad. P4(Cas) also informed anybody nominated as 'a person to be notified'.

Unit Commanding Officers (both home and abroad) were also required to send a letter of condolence to their casualties' next of kin. In these letters COs were permitted to give, in confidence, as much information as they felt appropriate about the incident. If a squadron commander was unable to write for any reason then the letter was to be sent by the Station Commander. Occasionally copies of these letters are found on P Files; these are primarily ones sent by overseas units and usually include a brief description of the funeral. Copies of letters sent by station padres or chaplains to next of kin are also sometimes found on the P Files.

Informing next of kin about non-fatal casualties

The Air Ministry also informed next of kin about non-fatal casualties. For personnel who were missing, wounded or injured the telegram sent began 'Regret to inform you'. Below is an example of the wording of a telegram sent to the relatives of a non-fatal casualty:

'Regret to inform you that your son (or husband/brother/ etc) Sergeant James Christopher GODWIN has been admitted to RAF Hospital Halton (or station sick quarters) on 18 May 1942 and placed on the seriously (or dangerously) ill list suffering from wounds (or injuries if flying accident) received as the result air operations (or as the result of a flying accident).'

The more seriously wounded went to hospitals, the less serious cases were often treated in RAF Station Medical Centres which had their own medical staff and wards. At home the hospital to which the casualty was admitted could be one of the RAF's own Hospitals (such as those at Halton, Ely, Wroughton, Branston and Rauceby), a wartime Emergency

Medical Service (EMS) hospital or a local civilian hospital. Overseas RAF personnel were admitted to RAF General and Field Hospitals, for example the 5th RAF General Hospital in Egypt, or to hospitals belonging to the Army or Royal Navy, for example in Malta RAF casualties went to the Army's 90th General Hospital at Imtarfa and sometimes to the Bigli Royal Naval Hospital.

The medical conditions of casualties were a given a classification:

- Dangerously Ill (DI) where the patient was very ill and there was an immediate possibility that they might die.
- Very Seriously Ill (VSI), where the patient might well die.
- Seriously Ill (SI) where the patient was seriously ill but there was no immediate likelihood of death.
- Slight – non-life threatening.

At home, when a casualty was classified as dangerously wounded or injured the unit concerned immediately informed the nominated next of kin by telegram and a copy of the message was sent to P4(Cas). The unit

A casualty in a British Field Hospital, North Africa 1942.

informed the next of kin where their relative was being treated so that the next of kin could visit the casualty. When the casualty's medical condition was classified as dangerous local civilian police throughout the UK were authorised to issue the next of kin with a free 3rd class rail warrant when the relatives showed them the RAF's notifying telegram. Free travel warrants were not available in cases were the casualty was not in a dangerous condition. However, qualifying relatives were able to travel with a half-price fare by using concession vouchers supplied by the casualty's unit. These concession vouchers were only available to wives or other relatives who were in receipt of a dependant's allowance.

Any change of condition from 'dangerous' to 'very seriously ill' or 'seriously ill' were notified to P4(Cas) by the hospitals. In the UK relatives were kept informed of any change either by the unit or by the hospital. Where relatives lived overseas or the casualty occurred overseas, P4(Cas) required weekly updates in dangerous cases and fortnightly in serious cases so that next of kin could be kept informed. P4(Cas) placed such information on the appropriate Casualty File.

Chapter 7

Funerals and Burials in the United Kingdom

Corporal Greenwood of the Fire Section, Wing Commander Mackie CO of 157 Squadron and Squadron Leader Brown, the Station Medical Officer, try to reach the crew of Mosquito DZ707 which crashed at RAF Predannack, Cornwall, on 26 February 1944 while on a training flight. Also in the picture are the station padre and fire crews. The pilot was killed but the navigator was rescued.

Civil Burial & Death Certificates

In the UK disposal of bodies cannot take place without the correct permissions to move, bury or otherwise dispose of the remains, which must be given by the Registrar of Births and Deaths for the district in which the death occurs. Permission is given through the issue of a Disposal (Burial) Certificate and a Death Certificate by the Registrar who registers the death by making an entry in the Register of Deaths (Death Certificates are certified copies of the registrar's entry in the Register of Deaths). In Northern Ireland a Registrar's Certificate was issued to confirm that information of the death had been received. The Disposal Certificate must be issued before a body can be buried or cremated. Proof of a death is also required before the heirs of the deceased can acquire the legal right (known as 'probate') to any money, property and possessions left (collectively called 'the estate') and be able to settle the deceased's estate. Similarly proof of death is needed for any claim concerning pensions or insurance etc that might be available.

During the Second World War when a person serving with the RAF died in the UK it was the responsibility of the RAF to provide information concerning the death to civil Registrars of Births and Deaths but it was the civil Registrar who was then responsible for issuing the Death Certificate to the next of kin. Copies of the civil Death Certificates issued by registrars are rarely found on RAF Casualty Files. However other documentation relating to the death is sometimes included, for example the information required by the civilian registrar on a death due to war operations was provided by the relevant commanding officer using the Air Ministry Form AFWD (Air Force War Death). Copies of these forms are occasionally found on Casualty Files and further information about them is provided below.

Civilian Coroners' Inquests

The spate of recent civil Coroners' Inquests held for repatriated casualties from the Iraq and Afghanistan conflicts have led some family researchers to assume that coroners' inquests were always held for members of armed forces killed during the Second World War. However, this was not the case; while some coroners' inquests were held for deaths in the UK which were due to aircraft accidents, coroners' inquests were not held when personnel were lost on operations.

The 1941 issue of AP1922 stated that His Majesty's Coroners could chose to hold an inquest where a death was due to an enemy air raid[1] and also stipulated that commanding officers must inform the civil coroner of accidental (including aircraft) or natural deaths. The 1943 edition also made

---

1. AP1922 *Notes on Casualty Procedure in War* dated 1941 Section IX note attached to para 83.

it clear that HM Coroners in England, Wales and Northern Ireland, and the Procurator Fiscal in Scotland, had the right to make the final decision as to whether or not a death was due to war operations.

Although HM Coroners had a duty to investigate the circumstances of sudden, unnatural, violent or uncertified deaths, they also had discretion as to whether an inquest was held or not. There are instances of inquests being held into Second World War aircraft accidents, but records of these inquests rarely appear in RAF Casualty Files. However, reports submitted to the Casualty Branch by RAF officers attending an inquest in an official capacity are sometimes included.

Records of HM Coroners' Inquests are civil records and (where they have survived) are normally held in the archives of the district in which they were held, such as County Archives. Another source of information on coroners' inquests are local newspapers as their reporters often attended inquests. It is sometimes possible to find these articles either through a local newspaper's own archives or through the British Museum's British Newspaper Library.

Death Due to War Operations

The Air Ministry Air Publication (AP) 1922 *Notes on Casualty Procedure in War* gave instructions on casualty handling, including on the subject of death certification. When the death occurred in the UK the commanding officer (CO) of an RAF unit could take action to certify the death of an officer, airman/airwoman or any other person employed by the RAF or subject to the Air Force Act if they were killed as a result of 'war operations'. In the 1941 edition of AP1922 the definition given of 'death due to war operations' was:

1. Death during action taken by any of the armed forces of the enemy.
2. Death during action taken by any of His Majesty's Forces in combatting or engaged on a flight against the enemy or in repelling an imagined attack by the enemy or
3. Death in the course of duty upon any warning of the imminence of an attack by the enemy.[2]

---

2. AP1922 *Notes on Casualty Procedure in War* 1941 edition Section IX para 83.

A later edition of AP1922, issued in 1943, extended the definition to cover aircraft accidents. The definition of 'death due to war operations' as given in the 1943 version of AP1922 was:

1. A death due to the operations of the armed forces of the enemy.
2. A death due to the operations of any of His Majesty's Forces while in action against the enemy (including death by friendly fire) or
3. While acting in the course of their duty on any warning of imminent attack by the enemy (for example air raids on airfields and RAF installations).
4. A death due to an accident involving an aircraft of a naval, military or air force or which was caused by the descent from such an aircraft.

The last cause of death had provisos: the deceased had to be a **male** member of HM Forces, be acting in the course of his duties, and the aircraft had to be operating under the orders of a naval, military or air force. The latter wording enabled the definition to cover accidents involving Allied personnel and personnel from occupied countries.[3]

The 1943 edition of AP1922 also stated that the Secretary of State for Air and the Admiralty had the power to issue an order that accidental death of **female** personnel in HM Forces (as at 4 above) could be deemed to be as the result of war operations. The death of a civilian in any RAF aircraft accident was not regarded as being due to war operations.[4]

Air Ministry Form AFWD – 'Air Force War Death'
The extended definition of 'death due to war operations' provided in the 1943 edition of AP1922 allowed deaths resulting from aircraft accidents during training to be classed as being 'due to war operations'. The use of this form normally dispensed with the need for a Coroner's Inquest to be held which enabled burial arrangements to be made without undue delay. The Form AFWD was sent by the RAF unit to the civil registrar responsible for the district in which the death had occurred. The registrar then registered the death by making an entry in the Register of Deaths and issued the Burial Certificate for the disposal of the body.

The definition of 'death due to war operations' provided in the 1943 edition of AP1922 was extended to allow deaths resulting from aircraft accidents

---

3. AP1922 *Notes on Casualty Procedure in War* 1943 edition Section VI para 180.
4. Ibid.

during training to be classed as being 'due to war operations'. This enabled the commanding officer to certify deaths resulting from such accidents by submitting the RAF Form AFWD to the appropriate civil Registrar of Births and Deaths. Although unusual, copies of Forms AFWD issued in these circumstances are sometimes found on RAF Casualty Files.

Funeral arrangements

Funeral arrangements for RAF personnel who died in the UK were made taking into account the wishes of the next of kin wherever possible. Correspondence with them concerning UK funeral arrangements is sometimes found in the P Files, primarily those concerning aircraft accident deaths. Some of the correspondence comes in the form of copies of telegrams from units to next of kin informing them of the arrangements made to transport the body back to the next of kin for a private burial. Other correspondence found between P4(Cas) and the next of kin relates to what next of kin could claim by way of expenses towards private funeral costs. Permissible funeral expenses were clearly laid down in a number of RAF directives (Air Publication 837 – *Manual of Administration in the RAF (War Edition)*[5] and Air Ministry Order A.835 of 1943) and varied according to what type of funeral had been selected by the next of kin. Headstones were provided at public expense through the Imperial War Graves Commission when a Service funeral was chosen. Private headstones were only permitted when the burial was not in an RAF cemetery or in an RAF plot in a public graveyard.

The units were responsible for informing the next of kin about the options for funeral arrangements. The next of kin of members of the RAF who were killed or died while serving in the UK were normally offered three options of funeral, details of which were provided in a leaflet. It was the responsibility of the RAF station where the body was held to send a letter and accompanying leaflet concerning funeral arrangements to the next of kin. The options offered before 1943 were:

- An RAF funeral with Service Honours, the funeral to take place at the RAF Station where the deceased was stationed or, if the person had died away from their home station, at the RAF station at which they

---

5. Held in National Archives reference AIR10/2264.

had died or the body was taken. Following the funeral the burial took place in the RAF station's local churchyard or cemetery. However, in 1943 RAF Regional Cemeteries were introduced which replaced the cemeteries or churchyards in the vicinity of RAF stations for service burials (see Regional Cemeteries below).

- A private funeral at a place chosen by next of kin. When this option was chosen the RAF would arrange for the body to be sent to the next of kin's home address by road or rail. If the body was moved by rail the next of kin were advised to arrange for an undertaker to meet the train. The relatives were sent the details of the transport arrangements and, when transport was by train, the train's arrival time by the RAF station despatching the body. These details were usually sent by telegram and copies of these are sometimes found on RAF Casualty Files.
- A funeral at the RAF Cemetery at Brookwood near Farnborough. This option was only available when the death had occurred within some eighty miles of London. The Imperial (now Commonwealth) War Graves Commission was responsible for the upkeep of this cemetery. Service honours would be accorded at the RAF station where the death had occurred and also, if possible, at the RAF cemetery itself.

The information leaflet was sent to the next of kin to help the relatives make an informed decision as quickly as possible and they were asked to notify the RAF station which had sent it of their decision.[6] The RAF did not offer cremation as a choice, although this option was sometimes chosen by next of kin who preferred a private funeral.

When the nominated next of kin lived abroad and it was impossible to ascertain their wishes regarding the funeral quickly enough, the RAF station concerned held a Service funeral and interment. This mostly happened when the casualty came from an Empire or Allied country and was serving either with the RAF or a Dominion Air Force. Overseas next of kin wishing to have the remains brought back were initially informed that any question of reinterment could only be considered at the end of the war. However, the question of repatriation was closed when the Dominions decided against the repatriation of their dead (see Repatriation).[7]

---

6. AP1922 *Notes on Casualty Procedure in War* Appendix F (i) (ii).
7. Ibid Appendix J.

An RAF Burial at Brookwood in April 1941.

Pre-1943 Funeral Costs – Other Ranks

Before 1943 when the next of kin of an airman or woman who died while serving (whatever the cause of death) chose the option of having a Service funeral, all the costs would be met by the RAF. If the next of kin could not afford the cost of a return rail journey to attend the funeral, two free rail warrants were available to them from their local police station on production of the telegram notifying the next of kin of the death.

If a private funeral was chosen by the relatives, the cost of transporting the body to their home address (provided this was not outside the UK) was paid for by the RAF. In addition a grant of £7 10 shillings was payable from public funds towards funeral costs. The RAF station handling the arrangements deducted any expenses incurred by them including the cost of the coffin, provided by the RAF, in which the remains were sent home. If the expenses incurred by the RAF station were less than the £7 10 shillings grant the remaining money was either credited to the deceased's service estate or paid to the next of kin. Any balance was usually very small and the costs of the private funeral had to be met by the next of kin. No assistance was available from RAF charitable funds to assist with private funeral costs, and families were expected to raise their own headstones.

Pre 1943 Funeral costs – Officers

The costs of officers' Service funerals were only paid from public funds if the officer died as the result of an aircraft accident or enemy action in the air or on the ground but not if they were on leave (e.g. killed in an air raid at home). Any funeral costs however, were not to exceed the amount allowed for the funeral of an airman. As with other ranks, two return rail warrants were available when relatives could not afford to travel to the RAF station for the funeral.

Where the next of kin chose to arrange a private funeral, the officer's body was transported to the home address at public expense. If the officer was killed flying, (either in an aircraft accident or by enemy action) the costs of a private funeral up to a maximum of £14 was paid from public funds. The cost of the coffin, which was provided by the RAF to transport the body, was deducted from the £14 before it was paid, or recouped from the next of kin if the deceased officer did not qualify for the grant.

No public money was paid to the next of kin of officers who did not meet the above criteria other than those to cover the costs of transporting the body to the home address for a private funeral.

Funeral Provision post-1943

In 1943 the government decided more should be done to help with the costs of funerals of serving members of the armed forces. For the RAF this decision was embodied in Air Ministry Order (AMO) A835 of 1943. The order declared that '*in future no distinction will be made in the matter of funeral entitlement between officers and airmen and others*'. The new rules would apply to all full time members of the Air Forces who died while serving, whatever the cause of death. Full time members were defined as:

a. An officer of the RAF serving on the active list.
b. An officer of the RAF Volunteer Reserve (RAFVR) (other than an officer of the Education branch[8]) who was mobilized during the war and was in receipt of service pay and allowances. The majority of wartime air crew served in the RAFVR.
c. An officer of the Reserve of Air Force Officers, the Auxiliary Air Force or the Auxiliary Reserve of Officers mobilized during the war and in receipt of service pay and allowances.
d. An airman of the RAF.
e. An airman of the RAF Reserve, the RAF Volunteer Reserve, the Auxiliary Air Force or the Auxiliary Air Force Reserve mobilized during the war and in receipt of service pay and allowances.

---

8. For status of Education Branch officers see Appendix I.

    f. A member of the Women's Auxiliary Air Force (other than a non-mobile member) mobilized during the war and in receipt of service pay and allowances.

    g. A member of Princess Mary's Royal Air Force Nursing Service not on the retired list.

    h. A member of Princess Mary's Royal Air Force Nursing Service Reserve mobilized during the war and in receipt of service pay and allowances.

    i. A full-time member of a Dominion or Allied Air Force operating with the RAF where the responsibility for funeral arrangements was taken by the RAF.

Further categories were included to cover members of Voluntary Aid Detachments employed with the RAF, RAF officers on half pay who died of causes attributable to RAF service, and full-time members of the Air Forces mentioned above who were discharged from service while undergoing treatment in hospital or another medical establishment and who died without leaving their place of treatment. AMO A835 permitted these latter individuals also to be classed as 'serving'.

In addition to extending eligibility, there was more generous funding available. All the costs of a Service funeral would be met and coffins of the same standard were to be provided for both officers and other ranks. A Service funeral was still not available when a serving member died at home on leave but now an allowance of £10 was payable towards the costs of a private funeral for the individual.

Burials

While only some RAF Casualty P Files contain information about funerals, most do contain information about place of burial. The exceptions are primarily files relating to personnel with 'no known graves'. In these cases the files will normally contain information as to where the individual is commemorated. This would usually be on one of the Air Forces' Memorials such the one at Runnymede which commemorates by name over 20,000 airmen (and women) who were lost operating from bases in the UK and North and West Europe and who have no known grave (see also Chapter 14).

Place of Burial
Private funerals and burials took place all over the UK and solitary RAF headstones can be found in many churchyards. Service burials, i.e. those

conducted by the RAF, were more restricted as to location. At the outbreak of the war the Imperial War Graves Commission (IWGC) made arrangements with burial authorities in the UK for special areas, known as Service burial plots, to be set aside in 1,236 local cemeteries. The IWGC took responsibility (and still does as the CWGC) for the maintenance of these plots and the graves they contained. The IWGC also provided permanent headstones to replace the temporary wooden ones erected by the War Office Graves Registration department immediately following a Service funeral.

The Air Ministry pointed out to RAF Stations that an RAF burial did not take place in the graveyard of an RAF station's local parish church by right but only with the agreement of the parish priest,[9] and made it clear that the Air Ministry would not fund the extension of parish graveyards even if the need for an extension arose because of the number of RAF burials which had taken place in the churchyard. The Air Ministry instructed units that, whenever possible, RAF burials in the UK should take place in these special Service plots except when the burial was to take place in an RAF cemetery or a private funeral had been chosen. Commanding officers were responsible for ensuring that Service burials did not take place at unapproved burial grounds. Although the RAF did not provide special facilities for burial observances of other faiths, RAF burial plots and RAF regional cemeteries were open to all Air Force personnel regardless of religion or creed.

RAF Regional Cemeteries

As early as 1940 the Air Ministry had encouraged the use of the RAF burial plots which would be under the care of the Imperial War Graves Commission. They planned a series of Regional Cemeteries within existing civilian cemeteries. The RAF cemetery within the private Brookwood Cemetery, near Farnborough, was already in existence and there were plans for three more RAF regional cemeteries. In 1943 it was announced that in fact a further five RAF regional cemeteries had been established within existing civilian cemeteries.[10] These were at:

1. Bath (RAF cemetery within Haycombe Cemetery) covering RAF stations in Somerset, Gloucestershire, Wiltshire, Devon, Cornwall, Dorset, Worcestershire, Herefordshire, and the Welsh counties of Monmouthshire, Glamorgan, Cardigan, Carmarthenshire and Pembrokeshire.

---

9. Air Ministry Order A.143/1942.
10. Air Ministry Order A600/1943 RAF Burial Scheme.

2. Cambridge (RAF cemetery within Newmarket Road Cemetery) covering RAF stations in Cambridgeshire, Bedfordshire, Norfolk, Suffolk, Lincolnshire, Rutland and Huntingdonshire.
3. Chester (RAF cemetery within the Blacon Cemetery) covering RAF stations in Cheshire, Lancashire, Cumbria, Staffordshire, Shropshire, and the Welsh counties of Montgomery, Merioneth, Caernarvon, Denbigh, Flintshire and Anglesey.
4. Oxford (RAF cemetery in the Botley Cemetery) covering RAF stations in Oxfordshire, Berkshire, Buckinghamshire, Warwickshire, Leicestershire, Nottinghamshire, Derbyshire and Northamptonshire.
5. Harrogate (RAF cemetery within Stonefall Cemetery) covering RAF stations in Yorkshire, County Durham and Northumberland. The already existing RAF cemetery at Brookwood was to cover Hampshire, Sussex, Kent, Surrey, Essex, Hertfordshire and Middlesex.

The Air Ministry decreed that all Service burials were now to take place in these Regional Cemeteries, however, exceptionally, they could continue in a churchyard which had already been extended specifically for RAF burials. Private burials could continue to take place anywhere.

Record of Burial

When a burial had taken place, whether it was a private or a Service burial, the RAF station involved was required to provide details about it to the Casualty Branch. These details were to include where and when the burial had taken place or, if a private cremation had taken place, where this had occurred. The details were provided on RAF Form 1755 the 'Burial Return' and these were added to the Casualty P Files. The Burial Returns contained in RAF Casualty P Files are a useful source of information, especially where a private funeral has taken place. Most RAF Casualty Files relating to individuals who died within the UK and those of personnel who died at RAF units abroad contain the RAF Form 1755. This small form provides the service number, name and unit of the individual, date of death, the place, date and time of burial, religion and the means by which the body was identified. Sometimes the name of the officiating clergyman is included. When relating to a cremation the information usually includes the name of the crematorium and date of cremation. On occasion the F1755 also includes a note of a memorial plaque erected following cremation. It should be noted that the RAF did not provide cremations as an option; all cremations were privately arranged by the next of kin.

The Burial Return (F1755) above is for Sergeant Malcolm Robertson of the RNZAF. He was killed when his Spitfire AR403 crashed in the grounds of Wedderlie House, Westruther, in the Scottish Borders. The Burial Return states that he was buried in Craigton Cemetery, Glasgow, in grave number 219 E. The Return also shows he was serving with 65 Squadron, which was designated 'East India', based at RAF Drem near Edinburgh. His rank is given as sergeant pilot. (A differentiation was made between air crew sergeants and the much more experienced ground trades sergeants). His religion is given as Presbyterian, the date of his death as 16 January 1943. The date of his burial was 26 January 1943.

The Return states that his remains were identified by his identity discs by the authorities at RAF Charterhall, the nearest RAF station to the crash site. The Burial Return also records that his personal effects were sent to the Standing Committee of Adjustment (see Chapter on Disposal of Effects) on 1 February 1943. The signatory of the Burial Return is the commanding officer of 65 Squadron, Squadron Leader J.E. Storrar.

In July 2012, a team of aviation archaeologists excavating the crash site of Spitfire AR403 found human remains. These were identified as leg bones belonging to Sergeant Robertson and were interred with his main remains (which had been recovered and buried in 1943) at a rededication service in August 2013.

89

Chapter 8

Overseas Funerals and Burials

An RAF burial at Hinaidi Military Cemetery, Bagdad, Iraq.

Funerals at Overseas Units

When a death occurred at overseas RAF bases or at units operating in the field, the next of kin were informed by the Air Ministry Casualty Branch, P4(Cas). In addition to the RAF permanent bases in various parts of the world there were many RAF air crew training at flying schools in Canada, Rhodesia, South Africa and America under various joint training schemes. Inevitably there were flying accidents at these Air Training Schools and P4(Cas) was notified of any casualties which resulted. The Casualty

Branch then relayed the information to the next of kin. There were also the operational casualties suffered by RAF units operating from temporary airfields in the various operational theatres. These units notified the Casualty Branch who then informed the next of kin.

Due to local conditions overseas and, sometimes, communication difficulties, funerals and burials very often had to take place without the next of kin being consulted as to their wishes. In these cases Service funerals and burials were held, and the commanding officer of the deceased, or the chaplain who conducted the funeral and burial, would send the next of kin a letter describing the funeral telling them where and when it had taken place, who attended, what military honours were rendered (for example that a bugler had played the *Last Post*) who had laid wreaths, and the place of burial. In addition to the details submitted by the overseas unit, some also enclosed photographs. These were passed on to the next of kin; only rarely are copies of these photographs found on Casualty P Files.

All overseas units, whether on permanent bases or operating in the field, were required to submit the Burial Return. The information required was the same as for Burial Returns submitted in the UK but RAF units in the field were required to state whether a durable grave marker had been placed

RAF and USAAF personnel line the road at the funeral of Wing Commander Lance Wade at Mirandola near Modena, Italy. A former hurricane pilot who was on the staff of the Desert Air Force, Wade was killed when the Spitfire he was piloting crashed on take-off at Foggia on 12 January 1944. Note the coffin covered in a Union Jack and the RAF and US chaplains. Wade was a US citizen who had joined the RAF and had turned down the opportunity to transfer to the USAAF when America entered the war. At some point Wade's remains were reburied in Texas. This is most unusual, as repatriation of remains of RAF personnel was not permitted.

or whether one needed to be supplied by the Army Graves Registration Unit covering their area. The overseas Burial Returns were not sent directly to the Casualty Branch but were sent through the Base Personnel Staff Officer (BPSO) who was responsible for administrative matters. If no BPSO was present, the unit sent the Burial Return to their Air Headquarters for onwards transmission to the Casualty Branch.

Burials normally took place in British military cemeteries which existed throughout the Empire and in various dependencies. For example, in the case of casualties suffered during the siege of Malta, the majority of Air Force dead were buried in the Capuccini Naval Cemetery, Kalkara. New British military cemeteries were also established during the war to accommodate the dead following a major campaign, for example those in Syracuse and Catania in Sicily created after Operation Husky (the invasion of Sicily) in July 1943. British military cemeteries were later established in Germany and the Far East. These were later handed over to the Imperial War Graves Commission. Now the Commonwealth War Graves Commission maintains them on behalf of the member countries of the Commission, which are the United Kingdom, Australia, New Zealand, Canada, India and South Africa.

Field Graves

There were occasions when it was not immediately possible to recover a body from a crashed aircraft for burial in a cemetery. The reasons for this included enemy activity in the area, nature of the terrain, and for air crew, the isolated location of their crash site. When this was the case air crew were often buried close to their aircraft in what is termed a Field Grave. It was hoped that at some future date the remains would be recovered for reburial in a proper cemetery. In the North African Western Desert campaign the remains of Allied and Axis air crew were found by ground forces of both sides as the battle ebbed and flowed over the same ground. Any remains, Allied or Axis, found by the Allied forces were buried and information on the location of the burial recorded and passed to the Army Graves Registration Units. This was done in accordance with the Geneva Conventions which required the graves of the belligerent forces to be recorded so that they might always be found. Information about the burial of Air Force personnel was passed by the Grave Registration Units to the Air Ministry Casualty Branch. The German Afrika Corps forwarded information about Allied bodies they found through the International Committee of the Red Cross and the Allies reciprocated with information on German and Italian dead.

Marking a field grave at a crash site in North Africa.

Field Grave of Squadron Leader P.R. Heath of 3 Squadron RAAF buried beside the remains of his Gloster Gladiator N5750 about a mile from Sidi Barrani in the Western Desert. He was killed on 19 November 1940 while undertaking escort duties for a low level reconnaissance aircraft when his aircraft was shot down by an Italian CR42 aircraft of 82 Squadriglia, 13 Gruppo. Sqn Ldr Heath's body was buried by Captain D.P.J. Lloyd of the 11th Hussars. His remains were later recovered from his field grave and he is now buried in Halfaya Sollum War Cemetery, Egypt.

Air Crew Dead in Occupied Europe and Germany

'They [belligerents] shall further ensure that the dead are honourably interred, that their graves are respected and marked so that they may always be found.' Geneva Conventions Chapter 1 Article 4 27 July 1929

The RAF burial of a Luftwaffe crew shot down over a Coastal Command airfield in the north of England. The coffins are draped in the flag of Nazi Germany. Note the civilians paying respects by removing their hats.

Post-war RAF and Dominion air forces graves in Europe were registered by the Army Graves Registration Service and the RAF Missing Research Enquiry Service (MRES). Wherever possible the MRES confirmed the identity of the occupants. The Form 1755 Burial Return was not used to record the burials of air crew in occupied Europe or Germany. Instead a Graves Registration Report Form (AFW3372) or a Schedule of Final Resting Place was sent to the Air Ministry Casualty Branch and are included on the Casualty File.[1] Sometimes 'Burial Detail Acceptance' forms are also found

---

1. See Chapter 13 Burial Documentation.

on Casualty P Files. Copies went to the Imperial War Graves Commission to provide the location of the graves which would come under their care.

Where Allied Air Force personnel were buried by the German or Italian authorities, information about the place of burial was usually sent through the International Red Cross Committee to the relevant authority. For RAF and colonial air crew the information was passed to the British Red Cross who forwarded it to the Air Ministry where it was placed on the relevant Casualty File. Post-war captured German Death Cards added to the information already held by the Allies on burial places. Burials were also conducted by the people of enemy occupied countries, either on the instructions of German authorities or sometimes secretly and without the Germans' permission. Information about these burials was passed to the Air Ministry by a variety of means. Some information arrived during the war, passed on by veterans' organisations or resistance movements, some came to light as the Allies moved through liberated countries after D-Day and some was not received until the end of the war. Whatever the source of the information about last resting places of members of RAF or Dominion Air Force personnel, and of foreign nationals serving with or under the umbrella of the RAF (e.g Polish Air Force (PAF)), it was passed to the Casualty Branch who were eager for any scrap of information to add to the Casualty Files.

In countries which were occupied by the Germans many of the Air Force graves remained in situ at the request of local people who gave undertakings to care for them, but some were moved to British Military or Imperial War Grave cemeteries for a variety of reasons. In France and the Netherlands graves of air crew can be found in many local cemeteries as well as in the larger plots used by the Germans to bury Allied casualties. An example of the latter is Guidel Communal Cemetery in western France which was used by the Germans as a 'regional' cemetery for Allied dead washed ashore or taken from crashed aircraft. Guidel Cemetery contains the graves of 115 RAF and Dominion Air Force dead in a section maintained by the Commonwealth War Graves Commission.

Many aircraft lost on operations in Europe crashed in Germany, some 1,577 in the Ruhr area alone. In Germany, all bar a very few air crew graves were moved into British military cemeteries which were later placed in the care of the Imperial war Graves Commission. RAF and Dominion air crew formed a large percentage of the British and Empire casualties who were buried in Germany. Within days of the war ending the Air Council discussed the question of the air crew who had been buried there. The Air Ministry's Principal Personnel Officers Committee wanted to make an Air Council approved recommendation about the future of these graves to the Secretary of State for War (Chairman of the Imperial War Graves Commission) so, at a meeting on 11 May 1945, the Air Member for Personnel presented the Air Council with three options for the Air Force graves in Germany and asked them which they preferred.[2] The options he gave were:

1. RAF war graves being maintained in permanent cemeteries.
2. The transfer of RAF war graves to territory west of the Rhine.
3. The removal of the RAF war graves out of Germany altogether.

There were worries that the adoption of the option of moving the graves out of Germany would spark requests for the repatriation of graves in other countries. Nevertheless the members of the Air Council were in favour of moving RAF war graves out of Germany back to the UK. In their view it was possible to differentiate between Germany and other countries.

The matter was discussed again at an Air Council meeting on 27 August 1945[3] when it was decided to canvass the views of the Dominions through their representatives at the Imperial War Graves Commission (the High Commissioners of each dominion). The Air Council were told that the Board of Admiralty (for the Royal Navy) supported the transfer of bodies back from Germany to the UK and that similar proposals were favoured by Canada and by the Americans. The War Office (for the Army) had yet to decide.

At a further meeting of the Air Council held on 2 October 1945 they were informed that on 6 September 1945 the Cabinet had discussed the question of what should be done about war graves in Germany and had decided that British war graves should be concentrated in the areas in which the casualties had occurred. The Air Council was not happy with this decision and a draft Cabinet Paper containing their alternative proposal that the RAF graves should be concentrated in one Air Force cemetery west of the Rhine was prepared for submission to the Prime Minister, Clement Attlee. There was a hope that the Prime Minister might approve the proposal without further Cabinet discussion. However, the Secretary of State for Air, Viscount Stansgate DFC (himself an RAF officer in both the First and Second World Wars and whose son Michael had been killed while serving with the RAF), suggested that the Air Ministry should get

---

2. National Archives reference AIR6/75 January 1944 – December 1945 Meetings. Air Council Minutes of 11 May 1945 paragraph 7.
3. AIR6/75 Air Council Meeting 27 August 1945 paragraph 4.

their proposal agreed by the War Office first. However, the War Office did not accept the Air Council proposal and in December the Air Member for Personnel informed the Air Council that a further report taking the War Office view into account had been submitted to the Secretary of State, now Mr Noel-Baker.[4] Nothing came of the Air Council's efforts and the Cabinet decision to concentrate the dead in Germany in the areas where they died was implemented.

A number of British military cemeteries were established in Germany and the Air Force dead were moved to these and buried in special Air Force sections of the cemeteries. These cemeteries are now in the care of the Commonwealth War Graves Commission. The cemeteries containing Air Force graves are:

- Berlin 1939-1945 War Cemetery with 3,204 known graves, 2,606 of which are Air Force
- Becklingen War Cemetery (85 Kilometres north of Hanover) with 2,303 known graves of which 848 are Air Force
- Celle War Cemetery with 208 known graves, of which 32 are Air Force
- Cologne Southern War Cemetery with 23 known Air Force graves.
- Durnbach (45 kilometres south of Munich) with 2,879 known graves, of which 2,588 are Air Force
- Hamburg War Cemetery with 2,096 known graves of which 705 are Air Force
- Hanover War Cemetery with 2,358 known graves of which 1,798 are Air Force
- Keil War Cemetery with 898 known graves of which 803 are Air Force
- Munster Heath War Cemetery with 588 known graves of which 50 are Air Force
- Reichswald Forest War Cemetery (Kleve) with 7,500 known graves of which 3,915 are Air Force
- Rheinberg War Cemetery with 3,183 known graves of which 2,791 are Air Force

There are only twenty-five air crew who remain buried in churchyards and civilian cemeteries in Germany. Some remain because searches for their bodies in the cemeteries were unsuccessful. Each of these burial sites have special memorial stones which read 'Believed To Be Buried In This

---

4. National Archives reference AIR6/75 Air Council Meeting 6 December 1945.

Cemetery'. The churchyards and cemeteries which still contain Air Force Graves are:

- Altdorf Protestant Cemetery where four crew of Stirling EH931 of 620 Squadron which was lost on the night of 5/6 September 1943 are buried.
- Burgoberbach Roman Catholic Churchyard where Flying Officer G.C. Warren who died on 16 March 1945 is buried. He has a memorial in Durnbach Cemetery.
- Parchim Cemetery where five members of the crew who died when Halifax MZ507 of 51 Squadron crashed on the night of 24/25 March 1944 are believed to be buried.
- Oberschleissheim Churchyard where six crew of Lancaster W4185 of 9 Squadron which was lost on 21 December 1942 are buried.
- Retzow Cemetery where there are nine Air Force burials, six are 'Unknown'. The three known burials are two crew members of Lancaster JB727 of 49 Squadron lost on the night of 2/3 January 1944 and one crew member of Lancaster DV376 from 50 Squadron lost on 16 February 1944. Two other members of this crew were concentrated to the Berlin 1939-1945 War Cemetery.

The Air Forces section of Reichswald War Cemetery near Kleve. It is the largest Commonwealth War Grave Commission Cemetery in Germany. (Copyright CWGC)

OVERSEAS FUNERALS AND BURIALS

Burials conducted by German Authorities

Burials of Allied air crew in Germany were conducted by both military and civilian authorities. Germany was divided into administrative areas called Kreis (district) and these were subdivided into Gemeinden (municipalities). It was the civilian authorities of these areas who were primarily responsible for the burial of air crew killed in their area if the German military authorities did not take responsibility. The Ruhr area, a centre of German heavy industry, was frequently bombed and inevitably many air crew were lost there. To cope with the numbers the German authorities in the Ruhr adopted a policy of moving deceased air crew from aircraft crash sites to one of thirteen major concentration cemeteries they set up. At least 3,000 casualties were taken from crash sites to these cemeteries. Post-war this German policy caused difficulties for the RAF Missing Research and Enquiry Service search officers looking for the missing as many of the bodies had been moved to cemeteries fifty to a hundred miles away from their crash site.

Initially the Germans observed the Geneva Conventions and accorded the Allied dead military honours. However, as the war progressed their treatment of the Allied dead became somewhat more perfunctory. Where the Luftwaffe or the Heer (German Army) was involved, burials still tended to follow military practice; however, when German civilian authorities conducted the burials they were very basic, especially those of the RAF bomber crews. This was for a number of reasons. Firstly German civil authorities were staffed by staunch members of the Nazi Party and a number of vindictive orders regarding the treatment of the air crew (who they called *Terrorflieger*) were issued. In addition there was the chaos which ensued from the large-scale Allied attacks on German cities together with a growing anger amongst the civil population induced by the heavy bombing raids and Nazi Party propaganda.

The bodies of Allied air crew were often buried without coffins by the civil authorities. Sometimes they were buried without any form of service and, on a number of occasions, unceremoniously thrown into craters caused by the bombing. There was an instance where a crew were buried in a Jewish cemetery; the Nazi authorities involved meant this to be an insult. Some air crew were buried where their aircraft crashed; this happened to the crew of Lancaster PD263 of 57 Squadron lost on the night of 11 December 1944 in an operation against Heimbach. An RAF search officer from 20 Section, No 4 Missing Research and Enquiry Unit, who was investigating information given to him by locals, found the graves of the crew in Gemünd Forest at a location given as SH3 GSCS 40421/250.000 –

064250 (see Chapter 12 for information on map references) which was near the aircraft crash site. The remains of the crew were recovered and reburied in Rheinberg British Military Cemetery on 1 April 1947.

Repatriation

Any question of a post-war repatriation of the remains of those killed during the Second World War was forestalled by the joint decision made in 1946 by the British and Dominion governments to follow the precedents about burial set in the First World War. In 1914 British remains could be repatriated from France at private expense which meant that only those families who could afford the transport and burial costs were able to bring home their dead. There were also concerns about the condition of the bodies which were being repatriated. In April 1915 this unequal (and some feared insanitary) practice was stopped on the orders of the Adjutant General of the British Army and the dead were buried in the areas in which they fell.[5] In 1917 the Imperial War Graves Commission was founded as it was feared that the graves amongst the battlefields might disappear. After the Armistice in November 1918 a report was presented to the War Graves Commission which recommended that remains buried in France and elsewhere should not be repatriated at public expense or returned to their families for burial. The War Graves Commission accepted this recommendation and, despite a public outcry and a heated Parliamentary debate, the decision not to repatriate bodies from graves in France, Belgium, Germany, Italy and the Middle East was not changed.

This difficult choice was made partly because of the numbers of graves involved, and because of the many dead who had no known grave. To repatriate all the bodies would have caused an enormous logistical problem; hundreds of thousands of bodies would require exhuming, identifying (where possible) and transporting. There was also a view that those who had fought and died together should lie together and have equal treatment in death. The newly created Imperial War Graves Commission was tasked with establishing cemeteries for the dead and now British and Commonwealth dead lie, officers and other ranks together, in large and

---

5. In the early 1960s repatriation of service personnel who died overseas was again permitted at private expense. It was not until the Falklands War of 1982 that next of kin were offered the choice of having their relative buried either in the Falklands British Military Cemetery or brought back to the UK for burial at public expense. The decision to allow repatriation at public expense was not back-dated. Today repatriation of the fallen is the normal practice for the British Armed Forces.

small Commonwealth War Graves Cemeteries scattered through northern France and Belgium (facing the line they gave their lives to defend) and in the other theatres of the First World War.

No decision as to whether or not this precedent was to be followed was made by the British government during the Second World War although the Australian government had announced in 1942 that permission for the exhumation of remains of Australian service personnel buried overseas for repatriation to Australia would not be permitted. Enquiries sent to the British Air Ministry about repatriation received the response that repatriation was not possible in the present circumstances, but the reply did not definitively rule it out at some future date. Any letters from next of kin asking about repatriation were placed on the appropriate P File together with the official response. In early 1946 the Air Ministry publicised the Cabinet decision against repatriation in an Air Ministry Order[6] which stated that '*His Majesty's Governments in the United Kingdom, Canada, Australia, New Zealand, South Africa, Newfoundland and India, have decided that the return to their homelands of bodies of His Majesty's Forces buried overseas shall not be undertaken or permitted.*' The war dead were to lie in cemeteries laid out and constructed by the Imperial War Graves Commission following the pattern established after the 1914-18 war. The Commission would be responsible for the upkeep and maintenance of these cemeteries in perpetuity.

---

6. Air Ministry Order A43/1946.

Chapter 9

Casualties Missing Presumed Dead

German service personnel at the crash site of a Halifax in occupied Europe.

Certification of Death

Certification of Death was required to administer the estate of deceased personnel. When a commanding officer knew that the death of one of his personnel had occurred in the UK as a result of war operations but the body had not been recovered or identified (or had been buried as an 'Unknown') he could report the death and the circumstances of it to the registrar of the district in which the death was believed to have happened. In England, Wales, Northern Ireland and the Isle of Man, the registrar would then notify his civil coroner who would investigate the case. If the coroner was satisfied that the death had taken place and was the result of war operations, he issued a certificate to the registrar which allowed the death to be registered.

In Scotland the local registrar reported the matter to the registrar General who would have the case investigated by the Procurator Fiscal. A certificate was issued if the Procurator Fiscal was satisfied about the death.

Death Certificates could not be issued for airmen who were known to have been killed (or went missing) on operational flights outside the UK, or who were lost at sea on training flights from the UK, or were killed in flying accidents overseas and their body not recovered. The physical absence of a body precluded their death being registered in the UK. Coroners and Procurators Fiscal could not investigate deaths occurring abroad unless the body was returned to the UK, and therefore no civil Death Certificate could be issued.

However, even when information was received from various sources which indicated beyond reasonable doubt that an officer or airman had been killed, the Air Ministry would not initially go further than to list them as 'Missing, Believed Killed'. Without direct and unquestionable evidence of the death from a BRITISH source the Air Ministry was not prepared to officially classify the officer or airman as dead. However, the Air Ministry was permitted to officially presume that the death had occurred. When presumption action was taken by the Air Ministry it enabled next of kin to settle the estate of the casualty. The Presumption of Death department of the Casualty Branch would instigate presumption action when it was believed air crew listed as missing on operations had been killed. However, before such action was taken it was considered essential to wait to see if there was further evidence of death or, if this was not forthcoming, to wait for a sufficient length of time before making the official presumption of death. The Air Ministry was anxious that incorrect presumptions of death were not made and to avoid next of kin being unnecessarily distressed. Documents relating to the taking of Presumption of Death action are often included in RAF Casualty files. These can range from copies of Notification of Death Certificates and official letters through to memos or notes on scraps of paper.

A Presumption of Death

Before 1977 there was no law in the United Kingdom which provided a single procedure to obtain a declaration of presumption of death which would cover all requirements. A Common Law Presumption of Death was available through a court application when there was no evidence that a person had been alive during a seven-year period and 'reasonable' enquiries had been made as to whether the person was alive or not.

This allowed relatives to administer the missing person's estate. This type of Presumption of Death was 'rebuttable' which meant if the person who had been presumed to be dead reappeared then the Presumption of Death was cancelled. The usual length of time required before an application for a Common Law Presumption was seven years. However, Common Law did allow for a Presumption of Death to be made before the seven-year point on 'the balance of probability'. In this case enough evidence was required which would lead a reasonable person to believe that the individual was dead. This was the provision which was used during the Second World War by the British armed forces.

The Air Ministry instituted Presumption of Death action in the following circumstances:

1. When a period of at least six months had passed since the date of the casualty.
2. When it had been confirmed with all likely sources of information that there had been no news of the airman concerned.
3. There was no evidence before the six-month point which would have justified an earlier presumption of death being made.

If there was sufficient evidence of an airman's death before the six-month point the Air Ministry would review the case for a Presumption being made but if any doubt existed presumption action would not be taken.[1]

Before Presumption of Death action was taken, the Air Ministry Casualty Branch would ask the next of kin, the squadron or unit and other agencies such as the International Red Cross, whether they had heard anything from or about the missing airman. Only when replies in the negative were received from all those contacted was Presumption action taken. The Air Ministry was at pains to make clear to next of kin that a death presumption was for official purposes only and did not mean conclusively that a person was dead.

Below are documents relating to the Presumption of Death action taken after Sergeant H.K. Green was killed in a flying accident while training in Canada. His body was not recovered. In this case the Presumption of Death was made by the Royal Canadian Air Force (RCAF); although Sergeant Green was a member of the RAF he was under the control of the RCAF while training in Canada and therefore they took the administrative action to presume death.

---

1. National Archives reference AIR2/9602 – Far East Casualties Death Presumption Policy. Letter to Air Officer Commanding Royal Australian Air Force HQ London from Wg Cdr Burgess, Air Ministry Casualty Branch, dated 7 October 1942.

To—	NONSECRET AIR MINISTRY KINGSWAY P4 CAS (R) RECORDS GLOS	Date		
			Receipt	Despatch
		Time of		/4
FROM—	HQ RCAF OTTAWA.	System		

Serial No. X.8241

RECEIVED A.M.C.S.1334B/HRS. 13TH JUNE 1943.

X568 U9859 11TH JUNE MY M 9796 15TH MAY. RE RAF 1321270
SGT GREEN H K UNIT ADVISES INTENSIVE SEARCH OF SUSPECTED
AREA BY BUSHMEN AND AIRCRAFT UNSUCCESSFUL FURTHER SEARCH
TO BE MADE BY SCOUTING PARTY TO LAC CHAPLEAU WHEN ACCESSIBLE
IN ABOUT 2 WEEKS. CHANGES OF DISCOVERING PILOT OR WRECKAGE
CONSIDERED REMOTE AS (GROUP MISSING) TERRAIN MUSKEG SWAMPS
SMALL LAKES AND DENSE UNDERGROWTH

TIME OF ORIGIN:-111910 Z.

COPIES TO:- P4 CAS(ACTION) (5 COPIES)

404272

14 JUN 1943

NOTE.—In the interests of economy, both sides of this sheet should be used.

Telegram from the Royal Canadian Air Force dated 13 June 1943 to the Air Ministry Casualty Section (P4(Cas)) to inform them Sergeant Green's aircraft could not be found.

7

P.404272/43/P.4.(B.6).

29 November 1943.

Madam,

      With reference to the letter from this department dated
June 11th 1943, I am directed to inform you, with deep regret,
that all efforts to trace your son, Sergeant K.H. Green ,
have proved unavailing. A report received from Royal Canadian
Air Force H.Q., Ottawa, states that an intensive search by
bushmen and aircraft proved unsuccessful and that owing to the
nature of the country over which he probably crashed, the chances
of discovering the wreckage were remote.

      In view of the time which has elapsed since he was reported
missing, it is now proposed to take action to presume his death,
and for this purpose I am to ask that you will be good enough
formally to confirm that you have received no further news or
evidence regarding him.

      A further communication on this matter will be sent to you
at a later date, but I am to assure you that this presumption
action is taken for official purposes only.

      I am to extend to you the sincere sympathy of the department
in your anxiety.

              I am, Madam,
                Your obedient Servant,

                         for Director of Personal Services.

Mrs. L. Green,
  1A Wolfington Road,
    West Norwood,
      LONDON S.E.27.

CC

*Letter to Sergeant Green's mother from P4(Cas) formally asking her whether she
has heard from her son and to inform her that Presumption of Death action is
proposed. In her reply Mrs Green formally confirmed to P4(Cas) that she had
heard nothing from her son.*

To— AIR MINISTRY KINGSWAY (P4 CAS)

From— HQ RCAF OTTAWA

Date · Receipt · Time of · Despatch · System

B6 7/12

Herbert,

Serial No. X.7?50

RECEIVED A...C.S. 1847 HRS. 16TH DEC. 43.

<u>IMPORTANT</u> 404272

X.462 M.9945 16TH DEC. MY M.9401 1?TH MAY 43. YOUR PCF68 6TH DEC. NON SECRET.
RAF 1321270 SERGEANT GREEN HENRY KENNETH PREVIOUSLY REPORTED MISSING IS NOW REPEAT NOW PRESUMED DEAD FOR OFFICIAL PURPOSES WEF 12TH MAY 43 RPT 12 MAY 43. NEXT OF KIN BEING INFORMED.

TIME OF ORIGIN: 161420 Z HRS.

COPIES TO: P.4. CAS (4 COPIES) (ACTION)

RECEIVED 16 DEC 1943 P.M. CASUALTY SECTION

NOTE.—In the interests of economy, both sides of this sheet should be used.

Telegram from Headquarters Royal Canadian Air Force, Ottawa, dated 16 December 1943 to Air Ministry P4(Cas) to inform them that the death of Sergeant H.K. Green had been presumed.

12

73-77 Oxford Street,

London, W.1.

P.404272/43/P.4.B.6.

21st December, 1943.

Madam,

    I am commanded by the Air Council to express to you their great regret on learning from the Chief of the Air Staff, Royal Canadian Air Force, that in view of the lapse of time and the absence of any further news regarding your son, 1321270 Sergeant K.H. Green, since the date on which he was reported missing, it must regretfully be concluded that he has lost his life, and his death has now been presumed, for official purposes, to have occurred on the 12th May, 1943.

    The Air Council desire me to convey their sympathy with you in the anxiety which you have suffered, and in your bereavement.

        I am, Madam,
           Your obedient Servant,

Mrs. L. Green,
  1A Wolfington Road,
    West Norwood,
      London, S.E.27.

Copy of the Air Council Letter of Condolence to Sergeant Green's mother sent when his death had been presumed.

Telephone :

GERRARD. 923 4.

~~HOLBORN 3434~~

EXTN. 3515

REF. P. 4.04272/43

AIR MINISTRY,

LONDON, W.C.2.

23. 12. 43.

SIR,

I am directed to inform you that the death of

1321270. SGT. K. H. GREEN.

who (was) reported missing on the 12TH MAY/43
~~(were)~~

is now presumed for official purposes to have occurred on

12TH MAY/43 (1. O P U Squadron).

OTTOWA.

I am, Sir,

Your obedient Servant,

for Director of Personal Services.

~~AIR OFFICER COMMANDING~~ ....(Group).

~~OFFICER COMMANDING~~ ....(Squadron).

RECORDS OFFICE, GLOUCESTER.

S.A.O. No. 1 DEPOT (N.E.), UXBRIDGE.

For Internal Ref. on (13096—9101) Wt. 26778—1604 100 Pads 9/43 T.S. **700**

Internal Air Ministry notification memo to inform other departments of the presumption of Sergeant Green's death.

Notification of Death Certificates

Once death was presumed the next of kin could request from the Air Ministry Casualty Section a 'Notification of Death' certificate. A copy of any Notification of Death issued was usually placed on the relevant P File. Below is the copy of the Notification of Death certificate sent by P4(Cas) at her request to Sergeant Green's mother to enable his estate to be settled.

P.4 4272/43/P.4.B.7.   18

NOTIFICATION OF DEATH

CERTIFIED that according to the records of this Department 1321270 Sergeant Kenneth Henry GREEN, Royal Air Force Volunteer Reserve, was reported missing and is presumed, for official purposes, to have lost his life on the twelfth day of May, 1943, as the result of an aircraft accident.

for Director of Personal Services.

Dated at the Air Ministry, London, this 29 day of February, 1944.

CASUALTIES MISSING PRESUMED DEAD

In England and Wales the Notification of Death certificate was generally accepted by insurance companies, banks etc as proof of death but problems arose in Scotland where the law is different. In England and Wales, before the estate of a deceased person can be settled, a grant of probate needs to be obtained from the Probate Registry. The Scottish equivalent of probate is 'confirmation', the grant of which enables an executor to distribute the deceased's estate. In 1940, Scottish law (which has separate courts and judiciary from England) required that an application to the courts for confirmation had to be accompanied by proof not only of the death of the person whose estate is in question, but also of the date of their death. These requirements had also caused a problem in the First World War and had led to the introduction in 1917 of the *Confirmation of Executors War Service Scotland Bill*. In the absence of both a body and a Death Certificate this Bill allowed applications for grants of confirmation to the estates of serving personnel who were reported as missing and presumed to be dead to be accompanied by a certificate, issued either by the Admiralty (Royal Navy), or the Army Council and later the Air Council. This certificate stated that the report of the death of the individual had been accepted for official purposes. There was a proviso that twelve months must have elapsed between the date of death and an application for confirmation or that six months had passed from the date that the certificate was issued. However, this arrangement ceased at the end of the First World War and so a similar Bill was introduced in 1940 to cover personnel serving in the Second World War.

The 1940 Bill largely followed the wording and provisions of the 1917 Act and allowed applications for confirmation of estates of personnel who died on war service to be supported by a certificate from the competent authority: Admiralty, War Office or Air Ministry as appropriate. The certificate was to state that either a report of the death of the person in question had been accepted for official purposes or that the person was listed as missing and must be 'deemed for official purposes' to be dead. The person applying for confirmation could then swear or affirm that they believed the individual to be dead and confirmation could be granted. As in the 1917 Act there was a proviso that twelve months from the date of death given on the certificate must have past. Before being presented to Parliament the Bill was approved by the three Services, and also the legal profession in Scotland.[2] The provisions of Confirmation of Executors (War Service) (Scotland) Act, 1940, were only to cover individuals reported missing during

---

2. Hansard Confirmation of Executors War Service (Scotland) Bill, House of Lords 13 June 1940 vol 116 cc571-3.

the 'war period', which was officially held to have ended on 24 February 1946, the date the Emergency Powers (Defence) Act, 1939, expired.

Despite this Act some judges in Scotland still refused to accept the Notification of Death certificates issued by the Air Ministry as sufficient proof of death and refused confirmation. In 1946 Scottish MPs in the House of Commons complained that problems 'have arisen in Scotland owing to the absence of statutory authority enabling the sheriffs of Scotland to accept as proof of death certificates from the Admiralty, War Office, or Air Ministry, that a sailor, soldier or airman, is reported missing'.[3] The subject came up again in 1948 when the sad case of Sergeant J.L. O'Rorke was raised. Sergeant O'Rorke had gone missing on 20 November 1942 while serving with 202 Squadron based in Gibraltar. He had been the Flight Engineer aboard Catalina FP153 lost while escorting a convoy to Oran. During a U-Boat attack on the convoy the Catalina was fired on by Merchant Navy ships in the convoy and crashed into the Atlantic off the coast of Portugal. There were no survivors.[4] The Air Ministry took Death Presumption action and issued the usual Notification of Death certificate to his next of kin on 23 October 1944, stating that Sergeant O'Rorke must be presumed, for official purposes, to have lost his life on 20 November 1942.

While the Notification of Death Certificate issued by the Air Ministry was accepted by Scottish authorities when his widow wished to remarry, it was not accepted by the Sheriff of Chancery when used by Sergeant O'Rorke's sister to support her application for title to some of her brother's property. The matter was raised in the House of Commons when Scottish MPs asked that the Air Ministry issue a certificate which would be acceptable to the Sheriff. In response, the Secretary of State for Air replied that the Air Ministry had issued a certificate on 23 October 1944 stating that Sergeant O'Rorke must be presumed, for official purposes, to have lost his life on 20 November 1942. The issue of the certificate had been in accordance with normal practice in cases when an airman was missing, and it was beyond all reasonable doubt that he had not survived. The Secretary of State went on to say, 'The certificate used is one which has been agreed by the Registrar-General, and which has always been acceptable in the English courts.'[5]

The subject of Sergeant O'Rorke was raised again in the House of Commons and this time the reply came from the Lord Advocate who said,

---

3. Hansard House of Commons Debate 19 November 1946 vol 430 cc76-7W.
4. The National Archives ADM199/2143 Survivors Reports Merchant Navy 1 Nov 1942 to 31 Dec 1942 and ADM199/1216 MKF and KMS Convoy Reports.
5. Hansard HC Deb 11 February 1948 vol 447 cc87 and 364.

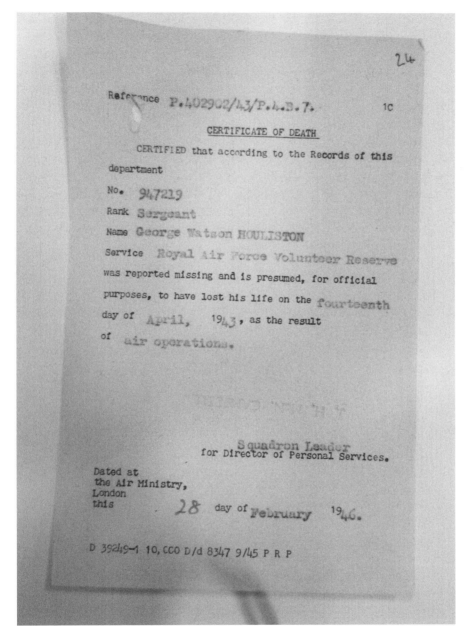

The 'Death Certificate' issued by the Air Ministry Casualty Branch in February 1946 for a Scot, Sergeant Houliston of 103 Squadron. He had been reported missing on 14 April 1943 when his aircraft, Lancaster W4828, failed to return. It had crashed near Le Mans, France.

'The certificate which the Air Ministry felt able to issue in this case stated that Sergeant O'Rorke was missing and that he was presumed for official purposes to have lost his life. I am aware that some Courts in Scotland do not accept such a certificate as sufficient evidence of death for the purpose of giving the Serviceman's heirs a good title to his heritable property. This is, of course, a matter for the discretion of the Court concerned in each case and it is not possible for the Executive to interfere.' He added that consideration had been given to introducing legislation to make the certificates of notification of death (issued by the armed forces) the equivalent to a certificate of actual death but it was decided that as the number of cases in which hardship had been suffered was small, and, bearing in mind that the normal timescale of seven years for a presumption of death would soon be reached, it had been decided not to introduce any appropriate legislation. There the matter rested.

1944 Post Presumption Memorandum raised after information was received from French War Organization.

CASUALTIES MISSING PRESUMED DEAD

When the grave or graves of those who had been officially presumed dead were found a Post Presumption Memorandum was circulated giving details of the grave sites. A copy of this Memorandum was placed on the Casualty P File.

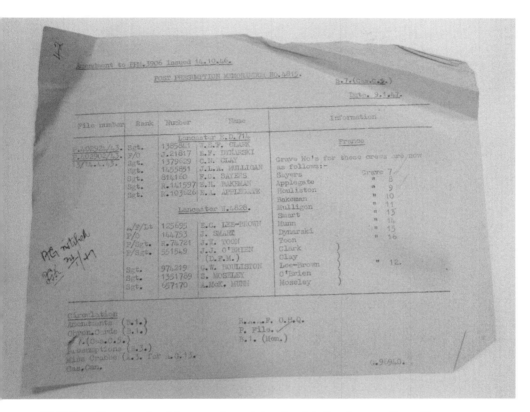

1947 Post Presumption Memorandum giving the details of grave sites of two crews found post-war. It was circulated in January 1947 to sections by S7 (Cas) the successor of P4(Cas).

Part 2

Tracing the Missing and the Identification of the Dead

Members of a RAF Missing Research and Enquiry Service (MRES) search team at an exhumation in France. The MRES was tasked with the tracing and identification of thousands of air crew listed as missing in all theatres of war. From small beginnings it developed into an organisation with search teams scouring areas in which air crew had been lost, from Europe to the jungles of the Far East. Reports and findings produced by the MRES are included on the relevant P Files.

Chapter 10

The RAF Missing Research and Enquiry Service

Enquiries into the fate of missing aircrew had been conducted by the RAF Casualty Branch since 1939 but the Missing Section was limited by circumstances in what it was able to do. The Section was largely confined to collating and evaluating information about missing personnel received in P4(Cas) through recognised channels. On occasion the Section was able to follow up on the information; they identified some airmen lost during the Battle of France and the consequent withdrawal from Europe and established their burial place. The Missing Section also had some success in identifying bodies washed ashore or picked up when aircraft were lost over the sea. However, as the workload increased with the ever-growing number of casualties, the short-staffed Section became too hard pressed to be able to follow up leads or instigate investigations; they had no official direction to do so.

Relatives of the missing were anxious to obtain any information they could about the fate of their loved ones, and the Casualty Branch was receiving an increasing number of enquiries asking for information about the circumstances of a loss. Many of these enquiries concerned casualties which had happened months previously. Next of kin hoped that any information withheld by the Air Ministry for operational reasons could be released with the passage of time. Relatives and others both wrote and called in person at the Casualty Branch, who operated an 'open door policy' to visits from enquirers seeking information about the missing. Sadly P4(Cas) usually had no further information to give them. The situation was becoming very difficult; the Casualty Branch wished to help next of kin but was hampered by lack of resources and official direction. In late 1941 the frustrated head of P4(Cas), Wing Commander Burges, wrote to his superior (the Director of Personnel Services) asking for guidance: *'May we be informed, please, of the policy to be followed? If the Casualty Branch is not to extend its work in this direction [the investigation of cases involving missing personnel] it will of course be necessary to decline to go on when asked to pursue enquiries.*[1]

Wing Commander Burges' query was passed up the chain in the Air Ministry through the Air Member of Personnel (Air Marshal Philip Babington) to the Permanent Under Secretary of State for Air (Sir Arthur Street) and the Parliamentary Under Secretary of State for Air (Lord Sherwood). A positive reply came back from Street, whose own son was serving with Bomber Command, which said:

'It would be bad for morale if the idea were to get abroad that the Air Ministry was disinterested in the fate of people who were of no further use to the Service. I agree, therefore, that we ought to do rather more than we do at present in the way of "Missing Research", though naturally we should only pursue enquiries within reasonable limits.'[2]

Lord Sherwood agreed with Street and in his reply said that the view of the public *'was largely due to the sympathetic understanding with which these cases had been dealt with by the Casualty Branch and to whom all credit is due.'*[3] In other words P4(Cas) was the victim of its own success!

Burges had the clarification he had sought and it was officially agreed that more needed to be done to establish the fate of the missing and hence a Missing Research Section should be established within the Casualty Branch. However, the department responsible for agreeing the manning of the new section quibbled. It agreed the establishment of a Flight Lieutenant post to undertake the missing research work but did not agree any clerical staff in support. Their opinion was that *'As the "missing" section of P4 already carries out enquiries as exhaustively and comprehensively as possible, the work of this officer would appear to be that of re-examination of all possible evidence to ensure no significant fact or any line of approach has been overlooked. If he takes over cases before the "missing" section admits it can go no further, there is a possibility of duplication of effort and of staff.'*[4] A seething Burges struck back, telling the manning department, *'We feel you would like us to point out that the*

---

1. National Archives reference AIR2/6330 Air Ministry Missing Research Section P4(Casualties) Branch Minute Sheet Minute 1 Wg Cdr Burges to DPS dated 31/10/41.
2. Ibid Minute 4 PUS dated 17/11/1941.
3. Ibid Minute 5 Lord Sherwood to AMP dated 18 November 1941.
4. Ibid Minute 8 S1 to DPS dated 19/12/41.

whole point of having a Missing Research Section is to go beyond the ordinary work of the Casualty Branch.'[5]

At first, the new Missing Research Section (MRS) established within P4(Cas) lacked stability. For most of 1942 officers were posted in but then rapidly moved on, and it was undermanned (having only one serving officer and two clerks) for the work it already had, let alone the increasing workload as casualties mounted. Despite this the MRS established the fate of a good number of missing personnel and informed their relatives. At the end of 1942 Flight Lieutenant Sinkinson, who had been doing missing research work in combination with other duties in P4(Cas), officially took over the MRS and remained in post until the end of the war. But while the MRS thus gained stability, it remained understaffed.

The new MRS was office-bound and therefore limited, as the Casualty Branch staff had been before, to following up any information received by letter or telephone. However, through their meticulous work the MRS was able to solve more cases and inform the next of kin of the fate of their relative. The MRS also built up a database of reported crash sites in enemy territory which was to prove invaluable. They recorded all the information received about each missing individual, building up a dossier for each one. The MRS received some invaluable clues as to the identity of missing personnel through reports about possessions found with or on bodies. These reports came through both German and other sources such as intelligence reports, which also included reports from evaders,[6] or national Red Cross organizations. The reports included information about items such as laundry labels, serial numbers on issued kit and aircraft components, photographs, personal letters etc all of which could be used to help identify the dead.

The MRS formed close associations with organizations who might help both within and outside the Air Ministry. Outside the Air Ministry, jewellers, tailors, and manufacturers of personal items assisted the MRS and close and highly useful links were formed. A particularly helpful relationship was established with the Institute of British Launderers and their associated journals which helped with the identification of laundry labels. Within the Air Ministry and in the Ministry of Aircraft Production (and its suppliers

---

5. Ibid Minute 9 Head P4(Cas) to S1 dated 23/12/41
6. Air crew who were brought down in enemy-held territory but evaded capture or who escaped from PoW camps gave a report about their experiences to British Military Intelligence Section 9 (MI9) on their return to UK. These reports contained information on other crew members, where their aircraft came down etc. MI9 Escape and Evasion reports 1940-45 are held by the National Archives under reference WO208.

such as Rolls Royce and Avro) there was a well-established practice to mark all items which were public property and aircraft parts with a serial number, and careful records were kept of where each item went. These laborious records proved to be an invaluable asset (both at the time and in later years) in identification cases.

The Establishment of the RAF and Dominion Air Forces Missing Research and Enquiry Service

Post D-Day there was an increasing clamour from relatives for information about the casualties in liberated areas and the MRS was receiving a flow of information and artefacts relating to missing air crew which had been given to the liberating forces. It was decided to establish a field operations element to search for missing air crew. It was known as the Missing Research and Enquiry Service (MRES) and its function was to find all the available information relating to the missing and pass it back to the Casualty Branch Missing Research Section. It remained the task of the MRS to sift and investigate the information it received both from the newly established MRES and from other sources. Much detective work was often required, but Flight Lieutenant Sinkinson and his staff became expert at this, building up an invaluable collection of contacts, databases and knowledge to assist them since their formation in 1942.

The groundwork already done by the MRS at their base in Oxford Street proved invaluable to their field units who began their work in France in early 1945. MRES officers were instructed by the Inspector of Missing Research to *'Find everything possible. Report clearly what you find. Remember that your most discouragingly sparse report may contain just one apparently insignificant item that will enable [the] Air Ministry to close a case.'*

The first field unit of the new MRES was No 1 Missing Research and Enquiry (MRE) Section which had been instituted in December 1944 but did not begin its work in France until the spring of 1945. It was soon joined by No 2 MRE Section, formed in Belgium in May 1945. The MRE Sections were staffed by volunteer search officers (mostly air crew) drawn from the RAF and Dominion Air Forces, and the investigation of all RAF, Dominion and Allied Air Force (other than those of the United States) burials fell within their remit.

Initially the MRS within the Casualty Branch in London sent specific casualty enquiries together with the relevant dossiers to the MRE Sections operating in France and Belgium. However, it soon became clear that the task in France was so large that a new approach was needed. Two new MRE Sections (numbers 3 and 4) were formed as Mobile Sections; each was given areas of France to sweep, looking for aircraft crash sites, information on the crews, and the graves of known and unknown airmen. Cases arising from these sweeps were classified as X cases and the details obtained by the sweeping MRE Sections were sent back to P4(Cas). The X annotation can be found on some of the MRES documents included on Casualty P Files. The sweep approach enabled missing crews to be traced and identifications made in cases where little information was held in the Casualty Branch.

The war in Europe ended on 8 May 1945 and that against Japan in August the same year. With the cessation of hostilities the search for the missing expanded and, by August 1945, eight MRE Sections had been established to search across Europe. The figure of exactly how many air crew were missing was not clear at this stage. It was not until the autumn of 1947, when nearly all prisoners of war had been accounted for, that more accurate figures began to emerge. The head of the Casualty Branch MRS, Squadron Leader Sinkinson, gave the Air Member for Personnel the following figures[7] for the RAF, Dominion and Allied Air Forces (bar those of the US):

Total missing in all theatres	42,000
Missing in Europe	37,000
Presumed lost at sea	17,000
Untraced (including those buried as unknowns)	9,000

Of this number, 16,000 missing had been traced in all theatres. Of the 15,200 traced in Europe, 10,000 were from the RAF. In 1949 a final figure of 41,881 missing (i.e. still unaccounted for) was agreed.[8]

Missing Research Enquiry Units

In an effort to locate missing air crew within a reasonable time scale, the MRES was reorganised and expanded in Europe. A revamped Missing Research and Enquiry Service was established with initially three, later

---

7. National Archives reference AIR20/9050 Sqn Leader Sinkinson to AMP dated 2 October 1947.
8. No definitive figure has been arrived at. Various numbers have been given by different sources and even official figures vary and sometimes do not add up.

increased to five, sub-units called Missing Research Enquiry Units (MREU). Each MREU had forty search officers split into search teams which replaced the existing MRE Sections. Their activities were coordinated by the Missing Research and Enquiry Service, North-West Europe under Group Captain Hawkins whose name appears on documents in many P Files.

The areas allocated to the MREU were:

No 1 MREU	France and Luxembourg
No 2 MREU	Belgium, Holland, Czechoslovakia and the French Zone of Occupied Germany
No 3 MREU	Norway, Denmark and the American Zone of Occupied Germany
No 4 MREU	British and Russian Zones of Germany (including Berlin), and Poland
No 5 MREU	was originally formed as the Middle East and Mediterranean Missing Research and Enquiry Service. In July 1946 it came under HQ North West Europe and operated in Italy and Austria

At its height the MRES had over 150 staff and mainly operated from August 1945 until 1947 with some reduced MREUs continuing to operate until 1948. The last element of the MRES to disband was the very small Berlin detachment which continued to operate until December 1951. That year the Casualty Branch was able to report that of the 41,881 missing at the end of the war, 23,881 now had known burials, 9,281 were formally declared lost at sea, and no information had been obtained as to the fate of another 6,745.

These figures leave some 2,000 air crew still unaccounted for. Some of them occupy graves marked as Unknown Airman/Airmen as with the crew of Lancaster JD211 which came down at Besançon on 16 July 1943. The remains of the crew were buried at Besançon in graves marked as being those of Unknown Airmen. Private research, together with the work of the RAF's Air Historical Branch, enabled the Ministry of Defence, in December 2013, to confirm the graves were those of crew members of Halifax JD211. The graves are now marked as such. The remains of other missing personnel are still being found, such as those of Sergeant John Bremner, whose remains were found in a wooded area outside Berlin and buried with full military honours in October 2008. Sergeant Bremner had been killed when his Halifax came down near Berlin on 20 January 1944.

The Policy of the Missing Research and Enquiry Service

In early 1946, the Inspector of Missing Research (Group Captain Burges, who was also the head of P4(Cas)) issued a Statement of Missing Research Policy,[9] which had been agreed by the Director of Personal Services and the Dominions' Air Forces Headquarters in London. The statement was primarily a summation of how the MRES operated. It said:

'1. The Air Ministry is impressed with the interest in the problem of searching for traces of missing airmen which is taken by the public generally, and especially by those who have lost relatives and friends whose fate remains uncertain. The anxiety of the bereaved, who have remained so long in doubt, is fully appreciated, and their wish to know the full story of the casualty is sympathetically understood. It is, none the less, most undesirable to foster their desire for complete information when it must, with the comparatively limited means available, often fall short of realisation, and may never be fulfilled. It is obvious that to search with full effect for personnel who became missing during a war of nearly six years duration which covered the whole continent of Europe, would require an organisation comparable in size to the whole Air Force – a project quite outside the realm of practical politics. With these considerations in view, it will be of interest perhaps to state the policy in conformity with which the RAF and Dominion Air Forces Missing Research Service is now operating.

2. The method of search adopted must depend on the means available. These are limited by the numbers of men and vehicles which can be spared from other important commitments.

3. To expect to search Europe yard by yard, whatever the type of country and terrain, whether wooded or mountainous or flat pastureland, would be unreasonable, nor with the means available would time permit of even a limited attempt to do so. Instead, a planned search system has been evolved, as described in the following paragraphs.

4. It is found convenient to organise the various search areas on national lines, using the national or local boundaries to limit the operational areas. A Missing Research and Enquiry Unit establishes

---

9. The National Archives AIR2/6474 *Air Ministry Report on RAF & Dominion Air Forces Missing Research and Enquiry Service Report 1944-1949 by Gp Capt E. Hawkins Air Headquarters BAFO dated March 1949 Part 3 Appendix D 1&2.*

its Headquarters in a suitable provincial centre, if possible where it can obtain rations and stores from a not too distant British or Allied formation: of its six Search Sections, each consisting normally of five Officers with vehicles and drivers, one or perhaps two are retained at Unit Headquarters to operate in the surrounding country, while the remaining Sections are quartered at small centres some of which may be as much as 100 miles away. At each Unit and Section Headquarters the localities of known crashes and special cases under enquiry are indexed and marked on a map, but these are usually only a small part of the work to be undertaken. The main part of the work is concerned with the investigation of reports provided by local police of crashes in the area, and of material discovered by the Sections themselves.

5. The principle is followed of placing reliance first of all on local reports, because it is assumed that the inhabitants must have known of a crash in their locality and the existence of any graves. Numerous such reports are received, and the intention is in every instance to visit the spot named and prosecute enquiries from it, though political and geographical factors will of course be considered when deciding the actual details of the methods of search to be employed.

6. In France, for example, each area of operations includes a number of 'Departments' or territorial divisions, and Search Sections take these one at a time: there are ninety in all. Search officers deal first with enquiries sent by the Air Ministry department in hand: local Police Reports are then investigated; and finally a 'sweep' ensures that the Mayor and Police Officials of every commune in the department are questioned, so that no known crashes or graves in their localities should be overlooked, before the Section takes in hand another department. On completion of the work in one area, Unit Headquarters moves to another and the process is repeated until the whole country has been covered. Other countries are dealt with in a similar manner, details depending on local conditions and intensity of casualties.

7. It is only when there are grounds for believing that an unreported crash or grave is in a defined and accessible position will it be permissible to search an area yard by yard. To justify such a search, the grounds must be very strong indeed.

8. Priority cannot be given to any particular enquiry: those which come outside an area of current operations must wait until the area concerned is reached. To despatch search officers on single enquiries

at great distances from Unit Headquarters, besides being wasteful of manpower, time and money, would be detrimental to search operations as a whole.

9. While it is recognised that both traces of personnel and the memories of witnesses will fade with the passing of time, and all possible speed is being used to cover Europe on the lines laid down, long delays must unfortunately be accepted. It is extremely unlikely, and results to date support this view, that Missing Research Operations can ever find traces of surviving aircrew, or do more than make certain the fate of the missing: were any of the latter to be alive, they would be found by other organizations formed with that object, and with different methods of working.

10. Where, in the light of experience, The Air Ministry decides that identification of a grave, a body, or an aircraft is sufficiently certain for the official record, further investigation will not be undertaken unless (a) a reasonable doubt can be thrown on the evidence or (b) there is strong likelihood of finding fresh evidence material to the case.'

In addition to the above, guidance notes for the search, officers of the MRES were sometimes issued by the Casualty Branch documents called Missing Research Memoranda. These gave new directions (as a result of lessons learnt in the field) or reinforced previous directives such as the necessity for good report writing, etc. The search officers mentioned by Gp Capt Burges, and other members of the MRES were all volunteers and came from both the RAF and Dominion Air Forces. It had been decided at the outset that the grisly nature of the work that the MRES staff would be required to do needed volunteers rather than 'pressed' men to do it. Part of the search officers work included witnessing exhumations and searching the skeletal or decomposing remains for evidence of identity. Until 1948 the MRES officers were not permitted to undertake exhumations themselves although they attended them as witnesses; the work itself was done by the Army Grave Registration Units often using local labour and German PoWs. The Exhumation Reports found on Casualty Files were signed by the army officer present and, sometimes, by the MRE Unit officer who was the witness.

Chapter 11

Sources of Information Available to the Missing Research & Enquiry Service Working in Europe

Casualty P File Information

Information received prior to Liberation
The Missing Research Section of the Air Ministry Casualty Branch had collated every scrap of information they received about the fate of missing aircraft and crew from whatever source. The collated information, stored on the relevant Casualty File, was passed to the Missing Research and Enquiry Service when a Casualty Enquiry was raised with them by P4. The information collected included the International Red Cross Committee (ICRC) telegrams forwarding information from the German authorities, German *Totenliste* information, information from organisations in German-occupied countries (such as the French veterans organisation *Anciens Combattants*) forwarded by the ICRC, reports from resistance organizations and allied agents in enemy or enemy-held countries, information sent by PoWs to their relatives, reports from Air Attachés and other sources in neutral countries such as Sweden, and the results of any enquiries sent to the ICRC. The amount of information obtained from these sources was often limited to dates of crashes, some indication of the location of the crash, and sometimes burial places of crews.

Another source which provided information were the Escape and Evasion Reports gathered by the Directorate of Military Intelligence department MI9 which was responsible for supporting resistance groups and for assisting and encouraging Service personnel to evade or escape capture.[1]

---

1. The work of MI9 is described in the book *MI9 Escape and Evasion 1939-1945* by M.R.D. Foot and J.M. Langley.

RAAF = AUS 419511 W/P/O RA ... Aus/429919 W/qt S G BURNS
" 422656 F/Sgt AG ... 422363
    N ... R   6256

<u>QUESTIONNAIRE for completion by returned evaders and escapers.</u>   35/3

NOTE   Please read the whole questionnaire before starting to
                write your answers.

QUESTION 1.   Approximately where did the aircraft crash?

                In Calais Area (South)

QUESTION 2.   Did you bale out? If so state (a) the number and, if
                possible, the identity of any other occupants of the aircraft
                whom you know to have baled out before you. Have you any
                evidence direct or hearsay of what happened to them subsequently?
                (B) the number and, if possible, identity of any other occupants
                whom you know to have still been in the aircraft when you left it.
                Give any details which may have a bearing on the probable fate
                of these men.

                I was first to bale out & saw three other 'chutes.
                We were informed that two RAF airmen were
                in hospital when it was hit by a bomb & they
                were killed. Our a/c was at approx 1500 ft
                when I went out & as two others (N aug Engineer)
                followed me it may have been too low for the skipper
                & W/O P Smith

QUESTION 3.   Have you any other information touching on what happened or
                what probably happened to the other occupants?

                No.

QUESTION 4.   Have you information of any Royal Air Force personnel other
                than members of your own crew?

                While at interrogation I saw an RAF A.G with
                a broken leg, & as far as I could gather he was one
                of the hospital patients.

NOTE   Information given in this report will be passed on to the
                next-of-kin only at the Air Ministry's discretion. Neverthe
                less details of a very secret nature such as identity or exact
                location of aiders are not required, but only such general
                remarks which may enable the Air Ministry Casualty Branch to
                assess the probable fate of the other occupants.

                In every case be careful, if the facts stated have been learnt,
                not by your own observation, but through any other person, e.g.
                the enemy or inhabitants, to say so.

                                           Signature S G Burns
                                           Rank   F/Sgt
copy to RAAF.   Squadron or Unit 467
                                           Date   4/10/44

An Escape & Evasion Questionnaire completed by Flt Sgt S.G. Burns RAAF.

All air crew who evaded capture, escaped from PoW camps in Europe back to the UK, or who returned from neutral territory, were debriefed by MI9. Any information from the debrief which could be of help in tracing lost aircraft or crew members was passed to the Air Ministry for P4(Cas) where it was added to the relevant P Files.

Escape and Evasion Reports of air crew give an account of what happened to them from the time the aircraft came down to their return to the UK. The report can include an account of how, where and when the aircraft was lost, what happened to other crew members, information about other Air Force personnel encountered or heard about, as well as accounts of help provided etc. Some reports take the form of answers to questions, others include a narrative account. There are instances of copies of Escape and Evasion Reports on the Casualty P Files but the main collection of Escape and Evasion Reports is held in the National Archives under reference WO208. Some selected RAF Escape and Evasion reports are held under AIR40/2467.

Information received post Liberation
After D Day the amount of information received about missing air crew increased. As the Allies moved through France the liberated French people gave information to Army and Air Force units they encountered about aircraft which had come down in their locality or about burials which had taken place in their cemeteries. In Normandy a Mother Superior of a hospital provided a list of 48 Allied servicemen who had been treated there since 1940, most of whom were air crew and some listed as missing. The Bureau des Successions, Paris where death records are kept, also provided dossiers and personal effects relating to missing air crew. An invaluable source of information about air crew lost in France was provided by Madame Germaine L'Herbier, a member of a special aviation section of the French Red Cross, the Amicale des Infirmières Pilotes et des Secouristes d l'Air (IPSA). When, in 1940, Madame L'Herbier found herself without an air ambulance to fly, she obtained permission from the Germans to tour hospitals in France to obtain information about members of the French Air Force. However, Madame L'Herbier went further, she used the information she got to search for aircraft crash sites and burial sites of French air crew and then she slowly extended her activities to secretly include Allied air crew. In November 1944, when Group Captain Burges, Head of the Casualty Branch, visited Paris she gave him a large number of carefully documented records relating to some 200 missing air crew, their fate

and burial places. She also hand over a large number of personnel effects. Post Liberation Madame L'Herbier was tasked by the Head of the French Air Force, General Valin, with searching for missing French air crew in other parts of Europe and thus she led the French version of the MRES. She was awarded the Legion D' Honneur by the French and an OBE by the British for her work.

As the Allies moved into Belgium and the Netherlands and then into Germany itself more information was gathered and sent to P4(Cas) to be added to the information held on the Casualty P Files. With the liberation of PoWs yet more information was forthcoming. The MRES did find that some of the information they received was inaccurate and accusations of war crimes against air crew were on occasion unsubstantiated.

Information also came from returning PoWs who were required to fill in a Repatriation questionnaire by MI9. This questionnaire asked the liberated air crew a number of questions about the loss of their aircraft and the ex-PoWs were also asked to provide any information they had about other members of their crew or any other Air Force personnel they had met while captured. The quality of information on Repatriation questionnaires varies: some liberated PoWs provide very little and others are much more forthcoming. These Repatriation questionnaires were forwarded to the Casualty Branch where they were added to the appropriate Casualty P Files. They were later used by the MRES to assist in their searches. Below is an example of a fairly typical Repatriation questionnaire. This one was submitted by Flight Sergeant R.V.C Witham, the flight engineer on Lancaster ME737 of 630 Squadron which was lost on the night of 11/12 May 1944 while on a mission to bomb a military camp at Bourg-Léopold in Belgium. The aircraft crashed near Herenthout and five of the crew were killed.

19

QUESTIONNAIRE for completion by repatriated personnel

NOTE I   We want you to give us any information you can about your air crew (or the officers and airmen captured with you) and what became of them after capture or casualty.

TYPE OF AIRCRAFT AND LETTER .. LANCASTER ..... S........

SQUADRON .. 630 ... EAST KIRKBY...............

CREW.

Position.	Name	Initials	Rank	R.C.A.F. R.A.A.F. R.N.Z.A.F.
1st Pilot	WATT	W.	P/O.	R N Z A F
2nd Pilot				
Navigator	THOMPSON.		SGT	R A F.
F/Engineer	WITHAM	R V C	SGT	R A F.
W./Operator				
Mid Upper	AMIES	A	SGT	R A F
Tail	ROW THORNE		SGT	R A F
Front Gunner	STUART	K.	F/SGT	R N Z A F.
Bomb Aimer.				
Additional Crew.				

QUESTION 1A   Did you bale out, crash, forceland, ditch or get blown out? If so, state:-   BALED OUT.

(a) Names of members of the crew who baled out before you:-
BOMB AIMER. F/S STUART.

(b) Names of those who were in the a/c when you left:-
Pilot. P/O Watt, NAV SGT THOMPSON   W/OP. ? Sgt ?   Mid upper. SGT AMIES
R.Gunner ? Sgt ROWTHORNE.

QUESTION 1B.   Approximately where did the aircraft crash?
10-11 miles outside of ANTWERP

QUESTION 1C.   Tell us all you know about your aircrew - what happened were they killed or injured- taken prisoner with you - or did the Germans give you any details. Where did you hear of them last - what prison camps where they at - do you know their home town - next of kin or county?

The Bomb Aimer was with me at the Prison Camp, & since he has been home has contacted the parents of the members of our crew (RAF); and the parents have had notification of the graves.

When I baled out, the main plane (Starboard side came off & there was very little chance for the remainder to get out.

Above and overleaf: Repatriation questionnaire submitted by Flight Sergeant Witham.

131

417074   Q6432

<u>QUESTION 2.</u> Have you any information of any Royal Air Force, Dominion
Colonial or Allied Air Force Personnel other than those already mentioned.
Do you know anyone who was shot, injured, died in hospital, escaped and
not heard of again, have you met any evaders who are not registered
P.O.W. - give any information which will help to account for missing
personnel.

Name and Initials . . . . . W.ITHAM . . . . . R.Y.C. . . . .

Rank . . . . . FLIGHT. SGT. . . . .

Service Number . . . . 1851909 . . . .

Unit at Time of Capture . . . 5. GROUP . . . . 630 SqD. . . . .

Date of Crash . MAY. 12th 1944 . . . Date of Capture . MAY. 12th 1944 . . .

German KE Reports

At the end of the War in Europe the Allies captured much German documentation, amongst which were files concerning Allied aircraft which had crashed in Germany or in German-held territory. Most of these documents had been raised by the German *Luftgaukommando* and contained information about aircraft and their crews which crashed in the various *Luftgaukommando* areas. The file series KU concerned USAAF aircraft losses and so was sent by the British to the American authorities. The Americans kept the constituent parts of the documents together and they are now held in the US National Archives in Washington. British bomber aircraft losses were covered in the **KE** file series but, unlike the Americans, the British authorities did not retain the files intact but broke up the KE files and gave their contents to interested departments. Thus information and material from the KE Files which could help trace missing aircraft and crew was passed to the Air Ministry Casualty Branch (P4(Cas)). Where the captured documents and material extracted from the KE files were placed on the relevant Casualty P Files. Neither the Ministry of Defence nor the UK National Archives hold complete KE files. These have ceased to exist but elements from them are still on Casualty P Files and what is on the P Files is all that remains of the original KE series.

The amount of KE-extracted information found on the P Files relating to bomber losses varies; some files contain considerably more than others. There are no translations of the German documents on the Casualty P File but often a handwritten summary in English of details which could help trace casualties (such as date, time, location of crash, type of aircraft, number of crew reported killed or captured) is on the P File. The information extracted from the KE files includes crash location, date and time of crash, aircraft type, equipment carried, cause of crash (e.g. Flak or *Nachtjäger* (night fighter)), aircraft markings, and any information on guns, engines etc. Also included in the KE files were German *Toten Karten* (death cards) for members of the crew killed and information about prisoners taken. There are lists of personal items found on the crew, dead and alive; sometimes items such as identity discs, known as 'dog tags', or RAF and Dominion Air Forces identity cards and pay books taken from the KE files are found on the Casualty P File. On occasion more personal items are included such as the passport-sized photographs of themselves in civilian clothes carried by the crews. It was intended that these photographs would be used on forged documents to aid escape and evasion. However, the information given on KE documentation was not always accurate, as can be seen in the examples I have included. Aircraft are sometimes misidentified, dates of crashes and deaths can be inaccurate, and the crew names given incorrect or the names of more than one crew muddled together.

Toten Karten

The German authorities logged air crew deaths on *Toten Karten* (death cards). These were often included with KE Reports and are now found in Casualty P Files. The brown cards were the originals and gave information which would be included in the *Totenlisten* sent via the Red Cross to the British. The pink cards which are also sometimes included on Casualty P Files were held by Dulag Luft, the transit camp for captured RAF and other Air Force personnel at Wetzlar. Dulag Luft had a colour-coded system of cards: pink for the dead, blue for the missing and white for prisoners of war.[2]

Examples of KE File documents

The card below relates to Sergeant Munn killed on 12 April 1943. The card states that he was the member of the crew of a Lancaster. The red annotation states that he was buried on 16 April 1943 in Le Mans. Sergeant Munn was a member of the crew of Lancaster W4828 which crashed on the night of 12/13 April 1943.

Front of Card

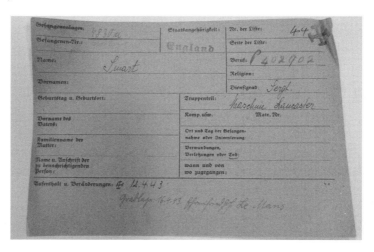

---

2. Air Ministry Report on Royal Air Force and Dominions Air Forces Missing Research and Enquiry Service 1944 to 1949 by Group Captain E. Hawkins HQ BAFO dated March 1949 Appendix K footnote.

Back of Card

There is an annotation stating that the information on the card was included on Totenliste 148.

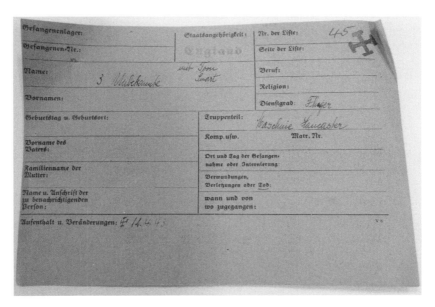

This Death Card refers to three unknowns and Troon and Smart, all members of the crew of Lancaster W4828 of 103 Squadron. The date of death is incorrectly given as 14 April 1943, not 12 April 1943.

Death Card relating to Flight Sergeant Justin Francis Loughnan RAAF who was killed on 14 October 1944. He was the WOP/AG on Lancaster HK599 of 115 Sqn which was brought down on a mission to attack Duisberg. The Death Card shows he is dead by underlining the word 'Tod' and, at the bottom, says that Flt Sgt Loughnan was buried at 9.05 on 17 October 1944 in Osterfeld Cemetery. He was later moved to Reichswald Forest British Military Cemetery. The rank given on his headstone there is Pilot Officer as he had been commisioned on 13 October 1944.

This Dulag Luft Wetzlar pink card relates to Sergeant P.R. Rowthorn of Lancaster ME737 lost on the night of 11/12 May 1944. The date of death is given as 12 April 1944 on the card. A time of 1.00 is given for the crash and a loction of 7 kilometres from Herenthout. The card also records that Sergeant Rowthorn was buried on 15 April in Antwerp.

Front of Card

Back of Card

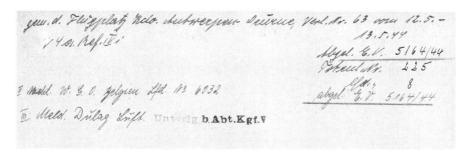

Dulag Luft Index card for Flying Officer C.F. Jelley DFC, killed when Lancaster PB228 of 635 Squadron was lost on the night of 6/7 January 1945. The aircraft loss location is given as Grossauheim where Fg Off Jelley is shown as buried (Grablage). He was later moved to Durnbach British Military Cemetery. The aircraft type (Flugzeugtyp) is incorrectly given as Halifax. Cotterell is shown as a crew member (Besatzungsmitlieder) but was actually on Halifax NR195 of 158 Squadron which also crashed at Grossauheim on the night of 6/7 January 1945. He too was buried at Grossauheim before being moved to Durnbach. Both aircraft were involved in an attack on Hanau about four kilometers from Grossauheim.

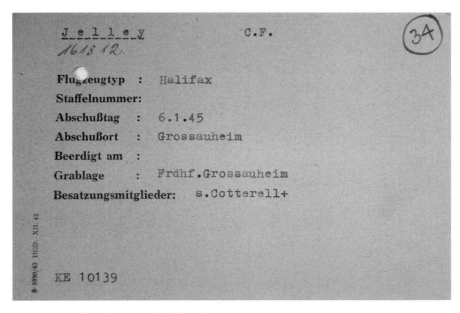

KE10139 is the German KE File reference.

Formblatt 2

KE 8078.

Nur für den Dienstgebrauch !

Angaben über die Erbeutung eines Feindflugzeuges.

Dienststelle: .... Fliegerhorstkommandantur ....

Ort: .... Berlin-Gatow ....

Zeit: .... 27.3.1944 ....

Verteiler:
Auswert.West
LGK.IIIIc
Gl./C-RÜ
Entwurf

Abschußzeit: .... 24.3.1944 um 22.32 Uhr ....
(Tag und Uhrzeit)

Aufschlagsort: .... Berlin NO, Friedrichshain und Umgebung ....

Art der Erbeutung: .... Nachtjäger ....
(Flak, Jäger, Nachtjäger, Notlandung)

Flugzeugmuster: .... Lancaster ....

Flugzeugkennzeichen: .... M Kokarde M ? ....
(Buchstaben vor und hinter dem Hoheitszeichen)

Zulassungsnummer: .... N D 581 ....
(Vor dem Leitwerk)

Bildgerät: .... nicht aufgefunden ....

F.T.-Frequenzen: .... An Kamerun, App. 35, gemeldet ....

Zustand des Flugzeuges: .... 99 % Bruch ....

Oberleutnant

138

Fliegerhorstkommandantur   Berlin-Gatow,den 27.3.1944
    Berlin-Gatow   Telefon: 80 85 01
<u>Übernahme-Kommando I</u>   App. 749

An

1.) Auswertestelle West, Oberursel,
2.) Reichsluftfahrtministerium, Gl./C-Rü.,
3.) Luftgaukommando III, Ic.,
4.) Kdo.Flugh.Ber.4/III,Abt.Ib/Beute.

Bergungsbericht
────────────────────

I. 1. Absturzort@ Berlin NO, Friedrichshain und Umgebung.
    2. Absturzzeit: 24.3.1944 um 22.32 Uhr.
    3. Flugzeugmuster: Lancaster.
    4.)Anzahl der Motore: 4.
    5. Das Übernahme-Kdo. traf an der Absturzstelle am 25.3.44 um
       08.30 Uhr ein.
    6. Das Übernahme-Kdo. der Flg.H.Kommandantur Berlin-Gatow setzte
       sich zusammen aus: Oblt. Uhde, Techn.Ob.Insp.(Fs/N) Pallaske,
       Flg.Ing. Kaczmarek, Waffenwart Stabsfw. Donath, eine Wachmann-
       schaft in Stärke von 1 Uffz. und 6 Mann. Dazu als Fahrzeuge
       1 Pkw. und 1 Lkw.

II.1. <u>Bewaffnung:</u>
     Es wurden 8 M.G."Browning" Kal.7,7 mm geborgen. Gürtungsver-
     hältnis: 3 Geschosse gewöhnlich, 1 Geschoß mit grauer Spitze,
     2 Geschosse mit hellblauer Spitze.
    2. <u>Panzerung:</u>
     Die Stärke der Panzerung konnte durch den Zustand des Flugzeuges
     nicht ermittelt werden.
    3. <u>Funkgeräte:</u>
      1. 1 Seenotsender.
      2. Receiver Unit 3554.
      3. Receiver Unit Type 25.
      4. Indicator Type 62 Ref.Nr.10 Q/13000.
      5. Receiver Type R 3090 Ref.Nr.10 D B/444.
      6. Controll unit 446 Ref.Nr.10 L 13/6053.
      7. Controll unit 444 Ref.Nr.10LB/6051.
      8. Receiver Type R 1124 A/Ref.Nr.10 D/5.
      9. Receiver Type R 1155 A Ref.Nr.10 D/820.
     10. Transmitter unit Type 22 Ref.Nr.10 R/23.
     11. Teil der Rotationsscheibe zum Rotterdamgerät.
    4. <u>Festgestellte Frequenzen:</u> Die festgestellten Frequenzen wurden
     bereits an Kamerun,App.35, durchgegeben. Die Quarze gehen mit
     den Geräten zum Ln.Vers.Rgt. Köthen.
    5. <u>Herstellungsmerkmale:</u> Von den sichergestellten Motoren konnte
     ein Typenschild bereits geborgen werden. Es handelt sich um
     Motore von der Type Merlin 38,Air Corps Nr.AF 42-244481 und die
     M.F.R.-Nr. A-9485. Die Typenschilder werden dem Gl./C-Rü, zuge-
     führt.
    6. <u>Flugzeugkennzeichen:</u> M Kokarde M ?. Die Werknummer ist N D 581.
    7. <u>Kraftstoffproben</u> können nicht mehr entnommen werden. Schmier-
     stoffproben werden dem Gl./C-Rü. zugesandt.

III.   Abwurfmunition war nicht mehr vorhanden.

                                          -2-

- 2 -

IV. Angaben über die Flugzeugbesatzung:

    1. Gefangene wurden nicht gemacht.
    2. Verwundete wurden nicht geborgen.
    3. Anzahl der Toten: Es wurden 7 tote Besatzungsmitglieder
       geborgen:
       1. unbekannt.
       2. Sgt. Doy,W. 1150863.
       3. Sgt.Grimes,G.L.,1119613.
       4. Sgt. unbekannt.
       5. Bain,D.T.,415814.
       6. Berrigan, Leonhard S.
       7. Mee, J.M. N.Z.416518.
       Die Leichen wurden dem Res.Laz.101 Olympisches Dorf Döberitz
       zur Beerdigung zugeführt.
    4. Es besteht kein Verdacht, daß Besatzungsmitglieder flüchtig
       sind.

V. Bemerkungen:

    Der Zustand des Flugzeuges ist 99 % Bruch. Die Teile liegen ver-
streut von Berlin-Neukölln, Hermannplatz über Kottbusser Tor,
Elbingerstr.,Friedrichshain, Greifswalderstr. bis zum Bahnhof
Weissensee. Die unter Ziffer II 3. angeführten Funkgeräte
       Receiver unit 35/54
       Receiver unit R 1124/A
       Controll unit 446 und
       Controll unit 444
wurden gemäß Weisung des Flg.H.Ing.Verres,Flg.Horst Wunstorf,
nach Berlin-Lübars, Hochbunker 1200, überführt. Besondere Merk-
male konnten an dem Bruch nicht festgestellt werden.

Oberleutnant

Gesehen:

Oberstleutnant und Stabsoffizier
    des Fliegerhorstes

October 2008 pall bearers from the Queen's Colour Squadron, RAF Regiment carry Sgt John Bremner to his grave in the CWGC 1939 – 1945 War Cemetery, Berlin. Sgt Bremner died when his Halifax crashed near Berlin on 20 January 1944. Sixty one years later his remains were found in a wooded area outside Berlin. Sgt Bremner's funeral was attended by his sister and other members of his family. It is the responsibility the MOD's Joint Casualty and Compassionate Centre to identify remains, trace relatives and arrange an appropriate funeral service and burial when historic RAF remains are found.

A set of air crew identity discs, commonly referred to as 'Dog Tags'. This set was issued by the Royal Canadian Air Force to F.G. Graham, retrieved from a German KE File, and placed on his Casualty File.

Gefangenenlager:	KE. 85 87	Staatsangehörigkeit:	England	Nr. der Liste:	☩
Gefangenen-Nr.:				Seite der Liste:	
Name:	Rowthorne, Rowthorn			Beruf:	
				Religion:	•
Vornamen:	F.			Dienstgrad:	Sgt.
Geburtstag u. Geburtsort:			Truppenteil:	Lancaster	
			Komp. usw.	Matr. Nr.	
Vorname des Vaters:				1 253 111	
			Ort und Tag der Gefangennahme oder Internierung:		
Familienname der Mutter:			Verwundungen, Verletzungen oder Tod:		
Name u. Anschrift der zu benachrichtigenden Person:			wann und von wo zugegangen:		

Aufenthalt u. Veränderungen: ✝ 12.5.44 / 1.00 Uhr bei 3 km. s.o. Herenthout 7 km s.o. Herenthals
Grabl: 15.5.44 Feindlichfr. Antwerpen-Deurne, Grab Nr. 156 u. 157

V 8   25

Dulag Luft, the transit camp for captured RAF and other Air Force personnel at Wetzlar, had a colour-coded system of cards: pink for the dead, blue for the missing and white for prisoners of war. This Dulag Luft Wetzlar pink card relates to Sergeant P.R. Rowthorn of Lancaster ME737 lost on the night of 11/12 May 1944. The date of death is recorded as 12 April 1944. A time of 1.00 (a.m.) is given for the crash and the location is given as 7 kilometres from Herenthout. The card also records that Sergeant Rowthorn was buried on 15 April in Antwerp.

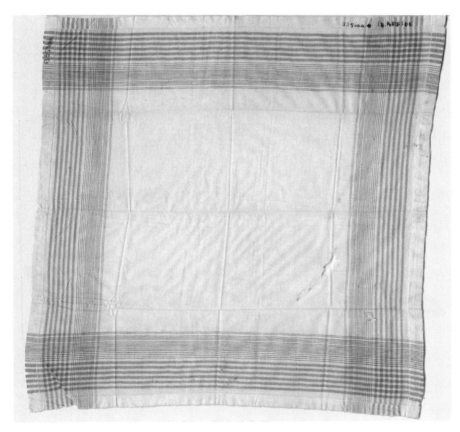

The back of the Dulag Luft Wetzlar pink index card for Sergeant Rowthorn.

The Mystery of the Handkerchief. It was found by a Dutchman on a body at a crash site in Holland. The handkerchief had a laundry marking showing the name Keeton and the Service Number 1239640 but Sgt A.E. Keeton had been the 2nd pilot of Wellington BK507 belonging to 199 Squadron when it crashed near L'Orient on 2 February 1943 and he was killed.

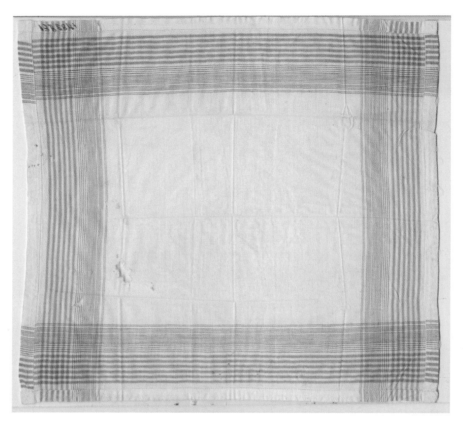

The other side of the handkerchief shows the Service Number 1385841. This belonged to Sergeant W.E.F. Clark who was the pilot of Lancaster ED714. This aircraft had crashed near Le Mans on 14 April 1943.

Air Crew brevets. Left to right: Top Pilot, Navigator, Bomb Aimer, Engineer, Bottom Wireless Operator/Air Gunner, Observer, Signaller. Note the blue wreath used by the Royal Australian Air Force instead of the brown used by the other Air Forces. (Copyright Author)

Pilot's brevets. Clockwise from top: Royal Air Force, Royal Australian Air Force, Royal New Zealand Air Force and Royal Canadian Air Force. (Copyright Author)

BOTTLE-IDENTIFICATION, BURIAL— STOCK No. 57-B-1000

Fill out GR Form No. 1, or write identifying information on any piece of paper, seal within the bottle, place bottle in left arm pit, and bury with body. Wrapping of the body should be secured to prevent movement of the bottle.

When immediate erection of a marker is impracticable, use second bottle containing like information, and place in the grave, in the center at its head; secure to prevent washing away by rain until a marker can be erected.

INSTRUCTIONS FOR CLOSING BOTTLE

To effect water-tight closure of the bottle, remove paper from cap and securely screw cap on bottle, forcing bottle into soft plastic material within cap.

American Graves Registration Service Burial Bottles which came in sets of 6. Instructions for use were on the lid of the box. Identifying information was to be sealed in the bottle. The bottle was to be placed in the left armpit of the body before burial or reburial.

Bomber crews 'escape' boots. The lower half was designed to looked like an Oxford-style lace-up shoe; the upper part was made of sheepskin-lined suede. The boots incorporated a hidden knife to be used by the wearer to cut off the upper part of the boot to leave the bottom half which would look like civilian shoes. (Photograph courtesy of Paul Laidlaw)

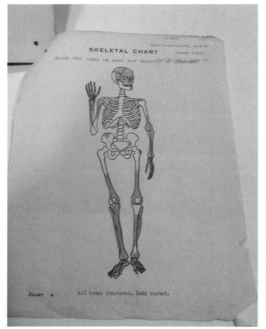

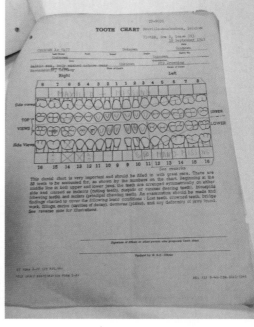

Above left: *US skeletal chart from a report raised at the US Central Identification Point at Neuville-en-Condroz, Belgium, on a set of RAF remains and forwarded by the RAF liaison officer there to the RAF authorities.*

Above right: *A US Tooth Chart from a CIP Neuville-en-Condroz report on an RAF casualty. Whereas the RAF dental records were poorly kept those of the US, Canadian and other forces were much more detailed.*

Above left: *A hand drawn map of the route (shown in red) taken by the search party from 9 Air Transit Section. They were looking for Liberator BZ952 of 357 Special Duties Squadron which crashed on the night 5/6 April 1944. The map was included in the report on the search/crash investigation by the CO of 9 Air Transit Section who had led the search party.*

Above right: *An example of a private headstone. Sergeant Walter Douglas RAF was killed in an aircraft accident off Hartland Point while training as a Wireless Operator/Air Gunner with Coastal Command's No 5 Operational Training Unit based at RAF Chivenor in North Devon. His body washed ashore at Pembroke Dock in Wales and his death was registered at Haverfordwest. Sgt Douglas was returned to his family for a private burial at Langholm in Dumfriesshire. The headstone records that he was killed on Active Service; everybody serving in the armed forces during a period of hostilities is regarded as being on Active Service, which is distinct from Operational Service. (Copyright Author)*

FILE No. P 374618/42

SURNAME: FITZGERALD, ~~Bryan~~. CHRISTIAN NAMES: DESMOND FRANCIS NUMBER: 121136 RANK: P/O.

(AMENDMENTS) EMPLOYED AS: FLYING DUTIES.

DATE OF ENLISTMENT DATE OF BIRTH: ✝ 26.2.1923 PLACE OF BIRTH: HASTINGS, SUSSEX UNIT: 115 Sqdn COMMAND: B.C. FORCE: R.A.F.V.R.

NEXT OF KIN

OTHER OCCUPANTS
S/Ldr. Wright
P/O Daintith   All missing.
Sgt Mollard
Sgt Wilde

REF. AND DATE	TYPE AND NO. OF AIRCRAFT	DATE AND PLACE OF CASUALTY	NATURE OF CASUALTY	CAUSE	NO.
A221 17/10/42	Wellington 111 Bk 312	Failed to return operations night 16/17.10.42. Moon.	Missing	F.B.	c/ℓ 967

✝ Enc: 88ᴬ   P.T.O. 3/11/42 16-10-42

INTERFOLD   P.T.O.

Above and below: *An RAF Casualty Card. Each casualty had their own Casualty Card which did not form part of the Casualty P File but recorded the Casualty File reference number. At the beginning of the War these were actual cards but the number of casualties and the shortage of materials reduced them to flimsy pieces of paper. Details of the casualty were recorded on the front of the Casualty Card; the reverse was used to record information about the fate of the casualty.*

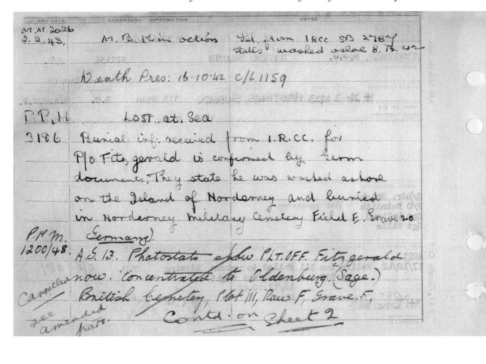

REF. AND DATE | SUBSEQUENT INFORMATION | NOTES

M.M.2026 2.2.43. — M. B. K. in action. Tel. from I.R.C.C. SB 2787 states washed ashore 8.B.42

Death Pres: 16-10-42 c/ℓ 1159

P.P.M.   Lost at Sea

3186 Burial inf. received from I.R.C.C. for P/O Fitzgerald is confirmed by German documents. They state he was washed ashore on the Island of Norderney and buried in Norderney military Cemetery Field E Grave 20 Germany)

P.P.M. 1200/48 A.G.13. Photostats show P/Lt.Off Fitzgerald now Concentrated to Oldenburg (Sage.) Cancelled British Cemetery, Plot III, Row F, Grave 5, see amended parts.   Contd. on Sheet 2

NE 8078-7

Formblatt 1
(gem.D(Luft)2606/07-Anlage 2)

Nur für den Dienstgebrauch!

Angabe über Gefangennahme von feindlichen
Luftwaffenangehörigen

Dienststelle: Fliegerhorstkommandantur   Verteiler:

Ort: .... Berlin-Gatow ....

Zeit: .... 27.3.1944 ....

        Abschuß ....

Betr.:   einer .. Lancaster ....

          Notlandung ....

          bei [1]. Berlin NO, Friedrichshain und Umgebung

          an   .24.3.1944 .... um 22.32 Uhr

Name: ...... Wee ....

Vornamen: J.M. ....

Dienstgrang: .. unbekannt, Erkennungsmarke: N.Z.416518 ..

Verbleib[2]: .. tot geborgen ....

Ort u.Zeit der Gefangennahme: ....

....

Bezeichnung des Lazaretts: ....

Ort u.Zeit der Beisetzung: ....
(Grablage evtl.nachmelden): ....

Leiche am 25.3.1944 im Res.Laz.101 Olympisches Dorf Döberitz
eingeliefert.

Zu [1]   Genaue Angaben des Aufschlagortes und dessen Lage
         zu größerem Bezugsort, bei Großstädten Angabe des
         Vorortes, Stadtteil oder der Straße.

Zu [2]   Ob gefangen, verwundet, vermißt, flüchtig oder tot
         geborgen.

                                         Oberleutnant

141

Formblatt 2
D Luft 2706/07, Anl.3

Flugplatzkommando
Antwerpen- Deurne
Kdo.Fl.H.Ber.22/XI

Nur für den Dienstgebrauch!

O.U., den 13. Mai 1944 **24. MAI 1944**

Abschliessende Meldung über Anfall von Lw.- Feindgerät
und gegnerischen Flugzeugbesatzungen

Verteiler: RLM, GL/C-Rü
F.Lg.Kdo.Belg./Nordfr. Ic/Vern.Offz.
Auswertestelle West, Oberursel i/Ts.
FU-Stelle 4 (Fp.Nr. L 22829, Fgpa. A'dam über Bentheim)
FU-Stelle 5 (Fp.Nr. L 50825, Fgpa. Brüssel)
Kommandeur der Lw.-Bergetruppen Paris-Nanterre

Tag des Absturzes: 12.5.44   Uhrzeit: 00.00 - 01.00 Uhr
Aufschlagort: 3 km SO Herenthout, 7 km SO Herenthals

Flugzeugmuster: Lancaster
Hin- oder Rückflug: Hinflug
Art der Bodenberührung: Aufschlag, Explosion mit Bomben
Bruch in Prozent: 100 %
Art der Erbeutung: verm. Nachtjäger

Buchst.-Kennz. ./.
Zulassungs-Nr. ./.

Bewachung des Flugzeuges wurde gestellt durch: Feldg. Herenthals

Verbleib der Besatzung

Tote, insgesamt - 4 - Mann
1. Sgt. T h o m p s o n L.   Erk.-N.1323406   Feindfr.Antw.-Deurne
                                                   Beisetzung 15.5.44
                                                   Grab-Nr. 155

2. Sgt. R o w t h o r n e.   " 853111   "   156
3. Sgt. A m i e s   P.   " 1445907   "   157
4.   unbekannt   "   158

    verm. Tote unter Trümmern im Trichter — {2

Bewaffnung

7,7 mm Browning Mach.Gun 303 Mk II   BI 86693 B
                                       " 85168 B
                                       " 88026 B
                                       " 95847 B

Technische Angaben

Motormuster: Merlin 24   keine Typenschilder

Die Ermittlungen u.Feststellungen führte:

                              Name:
                              (Fw.u.Führer d.Übernahmekommandos)

142

2.) Gross-Auheim, Exerzierplatz, -QS 6-, 18.50 Uhr, Halifax, 99 %, Kennz. DWG 5702 F 91, W.Nr. unbekannt, 99 %, 7 Tote.

...eldung über den Abschuß eines britischen Flugzeuges

Abschuß-Nr. ... 10139

Abschußtag und Zeit:	6.1.45 - 18.50	
Abschußort:	Grossauheim	
Flugzeugtyp:	Halifax	
Meldende Dienststelle:	Fl. H. Kdtr. Langendiebach	

Besatzung:

Name und Vornamen: Geburtstag und -ort:	Dienst-grad	Erk.-Marke:	gef.: verw.: tot:	Verbleib: welches Lager Art d. Verwundung Grablage
COTTRELL		xx85xx	tot	Frdhf. Grossauheim
KEMPER	John	429582	tot	dito
GORE		1021154	tot	dito
MORGAN		336722	tot	dito
JELLEY	G.F.	161312	tot	dito
WHIBROW	R.	1595362	tot	dito

Bemerkungen: ....

DULAG-LUFT, den .... 5. .45 Wo.

S 5858/44 He Heidelberger Gutenberg-Druckerei GmbH. V. 44.

143

Für Dienstgebrauch

Kdo. Flugh.Ber. 13/VII

KE- 10789 [KE]

Abschliessende Meldung über Abfall von Lw.-Feindgerät und gegnerischen
Flugzeugbesatzungen

Verteiler:

Feindgerät-Untersuchungsstelle .... 2 x
Luftgaukommando .... Qu./Lg.Ing .... 1 x
Kommando Flughafenber ich .... 1 x
Auswertestelle-West, Oberursel / Ts .... 1 x
Entwurf .... 1 x
Lw.-Stelle .... 1 x
Tag d. Absturzes 6.1.45   Uhrzeit: 18.50   aufsc l.Ort Gross-
                                              mit Bezugsort:auheim

---

Flugzeugmuster: Halifax   Buchst.Kennz. .... Kokarde
Hin- oder Rückflug: Anflug
Beschriftung oder Bemalung
am Bug   am Rumpf ./.   unten ./.
                                   höchst. ./.   in geometr ./.
                                 über Nummer ./.   Figur,Kreis,
                                                          Dreieck, Quadrat
                                 Zulassugs-Nr.   ./.

Dulag-Luft, Wetzlar
Eingang 2 6 JAN. 1945
Zentralkart. u. Meldest.

                                 (Buchst. und Zahl am Rumpfende oder slw.
                                  Buchst. unter Nummer ....)

1 Baumuster-Sch ild v. S.-Flosse: Halifax DWG 5702 F 91 SER: 37736/Z
1 "   "   Triebwerk-Auslauf: DWG 61114 B2. SER: 13694/Z
Auf der Qu-R-Bespannung: SER 34.782 in weiss TDS 3 A in rot aufschablonie
                                              C
Unter dem Triebwerk-Auslauf: 694/Z in rot aufschabloniert.
                             Z

Art der Bodenberührung: Art der Erbeutung:

Aufschlagbrand, Explosion   Flak
in der Luft

Bruch in Prozenten: 99%

Zur Aufnahme von Fahndungsaktionen nach flüchtigen oder vermissten Be-
satzungsmitgliedern wurden alarmiert: Polizeidienststelle Grossauheim.

Auswertestelle West
2 6 JAN 1945

- 2 -

Bewachung des Flugzeuges wurde gestellt durch:
dann: Flakabteilung 857/o, Untergruppe Hanau

Lichtbilder wurden gefertigt durch:
unter Kennzeichen:

Navigations-u. Funkunterlagen, Schriftstücke, Karten usw . wurden

Verbleib der Besatzung

Tote, insgesamt 7 Mann

Lfd. Nr.	Dienstgrad	Name	Vorname	Erk.-Nr.
1		Cotterell		
2		Kreften	John	8.4.1915
3		Gote		1021154
4		Morgan -		338722
5-7		unbekannt		

wurden in Grossauheim beerdigt

Gefangene insgesamt ./. Mann

Vermutlich flüchtig sind insgesamt ./. Mann

Die Ermittlungen und Feststellungen führten

Name ....

Dienstgrad ....

Fhr. d.Übernahmekommando

Technische Angaben:

Zelle: Rumpf: zerstört Fahrwerk:1 Laufrad Tragfläche: zerstört
Leitwerk: zerstört . Bauteile des Flugzeuges stürzten auf ein Haus in
Grossauheim, gr.-Kotzenburgerstr. 18 und verbrannten mit diesen. Leit-
werteil auf Exerzierplatz.

- 3 -

Motormuster: 14 Zyl. Doppelstern-Schiebermotor

Motormuster und Bruchprozente:

1. 24096/AMAC/ 3L/ 75%
3. noch nicht aufgefunden
Zu 1.: Auf dem Sitrngehäuse:HbR
149246/2, Nr. 117121 u.8632458
(sämtl. eingeschlagen)

2. SS 22686 SS 228603 Ca. 50%
4. noch nicht aufgefunden
Zu 2.: im Gartengrundstück Heimbachstr. 2 im Erdreich versunken.

Metall-Luftschraubenblattschr. .... Muster ....
      DRG.-Nr...........   Serial-Nr.........

1 Metallschraube im Grundstück Heimbachstr. 2 im Erdreich versunken.
Datenangaben nicht möglich.

Bewaffnung: nicht aufgefunden

Lfd.-Nr.   Kaliber   Muster und Hersteller   Einbauart starr oder beweg

Verwendete Visiere   ./.   ./.

Bordwaffenmunition:
(Kaliber, Menge, Gurt o. Trommel)
Mischungsverhältnis:
Angabe d.Bezeichnung auf d.Hülsenboden:

Abwurfmunition:
Art und Zahl: nicht aufgefunden
Art d.Bombenhänge: nicht aufgefunden
(Angabe nach Typenschild)
Art d. Bombenzielgerätes

Panzerung:
Stärke und Anbringungsart:
(mögl. Skizze als Anlage) nicht aufgefunden

146

Ft-Geräte : nicht aufgefunden

Antennenart und Einbauart: nicht feststellbar

Bildgeräte: Es ist anzugeben: Type, Ref.-Nr., Ser.Nr., Brennweite,
gr. Blende, Öffnung-Objektiv-Nr. und Zustand jedes Bild-
gerätes sowie Einbauart).

Flugbetriebsstoff und Hydraulik-Öle (Es ist die sichergestellte Menge
von Kraftstoff, Schmieröl und Hydraulik-Öle anzugeben)
Anzahl d. Kraftstoffbehälter: nicht aufgefunden

Anzahl der an Beuteauswertestelle d. Luftwaffe, Berlin, Adlerhof,

eingesandten Schilder : drei

(Von Flugzeugen, die zum Wiederaufbau bestimmt werden und von allen
Geräten, deren Einzelteile nach Anweisung der Feindgeräteuntersuchung-
stelle zu versenden, dürfen die Typenschilder nicht entfernt werden
sondern sind abzuschreiben.

Folgendes Gerät wird gemäss Anweisung der Feindgeräte -u. Untersuchungs-
stelle zum Versand gebracht:

....

....

....
Ing. d. Übernahmekommandos e. Stellv.

147

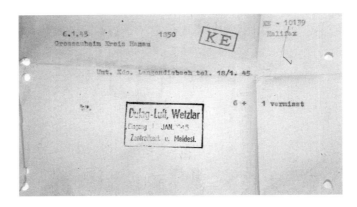

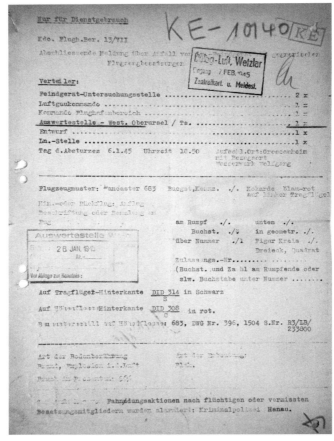

This Dulag Luft, Wetzlar, piece of paper records the crash of a Halifax taking place at 1850 hours on 6 January 1945 at Grossauheim, Kreis [District] Hanau. 6+ indicates six air crew are dead. One is listed as missing [vermisst].

- 2 -

Bewachung des Flugzeuges wurde gestellt durch:

dann: Flakabteilung 857/o Untergruppe Hanau

Lichtbilder wurden gefe tigt durch:

1 Combined operating Sign ls 1943. 1 Air for e A.P. 1027. 1 Secret/
Diversion schedule for Bomber command aircraft, 1 Air almal 1945.
Januar - April, 1 Karte England-Schottland, 1 Ausweis mit Passbildern
und an die Auswertestelle-West, Oberursel, weitergeleitet.

Lfd. Nr.	Dienst- grad	Vorname	Name	Erk.- Nr.
1			Jelley	161312
2			Thybrow	59536 2 G B
3		(Alexder, Thomas	Gladla	31.10.10 958.
4-6		unbekannt		

2 Tote in Grossauheim / 4 Tote in Langendiebach beerdigt .

Gefangene insgesamt ..../. .... Mann

Vermutlich flüchtig sind /insgesamt .... ein ... Mann

Die Ermittlungen und Feststellungen führten

Name ....

Dienstgrad ....

Fhr. d. Übernahmekommando

Technische Angaben:

Zelle : Rumpf: nur Mittelteil/Fahrwerk: 1 Laufrad/ Tragfläche: linker
gestört aufge-   verbrannt   tragflügel teilweise.
funden.
Leitwerk: teilweise.

- 3 -

Motormuster: 1 Stck 12 Zylinder Reihenmotor im Erdreich versunken

Metall-Luftschraubenblattschr...........Muster...........
DRG.-Nr........   Serial Nr......
1 Metallschraube im Erdreich versunken.

Bewaffnung: 2 MG 7,7 mm.

Lfd.Nr. 1   Kaliber 7,7 mm.   Muster und Hersteller MK II BS 250 900 SD
           1   7,7 mm.   303 MK II By, 88632

Bordwaffenmunition:
(Kaliber, Menge, Gurt o. Trommel)
Mischungsverhältnis:

Angabe der Bezeichnung auf d. Hülsenboden:

Abwurfmunition: nicht vorgefunden

Art d. Bombenhänge: nicht feststellbar
(Angabe nach Typenschild)
Art d. Bombenzielgerätes:

Panzerung:
(Stärke und Anbringungsart, mögl. Skizze als Anlage) nicht aufgefunden

Ft.-Geräte:
1 Transmitter -Receiver Type 1196 Ref.Nr. 10D/325 / Serial Nr. 027980
1 Junction Box Type 231 Ref.Nr. 10 AB 6370 Serial Nr. 292
1 Power Unit Type 87 Ref.-Nr. 10/2/301 Serial Nr. 14082
1 Receiving Unit Type E 25 Ref.-Nr. 10 P/II Serial Nr. 028266

Antennenart und Einbauart: nicht feststellbar

Bildgeräte: (Es ist anzugeben: Type, Ref.-Nr., Ser.-Nr., Brennweite,
             gr. Blende, Öffnung Objektive-Nr. und Zustand jedes Bild-
             gerätes sowie Einbauart). ./.

Flugbetriebsstoff u. Hydraulik-Öle (Es ist die sichergestellte Menge von
    Kraftstoff, Schmieröl und Hydraulik-Öl anzugeben)
Anzahl d. Kraftstoffbehälter: ./.

— 4 —

Anzahl der an Beuteauswertungsstelle d. Luftwaffe, Berlin, Alerhof, eingesandten Schilder: dreizehn.

(Von Flugzeugen, die zum Wiederaufbau bestimmt werden und von allen Geräten, deren Einzelteile nach Anweisung der Feindgeräteuntersuchungsstelle zu versenden sind, dürfen die Typenschilder nicht entfernt werden, sondern sind abzuschreiben.)

Folgendes Gerät wird gemäss Anweisung der Feindgeräte-Untersuchungsstelle zum Versand gebracht .

2 Fallschirme, 2 Schlauchboote.

....

Ing. d. Übernahmekommandos o. Stellv. Qu

Wertpapiere und Erkennungsmarken wurden durch Kurier an die Auswertstelle – West, Oberursel, weitergeleitet.

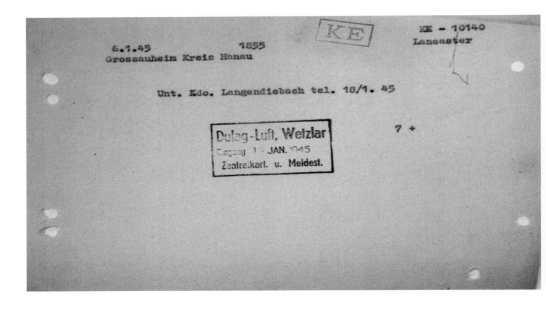

Wartime shortages made paper precious. Both the Germans and the British recycled paper and used any scrap of paper, including them in their records. The example below records the crash of a Lancaster at the waterworks [Wasserwerk Wolfgang] at Grossauheim on 6 January 1945.

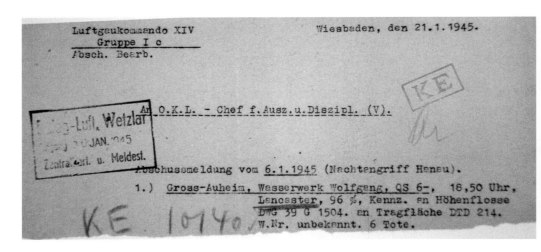

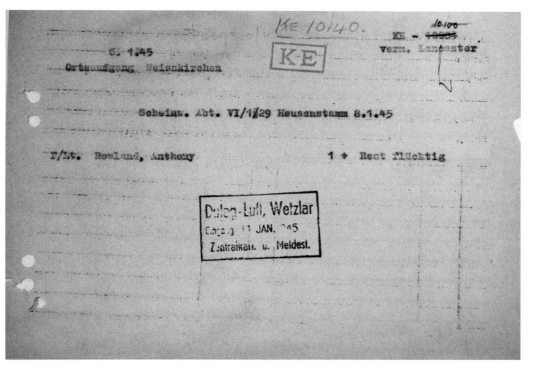

The Dulag Luft Wetzlar record of prisoner Flight Lieutenant J.A. Rowland RAAF pilot of Lancaster PB228 of 635 Squadron lost on the night of 6/7 January 1945. One or more (1+) of the crew are recorded as Fugitives (flüchtig) but in fact had been killed. On liberation Flt Lt Rowland said on his Repatriation Questionnaire that he believed his crew had got out before he left the aircraft. In 1975 Rowland became Chief of the Air Staff (RAAF). Note that the Dulag Luft Wetzlar record for Flt Lt Rowland was typed on the back of an old form and the lines on the reverse show through.

Chapter 12

Missing Research & Enquiry Service Documents Found in Casualty P Files

The Missing Research and Enquiry Service began an investigation either when sent a casualty enquiry (which normally came from the Missing Research Section of P4(Cas)) or as the result of a discovery made during a MRES sweep of an area. When a crew was largely composed of Dominion Air Force personnel (eg five Canadians, one RAF and one RNZAF) the casualty enquiry would originate from the overseas headquarters (based in London) of the Dominion Air Force whose personnel were involved, and copied to the Air Ministry Casualty Branch. With the enquiry came all the information P4(Cas) had gathered about the subject aircraft and crew.

Casualty Enquiries sent out by P4(Cas) were prompted either by information held in the Casualty Branch or resulted from information passed to P4(Cas) from other sources such as units serving in the liberated countries. One example of the latter is a case which began as a result of information sent to the Casualty Branch by 85 Group when it was based in Ghent, Belgium. The information passed on stated that two bodies had been found in the wreckage of an aircraft; the locals had buried the bodies on a hill overlooking Houffalize. It was known that a Lancaster had crashed there on 5 January 1945 and all the crew except the rear gunner were killed (the rear gunner became a PoW). The two graves were opened and the occupants identified. No 2 Missing Research and Enquiry Unit (MREU) was then tasked by P4(Cas) with tracing the four other crew members. The MREU search officer conducted a painstaking sweep of the crash site area. During a search of woods the remains of the bomb aimer were found and identified by the half-winged 'B' brevet on his jacket. More searching produced the remains of the pilot who was identified by his identity discs. Although thick undergrowth hampered his search the investigating officer also found the last two sets of remains. The bodies of all the deceased crew were recovered; four lie in Houffalize Communal Cemetery, Luxembourg and two in Hotton War Cemetery, Belgium.

Soon after No 1 MRE Section was established in France in 1945 it became clear that large areas needed to be checked so No 4 Missing Research and

Enquiry Unit was established to sweep areas of France searching for crash locations and burial sites. The information collected on the sweeps was sent back to the Casualty Branch who evaluated the MRES findings. When the Casualty Branch decided that further information was needed, a Casualty Enquiry was sent back to the MRES which requested an investigation of the crash site or grave. Copies of Casualty Enquiries are found on Casualty P Files.

AFW3372 Graves Registration Report Form

In addition to informing the Casualty Branch of sweep results the MRES also informed the Army Graves Registration of any unregistered graves found during a sweep. The information was sent to the Graves Registration Unit on Army Form W3372. This form was also used for sending any amended information. Copies of AFW3372 are found on Casualty P Files.

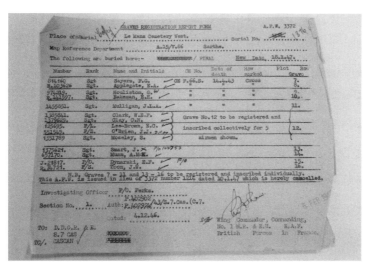

Graves Registration Report Form making an amendment marked 'Final' to previous burial information sent to the Army Graves Registration and Enquiry Service by the RAF No 1 Missing Research & Enquiry Unit, France, for graves in Le Mans Cemetery. The form is a local MRES reproduction of Army Form W3372. The investigating officer is given as Flying Officer Perks and the authority for the investigation is given as 2 Casualty Enquiries with the references P402520/43/S.7Cas and P402921/43/ S.7Cas (the designation of the Casualty Branch had changed from P4(Cas) to S.7 Cas)

Copies of this AFW3372 were sent to the Director of the Directorate of Graves Registration & Enquiry (DDGR&E) in the War Office, to the Air Ministry S.7 CAS and, as RCAF personnel were involved, to the Canadian Casualty Branch (CASCAN).

Missing Research and Enquiry Service Search Reports

When an investigation was concluded the MRES sent their recommendation as to the identification of the occupant of a grave to the Casualty Branch. It was the Air Ministry Casualty Branch who had the final say on whether or not an identification recommendation submitted to them by the MRES was accepted or whether the grave was to be registered for an Unknown Airman. The Casualty Branch also made the decision on whether a grave was to be a collective grave or an individual one.

The primary documents sent by the MRES containing the results of their investigations and recommendations (and which are included on Casualty P Files) are the MRES Search or Investigation Reports. The MRES Reports are variously addressed to Air Ministry P4(Cas), Air Ministry S14(Cas) and Air Ministry S7(Cas). These changes in the Casualty Branch designation were caused by post-war departmental reorganisations within the Air Ministry. They are not separate sections within the Casualty Branch.

The MRES Reports summarised the results of their investigation but the Search officers making the report were instructed that it should be full and 'include matters of human interest' which could be incorporated in letters to the next of kin.[1] However, irrelevant and unnecessary detail was not to be included as '*Local colour, when expressed too vividly, obscures the outlines of an account*'.[2] The report was to be confined to the specific Casualty Enquiry being investigated. The search officers were told that if, during their investigation, another crash or grave site was found they were to be the subject of separate reports. Search officers were also instructed to state whether or not they had personally visited the crash site, cemetery etc, and whether or not any existing cemetery records maintained by the local authorities had been scrutinized. The search officers were also expected to show initiative, especially when looking at possible exhumations. It was often the investigating officer on site who had the best handle on whether or not an exhumation would be worthwhile.

The quality of MRES Reports vary considerably: some are short and say little, others are long and detailed, and some give extremely gruesome

---

1. Air Ministry Report on Royal Air Force and Dominions Air Forces Missing Research and Enquiry Service 1944 to 1949 by Group Captain E. Hawkins HQ BAFO dated March 1949 Appendix A, Missing Research Memorandum 1.
2. Ibid Appendix B.1 Missing Research Memorandum 11.

details gathered from eyewitnesses. MRES Reports do not make easy reading; in one the search officer quotes a German eyewitness who described entrails hanging from trees and being eaten by farm dogs. Bodies were often fragmented, either by the impact of the crash or when a bomber blew up in mid-air; coffins or graves were quite often found to contain the skeletal remains or body parts of more than one individual. A fire on impact would also mean the remains were usually burnt, further complicating identification.

The remains of the crew lie amongst the wreckage of their aircraft which came down in occupied Europe.

MRES Investigation Report Format

MRES Reports have a standardized format, so much so that some units had the first page containing the 'administrative' information printed. All reports begin:

From: *The MRES unit submitting the Report*

To: *The Air Ministry (P4(Cas) later S14(Cas) and then S7(Cas))*

Copies to: *Dominion Air Force Overseas Headquarters when Dominion personnel involved.*

Date: *of the Report*

Your File Reference: *The P File Reference and Casualty Enquiry Reference*

Name of Search Officer & Number of Section: *The name of the individual search officer and the number of his Section*

Target: *The target that the aircraft was sent against.*

Aircraft Type & Serial No:

Date aircraft Reported Missing:

Place of crash with Map Reference:

Place of Burial with Map Reference:

Names of Crew/s:

Map References

The map references used by the MRES were taken from British Army maps in the 1:250,000 series. These were produced by the Geographical Section, General Staff and are known as GSGS maps. The GSGS series used by the MRES were GSGS 2738 and GSGS 4042 for France, Belgium, Luxembourg and most of Holland and GSGS 4346 for Germany. Each set of maps was used in conjunction with a gazetteer which gave full instructions on locating a particular place.[3]

Search officers were only required to give a figure reference. In the gazetteer of France, Belgium and Luxemburg, and Holland references on the map sheets of GSGS 2738 were started with the letter A, those on GSGS4042 series by the letter B, those on GSGS4346 series by the letter C and those of GSGS4230 series by the letter D. The grid letter indicated that the place was located within the *area of the grid letter* and in the grid *square* whose south-west corner was the intersection of numbered vertical and horizontal lines known as easting and northing with the easting given first. For example:

---

3. The extant set of GSGS maps has been given by the Ministry of Defence to the British Map Library of the British Museum and contains many Second World War maps together with the gazetteers. Copies of some GSGS maps are also held by other archives such as the Imperial War Museum.

Alençon was given as A8/Z.38 = Sheet 8 of GSGS2738 grid letter Z and in the grid made by 3 on the easting and 8 on the northing.

Abbeville was B4/M.78 = Sheet 4 of GSGS4042 grid letter M and in this grid 7 on the easting and 8 on the northing.

Altkirch was given as C.K48/A69 = Sheet K48 of GSGS4346 grid letter A and in this grid 6 on the easting and 9 on the northing.

In the Investigation Report below, the crash site and burial were at Lignières at map reference A21/P55 which equates to Sheet 21 of GSGS2738 grid letter P and easting of 5 and a northing of 5.

After the 'administrative' information comes the body of the report which can include descriptions of visits to crash sites and burial places, names of local persons and organisations contacted such as mayors, Burgomeisters (in Germany), the police, grave diggers, cemetery authorities, parish priests and details of eyewitnesses and brief descriptions of what they had seen. Search officers were also instructed to retrieve any identity discs or other identifying material together with any valuables or personal possessions found and which might have been kept. Anything retrieved was forwarded to the Casualty Branch but descriptions of items recovered sometimes appear in MRES Reports.

The example MRES Search Report given below relates to two Lancaster aircraft and their crews who were lost on 16 July 1944 over France. They were the subject of Casualty Enquiry F438. The MRES Report shows that the search officer, Flight Lieutenant Dawes (who was also the RAF liaison officer with the Army's No 57 Graves Concentration Unit) decided that an exhumation of the graves in the Le Mans cemetery would be of assistance. His report to the Air Ministry Casualty Branch (now designated S14) includes a summary of the results of the exhumations that took place and the objects etc that were found. As the crews included RCAF and RAAF personnel, copies of the report were sent to the Canadian Casualty Department in London (given as CASCAN on the report) and the RAAF Overseas Headquarters (given by RAAF o/s HQ), also in London. At the end of his report Flt Lt Dawes states that no Form AFW3372 will be sent to register the graves until after he has received the Casualty Branch's decisions.

R E P O R T

29 A.

FRO   : France Detachment Missing Research and Enquiry Service,
           Royal Air Force, British Forces in France.

TO   : Air Ministry (S.14 CAS), 2 Seville Street, Knightsbridge LONDON S.W.1. ✓

COPIES :   CASCAN
           R.A.A.F. O/S. HQ.

DATE   : 16 September 1947

YOUR FILE REF : P.420217/44/P4/104 dated 18.1.46

YOUR CASUALTY ENQUIRY NUMBER : F 438   DEPARTMENT : INDRE & LOIRE

OUR REF : OPS.8/CE.F.438 S/AIR

NAME OF SEARCH OFFICER & NO. OF G.C.U. : F/LT. E.J.DAWES, No.57

TARGET : NEVERS

AIRCRAFT TYPE & SERIAL NUMBER : LANCASTER ME 607 and ME 85

DATE REPORTED MISSING : 16 July 1944

PLACE OF CRASH : LIGNIERES   MAP REF : A21/P55

PLACE OF BURIAL : LIGNIERES Communal Cemetery   MAP REF : A21/P55

CREW :

	LANC. ME. 607			LANC. ME 85		
127737	F/LT.	G.L. JONES (RAF) Pilot	J.28935	F/LT.W.B.MURPHY RAF		Pilot
177620	F/O.	E. DALGLEISH (RAF) 2nd Pilot	1705245	SGT. E.CW.GOODE "		F/E
1394230	SGT.	B.St.J.WOOLLARD (RAF) F/E.	AUS.422342	F/S. W.H.E.WRIGHT RAAF		NAV
AUS.409772	F/O	F.R. TICKLE (RAAF) NAV.	AUS.423689	F/O. J.A.EWEN "		A/B
R.152727	W/O	F.G. GRAHAM (RCAF) A/B.	AUS.423870	F/S. W. PAUL "		WOP/AG
1581317	SGT.	J.H. FELLOWS (RAF) WOP/AIR	AUS.424764	F/S. A.H.JENKINS "		R/G
2220609	SGT.	R.A. GAUT (RAF) A/G.	AUS.427726	F/S. D.A.PATTERSON		
R.201588	F/SGT.M.J.W.CAMTWELL (RCAF) A/G.				RAAF,	MU/G

(ex R.95891)

RESULT OF INVESTIGATION AND FINDINGS :

1.   After reading through the relevant documents on this Casualty Enquiry prior to
commencing work in the Department of the Indre & Loire, I decided, considering the
presence of six RAAF and three RCAF personnel among the fifteen crew members, plus
the fact that there were thirteen coffins, that the opinion expressed in para 5 of
previous report dated 14.6.46 was somewhat pessimistic, and accordingly requested
permission to exhume. This was granted and the exhumation was carried out on the
8th and 9th inst.

2.   After having removed another body from the coffin containing the body of
F/SGT. PATTERSON and reburying same in row 2, Grave 3, all fifteen bodies were accounted for, as the small coffin in position Row B, Grave 2 contains the jumbled
remains of more than one body.

3.   Grave 1, row A was found to contain the body of F/SGT. JENKINS, from his
metal identity plaque.

4.   Grave 2, row A was found to contain the body of SGT. GAUT, this being substan-
tiated by his name and initials and "last three" being clearly inscribed on his shirt
collar.

5.   Grave 3, Row A was found to contain the body of F/SGT. PATTERSON, from his metal
identity plaque.

6.   In grave 4 of row A was found only the remains of a trunk plus a few scraps of
issue shirt. However the Maire assured me that at the time of death his name was
assumed to be PAUL from some papers which were removed from the body, hence the body
is undubitably that of F/SGT. PAUL. This is corroborated by the scraps of dark blue
pullover which were found, which were of the type issued by the Australian Comforts

29'2   ......

- 2 -

29/b

to men of the RAAF.

7. In grave 5 of Row A was found a fully dressed airman with RAF B/D, CANADA flashes W.O.II insignia and an "S" brevet. In spite of the discrepancy in this latter, this must have been the body of W/O GRAHAM as he was the only W/O in the two crews. Furthermore,Mairie records also show this to be the body of GRAHAM from identity discs found at the time of death, which were taken by the Germans. It seems probable that he had borrowed the tunic of a friend.

8. In the coffin in grave six, row A was found a body, probably that of an Officer. The shirt appeared to be new as there was no laundry mark whatsoever thereon. On the black tie was found a tie clip of somewhat unusual pattern. It consisted of an equilateral triangle with sides ½" long, and resembles bilck enamel on a brass backing. The outline was traced out with small imitation pearls inlaid at close inter- vals. In the centre of the triangle was an Aladdin's Lamp, surrounded by the initial A in the bottom left hand corner, the initial E in the bottom right hand corner, and at the apex, a small triangle. To the back was affixed a clip with a patent fastener. Attached to this brooch by a light chain about 1½" long was another, which was a minor replica of the other in respect of shape, but instead of any interior markings it represented the initial A, which was similarly traced out in the tiny inlaid pearls. To the back was affixed a clip of the same pattern as the other but on a smaller scale.Unfortunately the enamel had become tarnished, and cracked, and was impregnated with moisture from the decomposing flesh, the larger of the two brooches was cracked and the two clips were broken,as was the chain, and the article was not considered in a fit state to retain. It appeared to me not to be the general type of tie clip worn by a man, and gave me the impression that it was given to the wearer, probably as a souvenir or good luck charm, by a woman. I was thought at the time that this could possibly have been the body of F/O. J.A. EWEN , but later enquiries (see below) prove my observation above to be the more probable, and that the body was probably that of F/O TICKLE.

9. In the coffin in grave 7 of Row A were found the remains of a SGT.Engineer, and this must therefore be the body of either SGT. (then) WOOLLARD or SGT. GOODE. From enquiries I have made from several different people who witnessed the "mise en biere" I have been able to ascertain that, with the exception of WRIGHT & GRAHAM, who wereapparently thrown clear, the aircraft fell sufficiently far apart for the bodies to be picked up separately, i.e. the bodies were found either lying alongside the aircraft or were extricated from its wreckage. Although it was not possible to find any means of identification on this body at the time of the disaster, I am assured that he was a member of the same aircraft from which F/SGT. PAUL was extricated,hence it seems reasonable to assume that this was the body of SGT. GOODE.

10. Grave 8 Row A was found to contain an RCAF F/SGT. Air Gunner, and as F/SGT.CANTWELL is the only RCAF Sgt AG in the two crews, this was accepted as being his body, the "last four" of his personal number on his collar confirming this assumption.

11. The last grave in this Row A,number 9 was already shewn in the Mairie records as WRIGHT. The RAAF B/D "O" brevet and SGT's stripes confirmed this.

12. It will be clearer to summarise the contents of the coffins in Row B as below with the exception of Grave 2.

a) Grave 1. RAF B/D (scraps only) Non issue socks,Officer type shirt. Dental plate
b) Grave 3. " " right hand side missing, F/O braid.
c) Grave 4. " " (scraps only) Officer type shirt with mark W.133.
JW in black ink.
d) Grave 5. No B/D found, collar attached,shirt marked

WM....... WM(not clear)
283 or 253
and sewn on tab marked in embroidered figures 283.
pullover with label GENTKNIT FASHIONS. Evidently of heavy build.

Assuming that F/O TICKLE is in grave 6, row A as I will later show, then the F/O in Grave 3 above must be either F/O EWEN, or DALGLEISH. This leaves, then, three officers to be accounted for, viz F/LTS. JONES & MURPHY, and F/O EWEN or DALGLEISH. It would appear from the initials on the shirt in grave 5 that this might have been the body of F/LT. MURPHY,although the marks were admitedly faint. To strengthen thisbelief is the fact that he was wearing a shirt of a pattern much favoured by Canadians, who preferred collar-attached type shirts to those with detachable collars. If it can be found that the GENTKNIT trademark is not that of an English Establishment, then I am convinced

....

161

29 C

that this is indeed the body of F/LT. MURPHY, RCAF, if he was of heavy build.

13. It should prove possible to identify the officer in grave 1 from the unusual dental plate found in the lower jaw, as next of kin are doubtlessly aware of this.

14. After the above possibilities have been explored, it may be found that the remaining graves can be identified by elimination, i.e. should the dental plate be traced to one of the two F/Os, the other must be in grave 3, and the body in grave 4 that of the only officer unaccounted for, i.e. F/LT. JONES.

15. Grave 2 in row B contains a small coffin, in which were found scraps of issue clothing. If grave 7 is accepted as that of SGT. GOODE, then this must have been the remains of SGT. WOOLLARD & FELLOWS, there being at least the remains of at least two bodies therein.

16. In view of the fact that it was impossible to identify F/O. TICKLE at the time the exhumation was carried out, yet same had been done at the time of death according to Mme. SCHOUMACHER's letter, I returned to LIGNIERES on the 15th inst., and interviewed this woman, this having not been done by the investigating officer in the previous enquiry. Mme SCHOUMACHER was at that time one of the official Red Cross representatives in the dept., and went immediately from Azay le Rideau to the scene of the crash. I asked her if she could give me any information which might help in locating in which position F/O TICKLE had been buried. This she was unable to do, but took me to a woman friend of hers who was also a Red Cross worker and who likewise assisted in the "mise en biere". This second woman had no knowledge either of in what order the coffins had finally been buried. The only other possibility was a description of the body, and in this instance we met with more success. Mme SCHOUMACHER's friend definitely remembers a clip of some description she noticed on the tie of the body from which the disc inscribed "TICKLE" was removed. I gave her a description of the brooch, but although she admitted she could not remember any details of the brooch in question, she was very emphatic that there was a clip of some description on the tie on the body from which the disc marked TICKLE was taken. As we found no other tie with any clip on it, it would appear that the body in grave 6 row A was indeed that of F/O TICKLE. Furthermore, she added that the body was more or less intact with the exception that the side of the skull was smashed, and the lower part of the trunk had been badly crushed. This latter is certainly consistent with the type of injury a navigator might sustain, being thrown violently against, or being pinned against the navigation table, and tallies with description of body in the grave in question.

17. Every person whom I interviewed who actually saw the bodies, recalled that one was a man of abnormally heavy build "at least 100 kilos" was the average opinion. This apparently refers to the body in grave 5, row B which appears from the remains at the time of exhumation, to have been of very heavy build. This may prove of some assistance in identification.

18. I thanked Mme SCHOUMACHER on behalf of the relatives, for the care she had taken at the time of the disaster in ensuring that these airmen were accorded a proper burial. She washed the faces of the men before they were laid in the coffins, and had hard words with one of the Germans present who had removed the rosary found on the body of F/SGT. CANTWELL, which so shamed him that he gave it her back and she replaced it on the left wrist of this N.C.O., where it was found during the exhumation. The local Gendarmerie and all people whom I interviewed, spoke most highly of the efforts she made at the time to identify these unfortunate airmen, and I think under these circumstances she might be considered for the award of the Air Ministry Diploma for assisting in the identification of missing aircrews, or at least an official letter of thanks.

19. No 3372 will be submitted until your decision is given regarding the acceptance of :

a) Grave 6 row A as F/O TICKLE.
b) Grave 7 row A as SGT. GOODE.
c) The final marking for the whole of Row B.
d) Whether final 3372 should show GRAHAM as W.O or W.O.II.

which is now awaited.

20. Exhumation reports attached.

E. DAWES, F/LT. RAFLO 57 G.C.U.

[signature] F/L

Squadron Leader, Commanding
France Detachment M.R.E.S.
ROYAL   AIR   FORCE

Exhumation Documents

Air Force exhumations conducted by the Army Graves Registration Units (GRU) and Graves Concentration Units (GCU) in conjunction with the MRES were undertaken to establish or to confirm an identity or identities. The MRES Exhumation Officers worked closely with the Army GRUs and GCUs. They were expected to attend every exhumation done for identification or concentration purposes by these Army units and submit reports to the Casualty Branch. The MRES had been instructed that every 'Unknown' was to be exhumed unless the grave was registered by an airman's service number rather than his name or there was sufficient information available for the Casualty Branch to identify the individual without disturbing the grave.

An *exhumation* involves the removal of remains from a formal place of burial (graveyards, churchyards, and cemeteries both civil and military); a *recovery* of remains occurs when remains that have not been formally buried are discovered and removed[4] from crash sites etc. Bodies were sometimes exhumed and moved within cemeteries to fulfil the Air Ministry policy that crews should lie together. Mass exhumations were also conducted, either to obtain all the available evidence in investigations of cemeteries or areas or to concentrate air crew bodies in British military cemeteries. In Germany all known RAF and Dominion Air Force graves (bar twenty-five) were exhumed and concentrated into British military cemeteries. Mass exhumations were often complicated by a number of factors such as poor original records, by previous exhumations done by other nations looking for their own dead, or by the location of the cemetery.

One area which was badly affected in this way was the Döberitz collection of cemeteries which lay in the post-war Russian zone near Berlin. There are references and reports in Casualty P Files concerning cemeteries called 'Döberitz Standortfriedhof', 'Döberitz-Elsgrund' and 'Döberitz-Dallgow'. Many air crew whose aircraft came down in the Berlin area were buried in one or other of the cemeteries at Döberitz by the German authorities. The air crew dead from the western area of Berlin were initially taken by the Germans to a mortuary where they were examined to try to establish their identity and were then buried a few days later at Döberitz. In addition to RAF and Dominion Air Force casualties, American, Italian, and Russian casualties were also buried in the Döberitz area. In late 1946 a British Army

---

4. Definition provided by Commonwealth War Graves Commission.

GCU exhumed many of the bodies in the cemeteries. The MRES officers working with them found such German documentation as existed about the burials in Döberitz was largely inaccurate. During the exhumations many of the names and grave numbers in the German records were found to be wrong. Many bodies had been buried without uniforms, members of different crews had been mixed up while awaiting burial, and several hundred graves were unmarked and unrecorded. Many graves, especially in Döberitz-Elsgrund were found to contain two bodies.

The MRES and GRU officers had originally planned to only exhume graves recorded as being of RAF or Dominion Air Force air crew, but in view of the badly muddled state of Döberitz cemeteries and their poor records it was decided to exhume every grave in Döberitz Standortfriedhof and Döberitz-Elsgrund cemeteries. Some 530 graves were exhumed, but the MRES officers were unable to identify many of the remains. Of the 397 'Unknown' graves in the CWGC Berlin 1939-1945 War Cemetery over 200 contain remains exhumed from the Döberitz cemeteries.

Claims have been made that the Soviet military flattened the area containing the Döberitz cemeteries to use as a military training area, including tank training grounds. Nothing in the MRES Reports submitted by the Berlin Detachment (up to 1949), and held on the Casualty P Files, confirms this. Lengthy research by the RAF's Air Historical Branch has found no evidence of Soviet desecration of graves at Döberitz and indeed all the RAF and Dominion Air Force graves there had been concentrated elsewhere by the end of the 1940s.

Exhumation Reports
When an exhumation took place, copies of the Exhumation Reports raised were included with the MRES Search Report sent to the Casualty Branch. Until 1948 MRES officers were not permitted to undertake exhumations themselves; all exhumations were the remit of the Army Graves Registration Service and their Graves Registration Units (GRU) and Graves Concentration Units (GCU). In 1948 the army disbanded these units as their work concerning army casualties was felt to be complete. However, the search for air crew continued and the MRES began to conduct their own exhumations. While the army was in charge, GRU and GCU officers leading the exhumation produced Exhumation Reports. These were confidential documents, as was made clear by the RAF Inspector of Missing Research who stated that they were confidential documents belonging to the War Office and for which the Deputy Director, Graves Registration and

Enquiries was responsible. The original documents were held in the Deputy Director's office and Army Graves Units kept duplicates. MRES officers were banned from copying or circulating army-produced Exhumation Reports and MRES officers attending exhumations were instructed to make their own notes for identification purposes. The way these notes were recorded was not to be in a form similar to that used by the War Office.[5]

A separate Exhumation Report was sent for each grave exhumed. Four copies of each report were produced signed by the GRU officer, one of which was sent to the Air Ministry Casualty Branch and placed on the relevant Casualty P File. All pertinent local information relating to the grave was to be included in the Exhumation Report. Dates of death and the name or names recorded on the grave and/or in cemetery records were to be given. The original grave numbers were recorded at the top of the report, and if for any reason the body was moved from the original grave, the new grave number was given at the bottom of the report.

At air crew exhumations, once the grave was opened, it was the MRES Witnessing Officer who examined the contents. This was done on site and very often the search officer had to get down into the opened grave to conduct a thorough search for any clues. The remains were often not coffined; sometimes they had been buried wrapped in fabric shrouds, on other occasions the remains had been placed directly into the ground with no wrapping. Search officers were required to include in their report a description of the body/remains found. Often there was very little left to describe, but all details were to be given. Remains in some exhumed graves were found jumbled together. This was quite common and had occurred either because of the state of the remains recovered by the Germans at an aircraft crash site or because a crew had been buried together in a communal grave. Thus graves found marked for a single individual could in fact be those of two or more air crew. The MRES search officers were instructed to look carefully for any evidence that the grave might contain the remains of more than one person.

Any objects which could aid identification were prize finds. All air crew were issued with fibre identity tags giving their name, rank, service number and religion (C of E for Church of England, RC for Catholic, Pres for Presbyterian, Meth for Methodist etc) but these did not always survive the crash or were removed by the Germans or by the local authorities involved in the burial. In addition to the issued identity tags air crew often had their

---

5. Missing Research Memorandum No 1 c A dated 14.3.46 issued by Gp Capt R. Burgess, Inspector of Missing Research.

own privately purchased ones. These were often in the form of identity bracelets or necklaces and, being made of metal, often survived better than the issued tags. In the summer 2018 a group[6] working at the site of the former Natzweiler-Struthof concentration camp in eastern France found an ID disc belonging to Flight Sergeant F.H. Habgood who had been the Bomber Aimer on Lancaster NE164 which took part in an attack on Stuttgart on the night of 28/29 July 1944. The Lancaster was shot down by a night fighter on its return journey and came down at Ottrott Le Bas. Flt Sgt Habgood survived the crash but had the grave misfortune to fall into the hands of the Gestapo who, on 31 July 1944, took him to the nearby Natzweiler-Struthof Camp where he was immediately executed and his body cremated. Post-war an SAS major, searching for their missing personnel, discovered what had happened to Flt Sgt Habgood. He sent a report to the Air Ministry Casualty Branch which can be found on the Casualty P File for the crew of Lancaster NE164. In 1947 the Casualty Branch were able to write to Flt Sgt Habgood's father to tell him the tragic story of what had happened to his son and that those involved in his death had been tried for war crimes and punished.

The identity disc belonging to Flt Sgt Habgood found in the ash pit at Natzweiler-Struthof Concentration Camp in 2018. It is in remarkably good condition; even some of the blue enamel on the RAF wings has survived.

---

6. Members of the Centre Européen du Résistant Déporté.

Sometimes when an air crew grave was opened American 'burial bottles' were found. (The official version of these was green phials but, if these were not available, the Americans used any glass bottle to hand, often Coca-Cola bottles!) Such a find indicated that either the burial had been conducted by the American Graves Registration Service (AGRS) or, and much more usually, the grave had already been exhumed by a unit of the AGRS looking for their own dead. The green phials contained any identity tags or paper identification which the AGRS personnel had found. The information from the phials and any identity tags found were included on the Exhumation Report submitted by the RAF MRES.

When compiling their exhumation reports MRES officers were instructed to give an indication of physical descriptions. An assessment of height and build was required when remains were found that would permit this. This could be done through estimating the man's height from any discovered long bones (such as femurs) using the Brocca Scale or by using the height sizing indicated on any labels found on the remains of issued battle dress, for example a size 14 would be issued to a man of 5 foot 9 to 5 foot 10 inches. The colour of any remaining hair was recorded and search officers were to say whether it was thick or thin. This information could be compared with that held on the airman's personal records. Any information on teeth found in jaw bones was recorded, but as can be seen from the example Exhumation Reports, this was fairly basic and limited to 'filled' or 'missing' and a note of any unusual dental plate work. How the tooth information was recorded varies as different MRES Sections used different types of tooth charts.

The Casualty Branch required the dental information to compare it with the RAF and Dominion Air Force dental records of possible candidates for the grave. However, the Casualty Branch found that the dental information which should have been recorded on the RAF Form 48 on a man's enlistment was often missing. In his report[7] on the work of the Missing Research and Enquiry Service, Group Captain Hawkins did not mince his words: *'Identification of unknowns would often have been easier if the tooth charts for RAF personnel had been maintained up to date. Unfortunately, RAF dental histories have often proved useless and occasionally misleading, whereas in the cases of Dominion Air Force casualties up-to-date tooth charts have been of the greatest value in establishing identity.'* He demanded an improvement in the keeping of RAF dental records. The Dominion Air

7. Air Ministry Report on Royal Air Force and Dominion Air Forces Missing Research and Enquiry Service 1944-1949 by Gp Capt E.F. Hawkins DSO Air Headquarters BAFO March 1949.

Forces kept much more detailed dental information than the RAF and in cases involving their personnel the dental information supplied by the MRES search officers was of much more use for identification purposes.

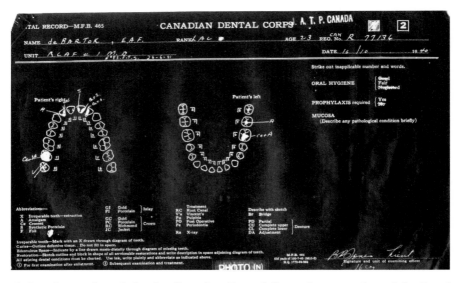

A dental record made by the Canadian Dental Corps for a member of the Royal Canadian Air Force.

In some cases the MRES found that the airman had had all his teeth removed and wore false teeth. Dental plates were not uncommon amongst young men during the Second World War. Dental health, especially amongst the less well off, was relatively poor; there was no National Health Service and treatments were not as varied as today. The removal of a tooth was often the only treatment offered so teeth were often pulled out or lost through disease and replaced with dentures. The Casualty Branch was able to identify some casualties because they wore dentures (see Exhumation Report 29M below).

Personal possessions, and any objects found in a grave which the search officer thought might help identify the deceased, were carefully removed, bagged, labelled and sent to the Air Ministry Casualty Branch Missing Section who used their accumulated knowledge and skill to investigate their ownership. This was not always straightforward, as is shown by this 'story of a handkerchief'.

The handkerchief arrived in the Casualty Branch accompanied by a letter from a Dutchman. The letter said that on 1 May 1943 at 0300 hours a large bomber force was over Holland. The weather was mild and it was cloudy. The Dutchman said he heard German aircraft approaching the bombers and then he suddenly heard an engine cut out and saw a red light and realised that a bomber had caught fire. He saw the aircraft crash to the ground and explode. The letter went on to say that the next morning at 0430 the writer and some other Dutch people found five bodies with their parachutes unopened; the pilot had apparently been hit when the German pilot attacked, as the writer says that a fire extinguisher close to the bomber pilot's head was riddled with bullets.

The Dutch writer reported that the Germans arrived at about 0700 and that the peasants in the vicinity had covered the bodies with sheets. The writer says he had burnt the logbook and maps before the Germans arrived. A German doctor examined the bodies, and the personal effects found were placed in a Red Cross sack. The Germans placed the bodies in plain wooden coffins and took them to the cemetery at Winterswijk where the funeral was held. The local people were allowed to place flowers on the graves. The writer says that he found the handkerchief, which he sent with his letter, on one of the bodies. He also reported that two members of the NSB Landwacht (a collaborationist Dutch paramilitary organisation founded by the Germans) had stolen silver cigarette cases from the dead.

When the Casualty Branch Missing Research Section examined the handkerchief they found it was marked with the service number 1239640 and the name Sergeant A. Keeton. However, the handkerchief had been found on the body of a crew member of Lancaster W4925 of 12 Squadron but there was no Sergeant Keeton amongst that crew. In fact 1239640 Sergeant A.E. Keeton had been the 2nd pilot of Wellington BK507 belonging to 199 Squadron when it crashed near Lorient on 2 February 1943 and he was killed. To add to the mystery, the other side of the handkerchief also had another service number on it. This service number – 1385841 – belonged to Sergeant W.E.F. Clark who was the pilot of Lancaster ED714 which had crashed near Le Mans on 14 April 1943. It was known he was buried in Le Mans West Cemetery.

So, how did the handkerchief come to be found on the body of a member of 12 Squadron on 1 May 1943 in Holland? The Casualty Branch managed to solve the puzzle: Keeton and Clark had been together in pilot training for several months, attending No 32 Elementary Flying Training School, then No 34 School of Flying Training, and finally No 30 Operational Training Unit together. Although they were sent to different squadrons when they graduated from their Operational Training Unit, their squadrons were based at RAF stations which were only a few miles apart. The handkerchief had apparently belonged originally to Sergeant Keeton of 199 Squadron but had somehow come into the hands of Sergeant Clark of 12 Squadron and from him it passed to another member of 12 Squadron on whose body it was found in Holland.

Exhumation Reports included descriptions of any clothing found, both Service and civilian. This information could provide important assistance for identification. Any rank insignia and Flying Brevets found were recorded as they could provide evidence of the rank and 'trade' of the deceased. The centred initials on a pilot's double wing brevet also showed which Air Force he belonged to: RAF, RAAF, RNZAF or RCAF. Uniform buttons could also assist with identifying whether the remains were those of a member of the RAF, RCAF, RAAF or RNZAF. The inclusion of information about the colour of any uniform found was important, a dark-blue uniform indicated that the body was that of a member of the RAAF (see example Exhumation Report 29D). A set of braces marked 'Police' could indicate the remains belonged to a member of the RAAF as their personnel frequently wore braces of this type. Any shoulder flashes found would also indicate the nationality of the deceased as the different nationalities flying in the RAF displayed their home country on such flashes.

Bomber Command air crew from round the world who were serving at an RAF airfield in the north of England. Their home country is shown on their shoulder flash, from left to right: South Africa, New Zealand, Newfoundland, USA, Australia, RNZAF and Canada. Those with national flash were serving in the RAF, the sergeant with the RNZAF flash was a member of the Royal New Zealand Air Force serving with the RAF. The patch which looks like a beetle on the sleeve of three of these men denotes they are qualified Wireless Operators (WOp).

Any uniform shirt remains found could be used to as a guide to whether the wearer had been an officer or other rank. The shirts were of different patterns; officers bought their own but NCOs' shirts were issued to them. However, this was not always a sure-fire method as NCOs who had been commissioned often retained and flew in their old issued shirts. A note of any laundry marks found on clothing etc was included in the Exhumation Report; search officers were instructed to say whether the mark was in ink, embroidered or sewn on. If the markings were indistinct they were cut out of the clothing and sent to the Casualty Branch Missing Section which had become expert in tracing laundry marks and labels. Not only had they built up a wide database of such marks but had also forged close links with the Institute of British Launderers and various trade publications. Search officers were advised that by washing the marks carefully in water and by holding the piece of cloth just below the surface of clean water, the magnifying effect made marks more readable. By early 1947 search officers were able to send laundry marks which were difficult to read to the RAF liaison officer with the American Graves Registration Command where a special infrared photographic technique was used to enhance the marks. The clues provided by the labels were followed up by P4(Cas). A Blenheim crew lost in May 1940 were identified through the tailor's label on the pilot's officers' uniform and the body of a dog found in the wreckage. The pilot's father confirmed his son's life-long passion for dogs and that it was highly likely he had taken his dog with him in the aircraft. Other pilots were known to have flown with dogs on board, including Flight Lieutenant Robin Sinclair, son of the wartime Secretary of State for Air, Sir Archibald Sinclair, who flew his Mosquito in the Far East accompanied by his dachshund Popsie.

When footwear was found in exhumed graves, details were recorded with type and size being given. Bomber air crew normally flew in one of two types of flying boot: either sheepskin-lined flying boots or the 'escape boot' which had been designed by a member of MI9 to assist in evasion. Fighter pilots flew either in flying boots or sometimes in their uniform shoes or, on occasion, their own shoes. Just as labels found on clothing remains such as shirts and underwear were useful, so were labels in non-issue flying footwear. These labels could provide names of makers or tailors and places/towns of origin; for example a company called D. Lewis made bespoke flying boots for officers. They were popular as a 10% discount was offered!

Non-issue items of clothing recovered from exhumed graves (such as a scarf from an old school or a silk scarf of a particular pattern, hand knitted jerseys, or underclothes) were also recorded and proved useful. Next of kin were often

Robin Sinclair and a tired Popsie in the cockpit of a Mosquito in the Far East.

able to confirm the deceased had owned a particular scarf and, similarly, non-issue jumpers and sometimes socks could be identified by family members.

Any equipment found in a grave was also recorded. This included Mae Wests (life jackets) which often had their wearers' names on them, flying suits whether inner or outer (with a note to say if heated), flying gloves, specialist equipment such as navigational items, and parachutes and the condition they were in. Some bodies were buried with pay books, ID cards, and passport photos of themselves in civilian clothes (designed to be used on forged documents to help escape and evasion), and sometimes personal photographs such as those of wives and girlfriends. These were removed from the bodies by search officers and sent to the Air Ministry Casualty Branch. Some Casualty P Files contain these types of items, either found during an exhumation or recovered from bodies by the Germans and later returned to the Casualty Branch.

Personal possessions of any value (such as silver cigarette cases, signet rings, inscribed lighters, non-issue watches etc) or those which could help in

Bomber Command air crew seen putting flying clothing on over their uniforms. Pieces of uniform and flying clothing retrieved during exhumations and crash site excavations helped identify remains.

identification as next of kin might recognise the articles, were forwarded by the search officer attending the exhumation, together with his report, to the Air Ministry Casualty Branch. A note of what was found was included in the Exhumation Report. When an article was found but not kept a note was made in the report to this effect, as was the case of the rosary mentioned in the Exhumation Report 29K below. Some of the personal items found at exhumation or recovered from other sources made their way onto the Casualty P Files.

Once the search officer was satisfied that no further evidence was to be found, the remains were reverently reburied. Outside Germany the graves would either remain in situ or, if the grave was isolated (which usually meant not in consecrated ground) or likely to fall into disrepair, the remains would be reinterred in a British military cemetery. When the grave was to be concentrated into a British military cemetery, (as were all but a few graves in Germany) the remains would normally be reinterred in their existing grave to await removal by the British Army Graves Concentration Units.

Below are examples of MRES Exhumation Reports which are fairly typical of the ones to be found on Casualty P Files. They are clearly marked as being RAF not Army Graves Registration Service Exhumation Reports.

EXHUMATION REPORT (R.A.F.)

29.D

Number : AUS.424764   Rank : F/SGT. Name : JENKINS A.H.   Service : R.A.A.F.

Cemetery or Place of Burial : LIGNIERES COMMUNAL CEMETERY   Map Ref : A21/P55

Plot :   Row :   4   Grave : 1

DESCRIPTION OF BODY :

HEIGHT :

BUILD :

HAIR :

TEETH :   jaw smashed

FINGERS AND HANDS :

IDENTITY DISCS :   metal type marked "JENKINS A.H. 424764 RAAF, C. of E."

DOCUMENTS OR/LETTERS OR RELICS :   red cloth bow

CLOTHING :

TUNIC :   R.A.A.F. battke dress "AG" brevet, F/SGT's insignia.

TROUSERS :

SHIRT :   khaki

UNDERWEAR :

SWEATER :   dark blue V- necked

SOCKS :

BOOTS :

MISCELLANEOUS :   braces, RAAF comfort scarf

EQUIPMENT :   M/WEST

DATE OF DEATH : 16.7.44.
DATE OF DEATH :
~~XXXXXXXXXXXXXXXXXXXXXXXXXXX3372XXXXXX705XXXXXXXXXXXX~~
CROSS SHOWS : Communal plaque for 15 as per 3372 ser. No.705 dated 3.9.46

CEMETERY RECORDS SHOW :   Unknown

REMARKS :   Accepted as F/SGT. JENKINS.

DATE EXHUMED : 8.9.47   EXHUMATION DONE B : CAPT. BLACK, 57 G.C.U.

CASE REFERS TO : F 438 s.   RAF WITNESSING OFFICER : F/LT. DAWES.

France Detachment M.R.E.S.
ROYAL   AIR   FORCE

EXHUMATION REPORT (R.A.F.)

29 E

Number : 2220609   Rank : SGT.   Name : GAUT R.A.   Service : R.A.F.

Cemetery or Place of Burial : LIGNIERES COMMUNAL CEMETERY   Map Ref : A21/P55

Plot :   Row : A   Grave : 2

DESCRIPTION OF BODY :

HEIGHT :

BUILD :

HAIR :   Brown, thick slightly wavy

TEETH :

FINGERS AND HANDS :

IDENTITY DISCS :

DOCUMENTS OR RELICS OR LETTERS :   NIL

CLOTHING :

    TUNIC :   R.A.F. B/D, "AG" Brevet, SGT's chevrons.

    TROUSERS :

    SHIRT :   issue, marked GAUT R.A. 609

    UNDERWEAR :   aircrew issue

    SWEATER :   issue aircrew and issue pullover

    SOCKS :   "

    BOOTS :   NIL

    MISCELLANEOUS : issue braces

EQUIPMENT :   heated inner F/suit

DATE OF DEATH :   16.7.44.

CROSS SHOWS : Communal plaque for 15 as per 3372 ser.No.705 dated 3.9.46

CEMETERY RECORDS SHOW :   Unknown

REMARKS :   Accepted as being the body of SGT. GAUT.

DATE EXHUMED :   8.9.47   EXHUMATION DONE BY : CAPT. BLACK 57 G.C.U.

CASE REFERS TO : F 428 s   RAF WITNESSING OFFICER : F/LT. DAWES.

                                  France Detachment M.R.E.S.
                                  ROYAL   AIR   FORCE

RECEIVED 6 OCT 1947 IN. S. 14. (CAS.)

<u>EXHUMATION REPORT (R.A.F.)</u>   29 F

Number :   Rank : F/SGT.   Name :   PATTERSON D.A.   Service :   R.A.A.F.
        AUS 427726

Cemetery or Place of Burial : LIGNIERES COMMUNAL CEMETERY   Map Ref : A21/P55

                                          Plot :   Row : A   Grave 3

DESCRIPTION OF BODY :

HEIGHT :

BUILD :

HAIR :

TEETH :

FINGERS AND HANDS :

IDENTITY DISCS :   Metal marked "PATTERSON 427726 RAAF" Pres."

DOCUMENTS OR LETTERS OR RELICS :   Metal UASTRALIA shoulder insignia

   CLOTHING :

            TUNIC :   R.A.F. B/D "AG" Brevet

            TROUSERS :

            SHIRT :

            UNDERWEAR :

            SWEATER :

            SOCKS :

            BOOTS :

            MISCELLANEOUS :

EQUIPMENT :   Parachute, outer flying suit

DATE OF DEATH :   16.7.44.

CROSS SHOWS :   Communal plaque for 15 as per 3372 ser.No.705 dated 3.9.46

CEMETERY RECORDS SHOW :   Unknown

REMARKS :   Accepted as F/SGT.PATTERSON. Second body in coffin removed and transferred
             to grave 3 row B

    DATE EXHUMED : 8.9.47   EXHUMATION DONE BY : CAPT.BLACK,57
                                                                    G.C.U.

    CASE REFERS TO : F 438 s   RAF WITNESSING OFFICER : F/LT.DAWES.

                                               France Detachment MRES
                                               ROYAL   AIR   FORCE

<u>EXHUMATION REPORT (R.A.F.)</u>   29 G

Number : AUS 423870   Rank : F/SGT. Name :   PAUL W.   Service : R.A.A.F.

Cemetery or Place of Burial : LIGNIERES Communal Cemetery   Map Ref : A21/P55

                                    Plot :   Row : A   Grave 4

DESCRIPTION OF BODY : Remains of trunk only.

HEIGHT : I.T.S.

BUILD : "

HAIR : NIL

TEETH : No head

FINGERS AND HANDS : NIL

IDENTITY DISCS : NIL

DOCUMENTS OR LETTERS OR RELICS : NIL

CLOTHING :

    TUNIC :   NIL

    TROUSERS : "

    SHIRT   : scraps issue

    UNDERWEAR: Non issue

    SWEATER : dark blue

    SOCKS : NIL

    BOOTS :   "

    MISCELLANEOUS : NIL

EQUIPMENT : NIL

DATE OF DEATH : 16.7.44

CROSS SHOWS : Communal plaque for 15 as per 3372 ser.No. 705 dated 3.9.46

CEMETERY RECORDS SHOW : PAUL

<u>REMARKS</u> : Identified by Mairie at time of death by papers taken from body,
             which were later seized by Germans.

DATE EXHUMED : 8.9.47   EXHUMATION DONE BY : CAPT. BLACK, 57 G.C.U.

CASE REFERS TO : F 438 s   RAF WITNESSING OFFICER : F/LT.DAWES,
                                        France Detachment M.R.E.S.
                                        <u>ROYAL   AIR   FORCE</u>

<u>EXHUMATION REPORT (R.A.F.)</u>   29 H.

Number : R152727   Rank : W.O.II   Name : GRAHAM F.G.   Service : R.C.A.F.

Cemetery or Place of Burial : LIGNIERES Communal Cemetery   Map Ref : A21/P55

                                        Plot :   Row : A   Grave : 5

DESCRIPTION OF BODY : Intact

HEIGHT :

BUILD :

HAIR :

TEETH :

FINGERS AND HANDS :

IDENTITY DISCS :   NIL

DOCUMENTS OR LETTERS OR RELICS :   NIL

CLOTHING :

     TUNIC : R.A.F. B/D. CANADA flashes, W.O.II insignia,"S" brevet.

     TROUSERS :

     SHIRT :   FULLY CLOTHED.

     UNDERWEAR :

     SWEATER :

     SOCKS :

     BOOTS :

     MISCELLANEOUS :

EQUIPMENT :

DATE OF DEATH : 16.7.44.

CROSS SHOWS : Communal plaque for 15 as per 3372 ser. No.705 dated 3.9.46

CEMETERY RECORDS SHOW : GRAHAM

REMARKS :   Body intact and fully dressed. Must have been W.O.GRAHAM, only W.O. in
          two crews. Exhumation confirms Mairie records.

DATE EXHUMED : 8.9.47   EXHUMATION DONE BY : Capt.BLACK,
                                                  57 G.C.U.

CASE REFERS TO : F 438 s.   RAF OFFICER WITNESSING : F/LT.DAWES.

                                        France Detacht. M.R.E.S.
                                        <u>ROYAL   AIR   FORCE</u>

RECEIVED
-6 OCT 1947
I.N.S. 14. (CAS.)

EXHUMATION REPORT (R.A.F.)   29 <u>c</u>

Number : U/K   Rank : U/K   Name :   U/K   Service : U/K

Cemetery or Place of Burial : LIGNIERES Communal Cemetery   Map Ref : A21/P55

                              Plot :   Row :   A   Grave : 6

DESCRIPTION OF BODY : Fairly intact, Skull smashed, appears to have been crushed.

HEIGHT : I.T.S.

BUILD :   "

HAIR : NIL

TEETH : NIL, jaw smashed

FINGERS AND HANDS : NIL

IDENTITY DISCS : NIL

DOCUMENTS OR LETTERS OR RELICS : Black triangular tie-clip with letter A attached
     by short chain, this latter also with clip. Broken and not considered in
     fit state to retain. See report for description.

   TUNIC :)
)   N I L
   TROUSERS :)

   SHIRT : Officer type VAN HEUSEN, 15½ collar, appeared new, no laundry marks.

   UNDERWEAR : non issue singlet, aircrew long drawers.

   SWEATER : NIL

   SOCKS : issue

   BOOTS : nil

   MISCELLANEOUS : black tie with clip as above

EQUIPMENT : Body wrapped in parachute

DATE OF DEATH : 16.7.44

CROSS SHOWS : Communal plaque for 15 as per 3372 ser. No. 705 dated 3.9.46

CEMETERY RECORDS SHOW : Unknown

REMARKS : Said by civilian who helped to arrange bodies for burial to be
            F/O. TICKLE.

DATE EXHUMED : 8.9.47   EXHUMATION DONE BY : Capt. BLACK, 57 G.C.U.

CASE REFERS TO: F 438 s.   RAF. WITNESSING OFFICER : F/LT. DAWES.

                                         France Detachment M.R.E.S.
                                         ROYAL   AIR   FORCE

EXHUMATION REPORT (R.A.F.)   29 J

Number :   Rank :   Name :   Service : R.A.F.

Cemetery or Place of Burial : LIGNIERES Communal Cemetery   Map Ref : A21/P55

                                        Plot :   Row A Grave 7

DESCRIPTION OF BODY :

HEIGHT : I.T.S.

BUILD   .   "

HAIR   :   "

TEETH   : NIL

FINGERS AND HANDS :   NIL

IDENTITY DISCS :   NIL

DOCUMENTS OR LETTERS OR RELICS : NIL

CLOTHING :

    .TUNIC : R.A.F. Battledress "E" Brevet, Sgt's chevrons.

    TROUSERS :

     SHIRT : issue

    UNDERWEAR : " (long aircrew)

    SWEATER : "

    SOCKS : "

    BOOTS : Suede type flying "REDFERN" size 8 or 9

    MISCELLANEOUS : issue braces

EQUIPMENT : scraps MAE WEST and harness Dinghy drogue F/Aid kit.

DATE OF DEATH : 16.7.44.

CROSS SHOWS : Communal plaque for 15 as per 3372 ser.No.705 dated 3.9.46

CEMETERY RECORDS SHOW : Unknown

REMARKS : Either SGT. WOOLLARD (later P/O) or SGT. GOODE.

DATE EXHUMED : 8.9.47   EXHUMATION DONE BY : CAPT.BLACK, 57 G.C.U.

CASE REFERS TO : F 438 s.   RAF WITNESSING OFFICER : F/LT.DAWES.

                                     FRANCE DETACHMENT M.R.E.S.
                                     ROYAL   AIR   FORCE

RECEIVED -6 OCT 1947 IN S. 14. (CAS.)

<u>EXHUMATION REPORT (R.A.F.)</u> *29K*

Number : R.201588   Rank : F/SGT.   Name : CANTWELL M.J.W.   Service : R.C.A.F.

Cemetery or Place of Burial : LIGNIERES COMMUNAL CEMETERY   Map Ref : A21 /P55

Plot :   Row: A   Grave 8

DESCRIPTION OF BODY :

HEIGHT : I.T.S.

BUILD : "

HAIR : Brown,thick

TEETH ; Jaw smashed

FINGERS AND HANDS : NIL

IDENTITY DISCS : NIL

DOCUMENTS OR LETTERS OR RELICS : Rosary (not retained)

CLOTHING : Battledress size 2 CANADA flashes, F/SGT's insignia."AG" brevet

   TUNIC :

   TROUSERS :

   SHIRT : issue marked 1588

   UNDERWEAR : aircrew long

   SWEATER : " over black non issue

   SOCKS : " (2 pr)

   BOOTS : NIL

   MISCELLANEOUS :

EQUIPMENT : silk gloves, heated inner suit, balaclava

DATE OF DEATH : 6.7.44.

CROSS SHOWS : Communal plaque for 15 as per 3372 serial No.705 dated 3.9.46

CEMETERY RECORDS SHOW : Unknown

REMARKS : Must be F/SGT. CANTWELL who was only RCAF F/SGT. in two crews. Number
on shirt confirms this.

DATE EXHUMED : 8.9.47   EXHUMATION DONE BY : CAPT. BLACK, 57 G.C.U.

CASE REFERS TO : F.438 s.   RAF WITNESSING OFFICER : F/LT.DAWES.

                  France Detachment M.R.E.S.
                  ROYAL   AIR   FORCE

RECEIVED 6 OCT 1947 IN S. 14. (CAS)

EXHUMATION REPORT (R.A.F.)   29 L

Number : AUS 422342 Rank : F/SGT. Name : WRIGHT W.H.E. Service : R.A.A.F.

Cemetery or Place of Burial : LIGNIERES Communal, Cemetery Map Ref : A21/P55

Plot :   Row : A Grave : 9

DESCRIPTION OF BODY :

HEIGHT : I.T.S.

BUILD   : I.T.S.

HAIR : Head missing

TEETH : NIL

FINGERS AND HANDS : scattered

IDENTITY DISCS : NIL

DOCUMENTS OR LETTERS OR RELICS : NIL

CLOTHING :

    TUNIC :)
)R.A.A.F. Battledress "0" Brevet, SGT's stripes.
    TROUSERS :)

    SHIRT : Non issue marked "WRIGHT 2342"

    UNDERWEAR : Cellular

    SWEATER : Dark pullover

    SOCKS : NIL

    BOOTS : "

    MISCELLANEOUS : NIL

EQUIPMENT : NIL

DATE OF DEATH : 16.7.44.

CROSS SHOWS : Communal plaque for 15 as per 3372 Ser No. 705 dated 3.9.46

CEMETERY RECORDS SHOW : WRIGHT

REMARKS : Exhumation confirms Mairie records.

DATE EXHUMED : 8.9.47   EXHUMATION DONE BY : CAPT. BLACK, 57 G.C.U.

CASE REFERS TO : P 438 s   RAF WITNESSING OFFICER : F/LT.DAWES.

France Detachment M.R.E.S.
ROYAL   AIR   FORCE

RECEIV
-6 OCT 1947
IN. S. 14.

EXHUMATION REPORT (R.A.F.)

29M

Number : . U/K   Rank : U/K   Name : Unknown   Service : U/K

Cemetery or Place of Burial : LIGNIERES Communal Cemetery   Map Ref : A21/P55

Plot : Row 1 B   Grave : 1

DESCRIPTION OF BODY :

HEIGHT :

BUILD :

HAIR :   I.T.S.

TEETH :   Complete top dental plate

LOWER :

FINGERS & HANDS :

IDENTITY DISCS : NIL   dental plate   dental plate

DOCUMENTS OR LETTERS OR RELICS :

CLOTHING :

    TUNIC. :   NIL

    TROUSERS : R.A.F. B/D.

    SHIRT :   Officer type

    UNDERWEAR :   long aircrew

    SWEATER :   NIL

    SOCKS :   Aircrew over non issue

    BOOTS :   NIL

    MISCELLANEOUS :   suspenders, black tie

EQUIPMENT : Para. pack.

DATE OF DEATH :   16.7.44.

CROSS SHOWS :   Communal plaque for 15 as per 3372 serial No.705 dated 3.9.46

CEMETERY RECORDS SHOW :   Unknown

REMARKS.

DATE EXHUMED : 9.9.47   EXHUMATION DONE BY : CAPT.BLACK, 57 G.C.U.

CASE REFERS TO : F 438 s.   RAF WITNESSING OFFICER : F/LT.DAWES.

France Detachment M.R.E.S.
ROYAL   AIR   FORCE

RECEIVED
6 OCT 1947
N.S. 14 (CAS)

183

<u>EXHUMATION REPORT (R.A.F.)</u>

29 N

Number : U/K   Rank : U/K   Name : U/K   Service : U/K

Cemetery or Place of Burial : LIGNIERES Communal Cemetery   Map Ref: A21/P55

Plot :   Row : B   Grave : 2

DESCRIPTION OF BODY :

HEIGHT :

BUILD :

HAIR :

TEETH :

FINGERS & HANDS :

IDENTITY DISCS :

DOCUMENTS OR LETTERS OR RELICS :

CLOTHING :

    TUNIC :

    TROUSERS :   scraps of rotted RAF B/D.

    SHIRT : Issue type

    UNDERWEAR :

    SWEATER :

                NIL ELSE
    SOCKS :

    BOOTS :

    MISCELLANEOUS :

EQUIPMENT :

DATE OF DEATH : 16.7.44.

CROSS SHOWS : Communal plaque for 15 as per 3372 ser.No.705 dated 3.9.46

CEMETERY RECORDS SHOW : Unknown

REMARKS : Small coffin badly deteriorated scraps of cloth and a few badly smashed
and jumbled bones, all mixed with a quantity of sawdust. Impossible to
state how many casualties involved, but certainly not less than two.

DATE EXHUMED : 9.9.47

CASE REFERS TO : F438as

EXHUMATION DONE BY : CAPT. BLACK, 57 G.C.U.

R.A.F.WITNESSING OFFICER : F/.T.DAWES,

France Detachment M.R.E.S.
<u>ROYAL   AIR   FORCE</u>

EXHUMATION REPORT (R.A.F.)

Number : U/K   Rank : U/K   Name : U/K   Service : U/K

Cemetery or Place of Burial : LIGNIERES Communal Cemetery   Map Ref : A21/P55

Plot :   Row   B   Grave : 3

DESCRIPTION OF BODY :

HEIGHT :

BUILD :

HAIR :   NO HEAD

TEETH :

FINGERS AND HANDS :

IDENTITY DISCS :

DOCUMENTS OR LETTERS OR RELICS :

CLOTHING :

TUNIC :   right hand side only of R.A.F. B/D, F/O braid.

TROUSERS :   Nil else

SHIRT :

UNDERWEAR :

SWEATER :   aircrew

SOCKS :

BOOTS :

MISCELLANEOUS :

EQUIPMENT :

DATE OF DEATH :   16.7.44.

CROSS SHOWS : Communal plaque for 15 as per 3372 ser.No.705 dated 3.9.46

CEMETERY RECORDS SHOW : Unknown

REMARKS : Originally in coffin with F/SGT. PATTERSON Row A Grave 3, Removed and
reburied as above.

DATE EXHUMED : 9.9.47   EXHUMATION DONE BY : CAPT. BLACK, 57 GCU.

CASE REFERS TO : F438 s   RQF WITNESSING OFFICER : F/LT.DAWES.

France Detachment M.R.E.S.
ROYAL   AIR   FORCE

RECEIVED
-6 OCT 1947

185

EXHUMATION REPORT (R.A.F.)

29 P

Number : U/K   Rank : U/K   Name : Unknown   Service : U/K

Cemetery or Place of Burial : LIGNIERES Communal Cemetery   Map Ref : A 21/P55

                                        Plot :   Row : B   Grave 4

DESCRIPTION OF BODY : skull smashed.

HEIGHT :

BUILD :

HAIR :

TEETH :

FINGERS AND HANDS :

IDENTITY DISCS :   NIL

DOCUMENTS OR LETTERS OR RELICS : NIL

CLOTHING :

    TUNIC :
                Scraps R.A.F. B/D.
    TROUSERS :

    SHIRT : Officer type, laundry mark in black ink W 133
                                                      +JW

    UNDERWEAR :

    SWEATER : aircrew

    SOCKS :

    BOOTS :

MISCELLANEOUS :

EQUIPMENT : scraps para. harness.

DATE OF DEATH : 16.7.44.

CROSS SHOWS : Communal plaque for 15 as per 3372 serial No. 705 dated 3.9.46

CEMETERY RECORDS SHOW : Unknown

REMARKS :

DATE EXHUMED : 9.9.47   EXHUMATION DONE BY : CAPT. W. BLACK, 57 G.C.U.

CASE REFERS TO : F438 s   R.A.F. WITNESSING OFFICER : F/LT. DAWES.
                                          France Detachment M.R.E.S.
                                          ROYAL   AIR   FORCE

RECEIVED -6 OCT 1947 IN S.14. (CAS.)

EXHUMATION REPORT (R.A.F.)

29 a.

Number : U/K   Rank : U/K   Name : Unknown   Service : U/K

Cemetery or Place of Burial : LIGNIERES Communal Cemetery   Map Ref : A21/P55

Plot :   Row : B   Grave : 5

DESCRIPTION OF BODY : Burned and badly smashed.

HEIGHT :
                see remarks
BUILD :

HAIR :
                Head smashed.
TEETH :

FINGERS AND HANDS :

IDENTITY DISCS : NIL

DOCUMENTS OR LETTERS OR RELICS :   NIL

CLOTHING :

    TUNIC :

    TROUSERS :

    SHIRT : Collar attached type marked   WM   WM (uncertain)   in ink & under-
                                                 283 .... WAD   neath sewn on tab
    UNDERWEAR :   or 253   marked 283 (Numbers
                                                                       in cotton)

    SWEATER : light coloured pullover with label "GENTKNIT FASHIONS,100% pure wool"

    SOCKS :

    BOOTS :

    MISCELLANEOUS :

EQUIPMENT :

DATE OF DEATH : 16.7.44.

CROSS SHOWS : Communal plaque for 15 as per 3372 serial no.705 dated 3.9.46

CEMETERY RECORDS SHOW : Unknown

REMARKS : From remaining bones appears to have been of heavy build.

DATE EXHUMED : 9.9.47

CASE REFERS TO : P438 s

EXHUMATION DONE BY : CAPT. BLACK,57 G.C.U.

R.A.F.WITNESSING OFFICER : F/LT.DAWES.

                France Detachment M.R.E.S.
                ROYAL   AIR   FORCE

RECEIVED
- 6 OCT 1947
I.S. 14. (CAS.)

187

American Involvement

Also found on a few Casualty P Files are American Identification Check Lists. These are an American form of exhumation/identity reports. They were either forwarded directly to the Casualty Branch in London by the RAF MRES liaison officer with the American Graves Registration Service or sent through MRES headquarters. Unlike the British who did graveside identifications the search teams of the American Graves Registration Service (AGRS), which was set up in the European Theatre in September 1945, exhumed and removed remains from graves and cemeteries, taking them to Central Identification Points (CIP) in either Strasbourg or Neuville-en-Condroz, Belgium. These CIPs had more technical means, such as infrared and fluorescent, to assist with the identification process.

The Americans were very active in looking for their war dead in all theatres and the US Government provided (and still do provide) considerable amounts of money and resources do to so. Unlike the British and Dominion governments the US Government repatriated many of their dead. From 1945 to 1951 the Americans ran 'The Return of the World War II Dead Program' under which 172,000 American dead were repatriated to the United States from a total of 281,000.[8] It was American military practice to bury in accordance with the wishes of the next of kin. Repatriation was at public expense. Some next of kin requested that the burial should take place in American Military Cemeteries (AMC) in the country where their relative died, some requested that they remain in the original isolated grave (for the Americans the term isolated covers any grave not concentrated into an AMC) and some requested repatriation. If the next of kin chose to leave the remains in an isolated grave they became responsible for the maintenance of the grave.

In December 1945 the AGRS in Europe reported that there were 27,780 unresolved cases, and a series of sweeps searching for US dead began in Europe. In 1946 a sweep to recover American dead in isolated graves and/or mass graves recovered 1,654 sets of remains. A further sweep in 1948 recovered a further 16,548 and a final sweep in 1949 another

---

8. World War 2 US Medical Research Centre Article on the Quartermaster's Grave Registration Service at www.med-dept.com

2,833. However, the American sweep teams were not always scrupulous in the way they operated. The American system of collecting up all unidentified bodies, including ones from aircraft crash sites, and taking them for temporary burial in one of their 'collection' cemeteries while they awaited identification, inevitably meant that some RAF and Dominion Air Force remains were also removed by the AGRS teams. Usually this was done unknowingly, but there were instances when the Americans had been well aware of the nationality of the bodies but had taken them anyway. The MRES search officers complained of problems with the Americans removing bodies other than their own dead and on at least one occasion accused the Americans of stealing them.[9] No doubt the AGRS would have argued that they were entitled to remove such remains, as they had been officially tasked by the Quartermaster General of the American Army with the retrieval, identification, transportation and burial of deceased American *and American allied personnel.*[10] However, some of the wrongly removed bodies were also misidentified as American at the CIP despite evidence to the contrary.

It was up to the RAF MRES Liaison Officers (RAFLOs) working with the American Grave Registration Command in Europe to 'rescue' the wrongly swept-up bodies when alerted to a case. They followed up the complaints from MREU search officers that RAF, Dominion or Allied (e.g. Polish) Air Force bodies had gone missing from graves known not to contain US dead. Sometimes the Americans had got there first but sometimes bodies were removed while the MREU search officer was investigating a case. One case where bodies were removed by the Americans and recovered by the RAFLO concerned the crew of Mosquito NS654 which went missing while on a photographic reconnaissance mission over the Stettin/Berlin area on 27 October 1944. The graves concerned were marked in German and Russian as being those of unknown American fliers. The mistake came to light when the MRES Berlin Detachment started to investigate a Casualty Enquiry sent to them by Squadron Leader Sinkinson, Head of the Casualty Branch Missing Research Section, in October 1946. The documents below tell the story.

---

9. *Missing Believed Killed* by Stuart Hadaway published by Pen & Sword 2008.
10. *The Graves Registration Service in World War II* by Edward Steere. QMC Historical Studies No 21 Historical Section of the Quartermaster General 1951.

From:-   Officer Commanding,
             BERLIN DETACHMENT M.R.E.S., RAF
             c/o H.Q. B.T.B. B.A.O.R. 2

To:-   American Graves Registration Command,
             European Area,
             Berlin, Germany

Copies to:- Air Ministry, 4 M.R.E.U., HQ R.A.A.F.,
             A.D.G.R.E., D.A.D.G.R.E.

Date:-   30th April, 1948

Ref.:-   BD/205/Ops.48

Report of Burial from Warnemünde.

Attached please find copies of reports re the 2 R.A.F. casualties found at Warnemünde Cemetery Row 1, Graves 1 and 2.

Para. 3 in P.424787/44/P.4/405 S. of 22 October, 1946 bears out your conclusions that the 2 R.A.F. bodies are x 6477 and x 6478 as these come from the location stated in the German records.

Your observation and information re the present location of the bodies of F/O. Holland and F/O. Bloomfield would be appreciated.

                                              F/Lt.

             for   Officer Commanding,
                 BERLIN DETACHMENT M.R.E.S.

20

INVESTIGATION REPORT

M.R.E.S.
FROM: BERLIN DETACHMENT ~~MAINENHOLDEN~~ R.A.F. (GERMANY)

TO: Air Ministry, S. 14. Cen., 2, Seville Street, LONDON S.W. 1

COPIES TO: H.Q. 4 M.R.E.U., H.Q. R.A.A.F., D.A.D.G.R.E., A.D.G.R.E., Files

DATE: 9th April, 1948

YOUR FILE OR FOLDER REFERENCE: P.494787/44/P.405 S.

YOUR CASUALTY ENQUIRY NUMBER: C. 866

OUR REFERENCE: 4 MREU/906/866

NAME OF SEARCH OFFICER: F/Lt. JOHN R. HUGHES, D.F.M.

TARGET: STETTIN and BERLIN Area

AIRCRAFT TYPE AND SERIAL NUMBER: Mosquito NS 654

DATE REPORTED MISSING: 27th October, 1944

PLACE OF CRASH, WITH MAP REFERENCE: Gut STEINFELD, E 55/0 82

PLACE OF BURIAL, WITH MAP REFERENCE: WARNEMUENDE, Neuer Friedhof, E 55/0 82
Grave: 1 and 2   Row: C.F.R.

CREW:
AUS.410234	F/O.	K.R. HOLLAND, D.F.C.	Pilot
151271	F/O.	G.J. BLOOMFIELD	Navigator

RESULT OF INVESTIGATION AND FINDINGS:

While on a "Search Trip" in Kreis ROSTOCK (Russian Zone) an attempt was made to visit Gut STEINFELD and obtain information re the crash of Mosquito NS 654, but owing to the fact that Gut STEINFELD was not on my list of "places to be visited", my request of the Russian Conducting Officer to visit the stated place was firmly refused.

However, I was allowed to have telephone communication with the present Burgermeister of Gut STEINFELD and obtain the following information:-

The Burgermeister stated that a twin-engined aircraft crashed at Gut STEIN-FELD on the 27th of October, 1944 during early afternoon. The aircraft exploded and burnt on impact, and the two occupants were badly burnt and charred.

German Wehrmacht recovered the bodies and conveyed them to WARNEMUENDE for burial.

After obtaining the above information a visit was made to WARNEMUENDE and the Friedhofsverwalter confirmed the statement of Gut STEINFELD's Burgermeister, when he said that two bodies had been brought to WARNEMUENDE for burial on the 30th of October, 1944.

16

-2-

PSS (b) 4999/5m/7.47

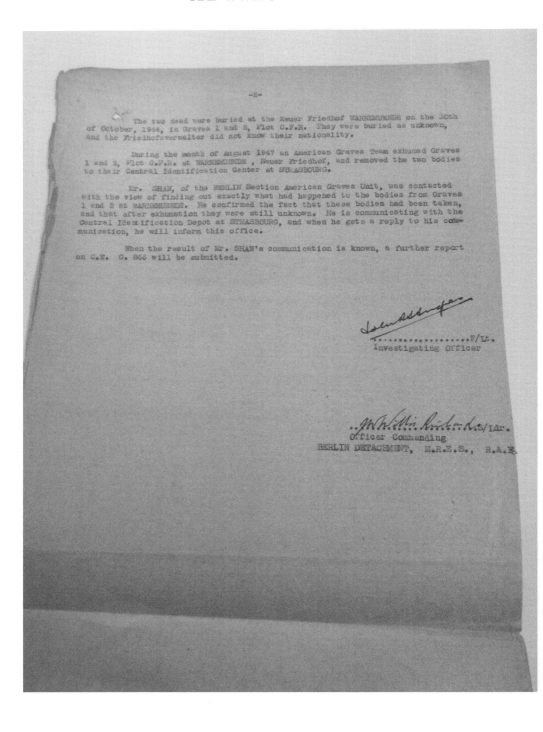

-2-

The two dead were buried at the Neuer Friedhof WARNEMUENDE on the 30th of October, 1944, in Graves 1 and 2, Plot C.F.R. They were buried as unknown, and the Friedhofsverwalter did not know their nationality.

During the month of August 1947 an American Graves Team exhumed Graves 1 and 2, Plot C.F.R. at WARNEMUENDE, Neuer Friedhof, and removed the two bodies to their Central Identification Center at STRASBOURG.

Mr. SHAW, of the BERLIN Section American Graves Unit, was contacted with the view of finding out exactly what had happened to the bodies from Graves 1 and 2 at WARNEMUENDE. He confirmed the fact that these bodies had been taken, and that after exhumation they were still unknown. He is communicating with the Central Identification Depot at STRASBOURG, and when he gets a reply to his communication, he will inform this office.

When the result of Mr. SHAW's communication is known, a further report on C.E. G. 865 will be submitted.

...................F/Lt.
Investigating Officer

..........................S/Ldr.
Officer Commanding
BERLIN DETACHMENT, M.R.E.S., R.A.F.

A2

FROM : F/Lt. PRIOR H.J., RAFID, AGRC Headquarters, European Area
APO 58, U.S. Army

TO   : AIR MINISTRY (S 14 Cas) 2 Seville St., London S.W.1.

ATTENTION : S/Ldr SINKINSON

DATE: 17/6/48

REF. : AGRC/Neuville/X-6477,X-6478/Air
A.M. REF. : P424787/44/P4/405/S

COPIES : 4MREU – RAAF – IWGC – DDGR & E – Berlin Detachment MRES – AGRC

SUBJECT : G.866 – A.410234 F/O Holland DFC
151271 F/O G.J. Bloomfield

1) Reference A.M. letter P424787/44/P.4/405/S dated 22/10/46 and
to letter from Berlin Detachment MRES reference BD/205/Ops48 dated
30/4/48 which was handed to me for investigation on the 4/6/48.by AGRC
Isolated Burial Section.

2) A check on X-6477 and X-6478 was then carried out and on checking
identification check list carried out by C.I.P. team AGRC on 17th September
1947. Nothing definite was shown to prove remains to be British. However
a joint disinterment was arranged and this took place last week in my
presence and the following points found proved remains to be members of
the R.A.F.:

X-6477: Rem. Blue BATTLEDRESS
         Rem. Silk Civilian Scarfs
         Rem. RAF Parachute Harness
         Rem. of Civilian type underwear
X-6478: Rem. Officer type Blue Shirt
         Rem. RAF issue underwear
         Rem. RAF type Parachute Harness

3) In view of the evidence contained in Air Ministry letter dated
22/10/46 and F/Lt Hughes report dated 9/4/48. I am certain that X-6477
and X-6478 contained the bodies of F/O HOLLAND and F/O BLOOMFIELD res-
pectively and immediately arranged for their release from USMC Neuville-
en-Condroz. In view of evidence held on American Check List in respect
of physical particulars plus tooth chart. I am certain that individual
identifications will be made and on my return requested by telephone for
S/Ldr Sinkinson to obtain a tooth chart of the Australian namely F/O
HOLLAND.

4) As the Army G.C.U. are shortly terminating their work I registered in Heverlee British Cemetery Louvain, Belgium Plot VI, Row E
Grave 5 as A.410234 F/O K.R. HOLLAND (DFC) based on the finding of a
full upper Denture, which are fairly common to Australian and New
Zealand personnel and in Plot VI, Row E, Grave 4 as 151271 F/O G.T.
BLOOMFIELD. No doubt if my assumption is incorrect an ammendment can
be notified to I.W.G.C. Brussels for the Graves to be reversed. Thus
I trust all urgency in obtaining dental particulars from RAAF Headquarters will be taken in order to accurately finalise case.

5) X-6478 - Removed from Warnemunde Cemetery Russian Zone on 26/8/47
from Row 1, Grave 2 to Neuville-en-Condroz USMC Plot BB, Row 8, Grave 194
now reburied in Heverlee British Cemetery Louvain, Belgium Plot VI, Row E
Grave 5 and accepted as A 410234 F/O K.R. HOLLAND (DFC)

X-6477 - Removed from Warnemunde Cemetery (Russian Zone) on 26/8/47
from Row 1, Grave 1 to USMC Neuville-en-Condroz Plot BB Row 8, Grave 193
now reburied in Heverlee British Cemetery Louvain Belgium Plot VI, Row E
Grave 4. and accepted as 151271 F/O G.J. BLOOMFIELD.

6) American Check Lists are attached for Air Ministry, RAAF Headquarters, 4MREU Berlin Detachment only. Please give the checking of
this case every priority in case an ammendment should have to be made.

H.J. PRIOR F/Lt.
RAFLO,   AGRC

AGRC FORM No. 11
Revised 30 Sept. 1946
Formerly "Check List
of Unknowns")

IDENTIFICATION CHECK LIST 1F-9035

(To be completely filled out and attached to each copy
of Report of Interment WD QMC Form 1042)

Unknown X___-6478_____

Cemetery Neuville en Condroz, Belgium

Plot ___BB___ Row ___8___ Grave ___194___

1. Date Processed: 17 September 1947
   ~~Examined at cemetery~~
   (Hour)   (Date)

2. Place of death Baltic Sea body washed ashore near Warnemuende, Germany
                   (Name of closest town)   (Coordinates and letter Prefix, maps)
   N 55/082 1/250000
   (Sheet, scale and serials used)

3. Remains recovered or disinterred by _____ 95th QM Bn A.G.R.C. _____
                                              (Name and organization)

4. Evacuated to Cemetery by Subordinate Identification Point #2, Neuville en Condroz,
                            (Name and organization)   Belgium

5. Description of clothing and equipment: (if clothes do not fit, obtain size from body measurements)

Item	Clothing Markings	Sizes	Indicate unusual markings color, wear, tear, repairs, etc.
* Headgear	None (Type)		
Raincoat	None		
Overcoat		None	
Jacket, Field		None	
Jacket, Combat		None	
Mackinaw		None	
Sweater		None	
Jacket, HBT		None	
* Shirt, Wool OD		None	
Undershirt, Wool		None	
Undershirt, Cotton		None	
Trousers, HBT		None	
* Trousers, Wool OD		None	

— 1 —

1F-9035

Belt, web	None		
Drawers, wool	None		
Drawers, cotton	None		
Leggings, wool	None		
Socks, cotton	None		
* Shoes	None	(type)	None
Overshoes	None		
Web Equipment	None	(type)	None
(Other item)	None		
(Other item)	None		

* If body is nude, sizes of these items should be computed by measuring the remains

Chevrons or
Insignia _____ None _____
(Type & location; shirt, jacket, coat, helmet)

Shoulder Patch _____ None _____

Does clothing indicate that deceased was a member of the Air, Ground or Naval Force?
UTD

6. Description of Remains :
       Est
    Age Utd _____ Height 5'6 7/8" Weight _____ Utd _____ Description of wounds _____ Utd _____

    Bandages or dressings _____ Utd _____ Scars _____ Utd _____
    (Length, width, location)

    _____ Utd _____ Tattoos
    (Number, location — illustrate on separate page)

    Outstanding moles, warts or birthmarks _____ Utd _____
    (Yes-no; description, location)

    Sunburn or tan, other than hand and face _____ Utd _____

    Complexion _____ Utd _____
    (Light, medium, dark, clear, pimples, pocks, freckles)

    Build _____ Utd _____
    (Large, fat, thin, muscular)

    Hair _____ None _____
    (Color, length, quantity, curly, wavy, straight, whorls, or definite parting)

    Hair _____ Utd _____
    (Baldness, widows peak, distinctive cutting or other characteristics)

Sideburns _____ Utd _____ Mustache _____ Utd _____ Beard or _____ Utd _____
(Color, setting, shape)   (Color, size, shape)   (Length, heavy)

— 2 —

196

1F-9035

Goatee ___Utd___
(Light, color, extent)

Eyes ___Utd___
(Color, setting, shape)

Eyebrows ___Utd___
(Color, bushiness, extent across nose)

Nose ___Utd___
(Size, shape, straight)

Eears ___Utd___
(Size, set close to or far from head)

Mouth ___Utd___
(Large, medium, small)

Lips ___Utd___
(Small, large, full)

Teeth ___See Tooth Chart___
(White, size, unevenness, spacing, noticeable crowns, fillings, extracts)

Chin ___Utd___
(Prominent, receding, pointed, dimples, double)

Jaw ___Utd___
(Large, small, normal)

Circumference of head in inches ___Crushed___
(Hat band)

Neck ___Utd___
(Size, length, short, normal, wrinkled)

Larynx ___Utd___
(Prominent, normal)

Shoulders ___Utd___
(Broad, straight, small, rounded)

Arms ___Utd___
(Length, muscular, color, extent and quantity of hair)

Hands ___Utd___

Fingers ___Utd___
(Short, thick, long, slender, size of knuckles, missing fingers or joints)

___Utd___
(Unusual characteristics of fingernails)

Chest ___Utd___
(Size of nipples, color, quantity and extent of hair, large, small, normal)

Waist ___Utd___
(Size of navel, appendectomy, amount, quantity, and color of hair)

Back ___Utd___
(Quantity and extent of hair)

Circumcision ___Utd___
(Yes-no)

Pubic Hair ___None___
(Color)

Herniaplasty ___Utd___
(Yes-no; location)

Legs ___Utd___
(Inseam, muscular, knock-kneed, bowed, normal, quantity, color and extent of hair)

Feet ___Utd___
(Size, corns, callouses, flat)

Toes ___Utd___
(Slender, straight, crooked, overlap)

Evidence of healed fractures ___Utd___
(Nose, arms, legs, etc.)

NOTE: Use attached charts "A" and "B" to indicate parts not received.

— 3 —

1F-9035

7. Have finger prints been placed on Report of Interment? ___No___ (Yes-no)

If not, explain ___Missing and decomposed___

8. Has tooth chart been prepared? ___Yes___ If not, explain _____ (Yes-no)

9. Remarks ___Remains disarticulated, fractured-Small amount of flesh in final sstage of decomposition- No clothing-Bones show evidence of having been burned. Estimated weight of remains 12 lbs. Metal grave marker lettered in Russian and German with remains.(See below). Fluoroscopic Examination Negative. Nothing found to warrant chemical laboratory examination.___

I certify that I have personally viewed the remains of subject deceased and all resulting information has been recorded to the best of my knowledge.

As processing revealed no positive identifying clues, this case is classified Unknown.

s/t ERNEST C. GADDY
(Officer's Name)

Grave marker (metal)

Same in   Heir Ruht
Russian   ein Unbekannter
            Amerikanischer
            Flieger
  30.10.1944
  (F.R.I.Nr 2)

CWO   USA
Rank   Service

Central Identification Point
(Organization)

— 4 —

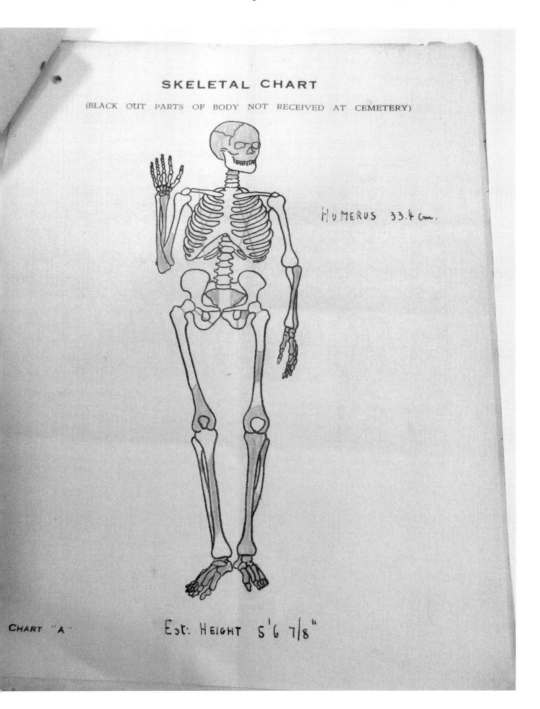

SKELETAL CHART

(BLACK OUT PARTS OF BODY NOT RECEIVED AT CEMETERY)

HUMERUS 33.4 cm.

CHART "A"

Est. Height 5' 6 7/8"

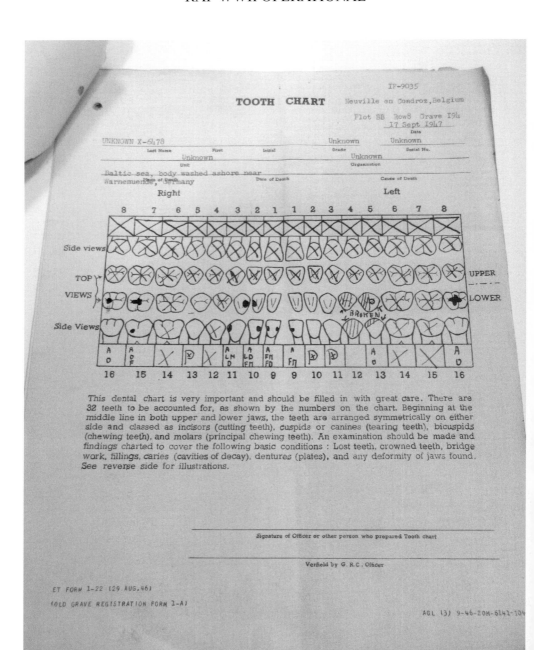

IF-9035

TOOTH CHART   Neuville en Condroz, Belgium

Plot BB   Row8   Grave 194
17 Sept 1947
Date

UNKNOWN X-6478   Unknown   Unknown
Last Name   First   Initial   Grade   Serial No.

Unknown   Unknown
Unit   Organization

Baltic sea, body washed ashore near
Warnemuende, Germany
Place of Death   Date of Death   Cause of Death

Right   Left

This dental chart is very important and should be filled in with great care. There are 32 teeth to be accounted for, as shown by the numbers on the chart. Beginning at the middle line in both upper and lower jaws, the teeth are arranged symmetrically on either side and classed as incisors (cutting teeth), cuspids or canines (tearing teeth), bicuspids (chewing teeth), and molars (principal chewing teeth). An examination should be made and findings charted to cover the following basic conditions : Lost teeth, crowned teeth, bridge work, fillings, caries (cavities of decay), dentures (plates), and any deformity of jaws found. See reverse side for illustrations.

_____
Signature of Officer or other person who prepared Tooth chart

_____
Verfield by G. R.C. Officer

ET FORM 1-22 (29 AUG. 46)
(OLD GRAVE REGISTRATION FORM 1-A)

AGL (3) 9-46-20M-6141-104

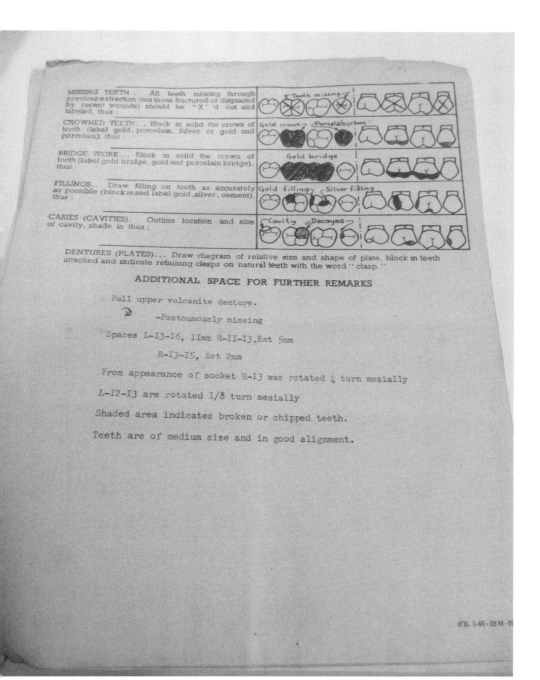

MISSING TEETH . All teeth missing through previous extraction (not those fractured or displaced by recent wounds) should be "X"'d out and labeled, thus :

CROWNED TEETH... Block in solid the crown of tooth (label) gold, porcelain, Silver or gold and porcelain), thus

BRIDGE WORK... Block in solid the crown of tooth (label gold bridge, gold and porcelain bridge), thus :

FILLINGS.. Draw filling on tooth as accurately as possible (block in and label gold, silver, cement), thus :

CARIES (CAVITIES). Outline location and size of cavity, shade in thus :

DENTURES (PLATES)... Draw diagram of relative size and shape of plate, block in teeth attached and indicate retaining clasps on natural teeth with the word " clasp "

ADDITIONAL SPACE FOR FURTHER REMARKS

Full upper vulcanite denture.

    —Posthumously missing

Spaces L-I3-I6, IImm R-II-I3,Est 5mm

    R-I3-I5, Est 2mm

From appearance of socket R-I3 was rotated ¼ turn mesially

L-I2-I3 are rotated I/8 turn mesially

Shaded area indicates broken or chipped teeth.

Teeth are of medium size and in good alignment.

d'H. 1-46-25 M -T

AGRC FORM No. 11
Revised 10 Sept. 1946
Formerly "Check List
of Unknowns")

IDENTIFICATION CHECK LIST   1F-9036

(To be completely filled out and attached to each copy
of Report of Interment WD QMC Form 1042)

38

Unknown X -6477

Cemetery Neuville-en-Condroz, Belgium

Plot BB Row 8 Grave 193

Date Processed: 18 September 1947
1. ~~Name of Cemetery~~
   (Hour)   (Date)

2. Place of death Baltic Sea, body washed ashore near Warnemuende, Germany
   (Name of closest town)   (Coordinates and letter Prefix, maps)
   M 55/ 082 1/250000
   (Sheet, scale and serials used)

3. Remains recovered or disinterred by 95th QM Bn A.G.R.C.
   (Name and organization)

4. Evacuated to Cemetery by Subordinate Identification Point #2,Neuville en Condroz,
   (Name and organization)   Belgium

5. Description of clothing and equipment: (if clothes do not fit, obtain size from body measurements)

Item	Clothing Markings	Sizes	Indicate unusual markings color, wear, tear, repairs, etc.
* Headgear	None (Type)		
Raincoat	None		
Overcoat	None		
Jacket, Field	None		
Jacket, Combat	None		
Mackinaw	None		
Sweater	None		
Jacket, HBT	None		
* Shirt, Wool OD	None		
Undershirt, Wool	None		
Undershirt, Cotton	None		
Trousers, HBT	None		
* Trousers, Wool OD	Nonw		

— 1 —

202

MISSING RESEARCH & ENQUIRY SERVICE DOCUMENTS

1F-9036

Belt, web _____ None

Drawers, wool _____ None

Drawers, cotton _____ None

Leggings, wool _____ None

Socks, cotton _____ None

* Shoes _____ None _____ (type) _____ None

Overshoes _____ None

Web Equipment _____ None _____ (type) _____ None

(Other item) _____ Burned remnant Civilian type silk scarf

(Other item) _____ Small burned remnant collar of electrically heated flying suit
* If body is nude, sizes of these items should be computed by measuring the remains

Chevrons or
Insignia _____ None
(Type & location; shirt, jacket, coat, helmet)

Shoulder Patch _____ None

Does clothing indicate that deceased was a member of the Air, Ground or Naval Force?

6. Description of Remains:

Age _Utd_ Height _Utd_ Weight _Utd_ Description of wounds _Utd_

Bandages or dressings _____ Utd _____ Scars _Utd_
(Length, width, location)

_____ Utd _____ Tattoos
(Number, location — illustrate on separate page)

Outstanding moles, warts or birthmarks _____ Utd
(Yes-no; description, location)

Sunburn or tan, other than hand and face _____ Utd

Complexion _____ Utd
(Light, medium, dark, clear, pimples, pocks, freckles)

Build _____ Utd
(Large, fat, thin, muscular)

Hair _____ Brown 1½" long
(Color, length, quantity, curly, wavy, straight, whorls, or definite parting)

Hair _____ Utd
(Baldness, widows peak, distinctive cutting or other characteristics)

Sideburns _Utd_ Mustache _Utd_ Beard or _Utd_
(Color, setting, shape) (Color, size, shape) (Length, heavy)

— 2 —

203

1F-9036

Goatee ____Utd____
(Light, color, extent)

Eyes ____Utd____
(Color, setting, shape)

Eyebrows ____Utd____
(Color, bushiness, extent across nose)

Nose ____Utd____
(Size, shape, straight)

Ears ____Utd____
(Size, set close to or far from head)

Mouth ____Utd____
(Large, medium, small)

Lips ____Utd____
(Small, large, full)

Teeth ____See tooth chart____
(White, size, unevenness, spacing, noticeable crowns, fillings, extracts)

Chin ____Utd____
(Prominent, receding, pointed, dimples, double)

Jaw ____Utd____
(Large, small, normal)

Circumference of head in inches ____Crushed____
(Hat band)

Neck ____Utd____
(Size, length, short, normal, wrinkled)

Larynx ____Utd____
(Prominent, normal)

Shoulders ____Utd____
(Broad, straight, small, rounded)

Arms ____Utd____
(Length, muscular, color, extent and quantity of hair)

Hands ____Missing____

Fingers ____Missing____
(Short, thick, long, slender, size of knuckles, missing fingers or joints)

(Unusual characteristics of fingernails)

Chest ____Utd____
(Size of nipples, color, quantity and extent of hair, large, small, normal)

Waist ____Utd____
(Size of navel, appendectomy, amount, quantity, and color of hair)

Back ____Utd____
(Quantity and extent of hair)

Circumcision ____Utd____
(Yes-no)

Pubic Hair ____None____
(Color)

Herniaplasty ____Utd____
(Yes-no; location)

Legs ____Utd____
(Inseam, muscular, knock-kneed, bowed, normal, quantity, color and extent of hair)

Feet ____Utd____
(Size, corns, callouses, flat)

Toes ____Utd____
(Slender, straight, crooked, overlap)

Evidence of healed fractures ____Utd____
(Nose, arms, legs, etc.)

NOTE: Use attached charts "A" and "B" to indicate parts not received.

— 3 —

1F-9036

Have finger prints been placed on Report of Interment? __No__

(Yes-no)

If not, explain __Missing__

8. Has tooth chart been prepared? __Yes__ If not, explain _____

(Yes-no)

9. Remarks Case consists of a small mass of fractured burned bones. A little

flesh in final stage of decomposition. A few charred pieces of clothing

that could not be recognized. No bones for measurement. Fluoroscopic

Examination Negative. Nothing found to warrant chemical laboratory

Examination. Estimated weight 10 lbs. As processing revealed no positive

I certify that I have personally viewed the remains of subject deceased and all resulting information
has been recorded to the best of my knowledge.

Identifying clues, this case is classified Unknown.

s/t ERNEST C. GADDY

(Officer's Name)

CWO   USA

Rank   Service

Same in   Hier Ruht
Russian   ein unbekannter
                 Amerikanischer   Central Identification Point
                 Flieger   (Organization)
   30.10.1944
   (CFr INr)

Metal Grave Marker.

- 4 -

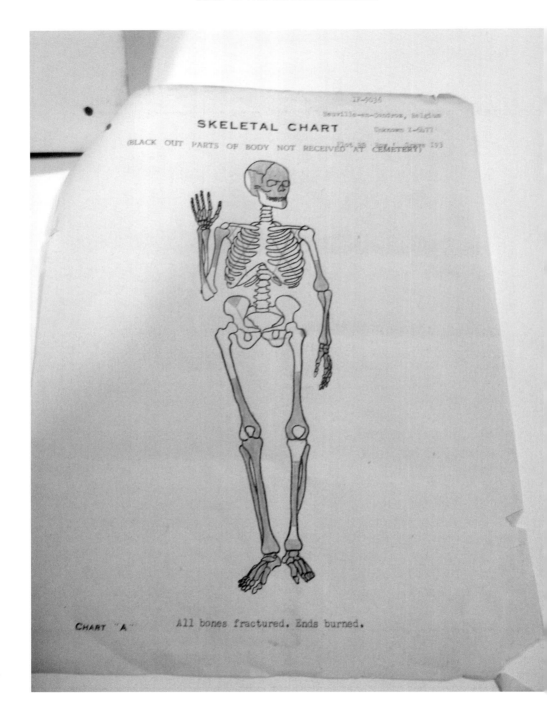

SKELETAL CHART

(BLACK OUT PARTS OF BODY NOT RECEIVED AT CEMETERY)

CHART "A"   All bones fractured. Ends burned.

MISSING RESEARCH & ENQUIRY SERVICE DOCUMENTS

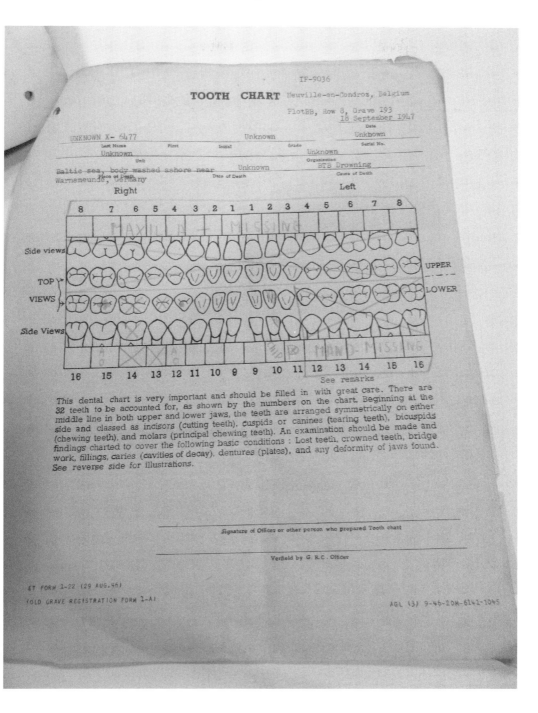

207

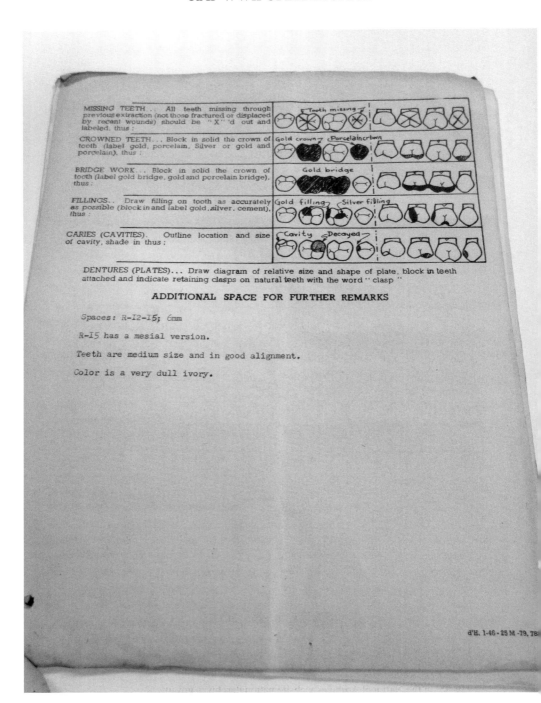

MISSING TEETH . All teeth missing through previous extraction (not those fractured or displaced by recent wounds) should be "X" 'd out and labeled, thus :

CROWNED TEETH . . Block in solid the crown of tooth (label gold, porcelain, Silver or gold and porcelain), thus :

BRIDGE WORK . . Block in solid the crown of tooth (label gold bridge, gold and porcelain bridge), thus :

FILLINGS . . Draw filling on tooth as accurately as possible (block in and label gold, silver, cement), thus :

CARIES (CAVITIES). Outline location and size of cavity, shade in thus :

DENTURES (PLATES)... Draw diagram of relative size and shape of plate, block in teeth attached and indicate retaining clasps on natural teeth with the word " clasp "

ADDITIONAL SPACE FOR FURTHER REMARKS

Spaces: R-12-15; 6mm

R-15 has a mesial version.

Teeth are medium size and in good alignment.

Color is a very dull ivory.

d'H. 1-46 - 25 M -79, 78

Post Mortem Reports

Post Mortem Reports are occasionally found on P Files. Generally these have been produced after post-mortems conducted when there was a suspicion that a war crime may have been committed. War crimes claims and accusations were investigated by the War Crimes Commission of the Judge Advocate General (JAG) and, when the MRES were involved, copies of documents sent by the MRES to War Crimes (JAG) were copied to the Air Ministry Casualty Branch. In keeping with the P4(Cas) practice of filing all information received on the relevant P File, the copies of Post Mortem reports were included on these files by the Casualty Branch. The War Crimes Commission passed to the Casualty Branch any information they uncovered which could help trace missing personnel and in return the MRES passed to the War Crimes investigators instances of possible war crimes.[11]

The pathologist report below concerns a case where it was thought that a war crime might have taken place. No 13 Missing Research and Enquiry Section had the body exhumed and the post-mortem (or autopsy) examination was undertaken by an American pathologist belonging to the US Army Medical Corps at an American Army Hospital in Stuttgart. The report was then forwarded by 13 Missing Research and Enquiry Section to the Missing Research and Enquiry Unit. They were members of No 3 MREU and copies were also sent to the British War Crime investigators of the JAG section of the British Army on the Rhine (BAOR) for their comments, to P4(Cas), and to the British Army's No 85 Graves Concentration Unit (85GCU).

Two officers are named as making the identification of the body. These are the MRES Investigating Officer (Parsons) and the Captain in charge of 85GCU (Fowler).

---

11. The National Archives hold various records about 1939-45 war crimes. Records for NW Europe are held in series WO 309. There is an online guide to war crimes records 1939-45 on the National Archives website nationalarchives.gov.uk

FROM : No 13 MRES, APO 403

      : No 3 MREU HQ, RAF APO 403
         Copies to War Crimes (JAG Sect),BAOR,Air Ministry P4 (Cas) 85 GCU.

DATE : 30th July 1947

REF   : 13MRES/G 1710

37A

                Exhumation and Autopsy
                1710052   Sgt Brown, J.W.

1.   As the case G 1710 was one in which a suspicion of War Crimes arose, the exhumation was performed in the company of a pathologist who removed the body to 387th Station Hospital Stuttgart for a full autopsy. The report of the pathologist, Capt. W.A. Griest, Army of United States, is appended with these papers.

2.   Certain contradictions appear between evidence collected from local inhabitants of Bondorf and at the autopsy, although there has been uncovered no proof of War Crimes. Sgt. Brown was found about nine kilometers from the reported crash point, and according to the ex-Buergermeister, without parachute or harness. From conversation with Captain Griest, it is not considered possible that the injuries to bones could have been occasioned by a fall from a great height without a parachute, but neither is it considered very possible that with the three fractured limbs referred to in the autopsy report, Sgt. Brown could have buried his parachute and moved any distance before being found.

3.   It is possible, however, and very probable, that in the event of a satisfactory theory or explanation appearing to account for the types of bone fractures discovered, Sgt. Brown could have died through shock, loss of blood, or exhaustion and exposure during the seven days between the crash and the finding of his body. Final comments and/or action are requested from War Crimes (J.A.G. Section) B.A.O.R.

                                    Investigating Officer

                                Officer Commanding
                                  No 13 Section

37b

PATHOLOGIST'S REPORT

28 July 1947

in the case of

     Brown, J. W.   Sgt   (Ref G-1710)
     1710052

A. Date of death: 24 - 2 - 1944

B. Place of burial: German Cemetery,
                        Bondorf, Germany
                        Kreis Böblingen

C. Type of cross: Plain wood

D. Marker on cross: Sergt. Brown engl.Flieger t März 1944.

E. Type of Grave: single grave. Body in wooden coffin.

F. Persons making identification:

                1. Parsons, W.B. F/Lt
                2. Fowler, R.   Capt

G. Identification made by means of:
                Identification made previously by means of German
                documents.

H. Items covering body:

                1. Inner flying suit
                2. W S D tunic, brevet and stripes torn off.
                3. W S D trousers
                4. Issue type sweater.
                5. O R type shirt, with collar and collar bones
                   missing.
                6. Cotton vest, no markings.
                7. Remains of cotton drawers.
                8. Blue issue socks.

I. Other items found with body: None.

J. General Examination. The body, examined three years and five
  months after death is that of a human being showing extremely
  far advanced decomposition. All the soft tissues have been
  converted into an amorphous mass whithout structure. The clothing,
  though still recognizable, is soft and can be torn with ease.

211

37c

K. Head. A moderate amount of brown wavy hair clings to the skull.
The scalp from which it arises is the consistency of mush. When the
debris covering the skull is removed, there is revealed an intact
calvarium without defect of any kind. The brain within the cranial
vault is a soft structureless mass. Amorphous tissue, the remains
of the soft tissue of the face, partly covers the facial bones;
in the eye sockets there is on either side a pyramidal structureless mass representing the eye and surrounding tissue. The facial
bones are intact. No foreign objects are present in the head.

L. Neck and vertebral column. The vertebrae of the neck are all
present and intact. The soft tissue of the neck has been changed
into soft mass in which details cannot be recognised. The
remainder of the vertebral column is not remarkable.

M. Shoulder girdle and upper extremities. The bones of the shoulder
girdle are intact. There is a complete oblique fracture of the
Right radius at the junction of the proximal and middle thirds;
the remaining bones of the upper extremities are negative. The
tissue of the shoulder girdle and extremities is so soft that
it can be stripped from the bones with the finger.

N. Thoracic Cage and abdomen. All soft tissue of the body cavities
is amorphous and no structure can be made out. The ribs are
oriented right and left, but are jumbled with respect to order.
One rib on the left shows a simple oblique fracture in the
anterior axillary line. The number of this rib is not determined.
Otherwise there is no abnormal finding in the thorax and abdomen.

O. Pelvic girdle and lower extremities. The pelvic girdle shows no
abnormal change. There is an inter-trochanteric fracture of
both femurs, and the left femur in addition, shows a simple
transverse fracture complete, in its middle third. The remaining
long bones and small bones of the lower extremities are unremark-
able. As in other parts of the body, the soft tissues of the
pelvic girdle and lower extremities show a far advanced state of
decomposition.

P. Summary. An autopsy was performed on the body of an individual
who had been dead for three years and five months. The soft
tissues showed a far advanced stage of decomposition. Several
fractures were demonstrated. They include:
      1. Fracture, radius, rt. oblique, simple, complete, junction
         of proximal and middle thirds.
      2. Fracture, rib, lt. oblique, simple, located in anterior
         axillary line, number of rib not determined.
      3. Fracture, intertrochanteric, bilateral.
      4. Fracture, femur, left, transverse, complete, in
         middle third.

No other abnormalities were demonstrated. No foreign objects
were present in the body.

2

3 D.

Q. Comment.
The advanced stage of soft tissue decomposition prohibits
evaluation of the existance or not of soft tissue injury.

Although a number of fractures were observed, these are
insufficient to serve as a primary cause of death.
The manner in which these fractures were incurred cannot be stated
from the autopsy.
A report in this case indicates that this individual was observed
to have a large hole in his head. No such hole was found at
autopsy. It is suggested as a possibility only that this hole in
the head was a scalp laceration which was not further examined
by the person first reporting it. Because of the far advanced
decomposition of the scalp, no statement as to whether or not
a scalp laceration was present can be made, however.

R. Conclusion:

The autopsy does not reveal the exact cause and manner
of death in this case.

WALTER D. GRIEST
Capt, Medical Corps
Army of the United States

213

Eyewitness Testimony

In addition to including information provided by eye witnesses on their Search/Investigation Reports MRES Search Officers sometimes submitted separate reports about information provided to them by local inhabitants concerning unidentified aircraft crashes. These would be sent to the Search Officer's Unit for onwards transmission to the Air Ministry Casualty Branch. Below is an example report about an aircraft crash sent by Flying Officer Rowlinson, a Search Officer with 21 MRE Section, to his commanding officer after he was given eye witness information about it whilst working in the Doberitz cemeteries in the Russian Zone.

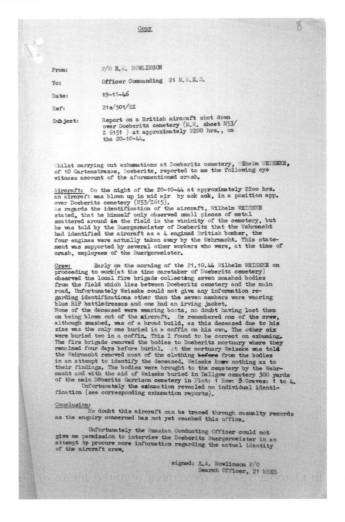

Chapter 13

Burial Documentation

Until the autumn of 1948 the RAF Missing Research and Enquiry Service (MRES) and their Missing Research Enquiry Units (MREU) worked in conjunction with the Army Graves Registration Directorate (Europe) through their Army Graves Registration Units (GRUs) and Graves Concentration Units (GCUs). From mid-1947 RAF MRES liaison officers had been attached to Army GCU units. It was the responsibility of the Army GRS and GCU to register graves, conduct exhumations, concentrate the remains of British and Empire dead into British Military cemeteries, move bodies within cemeteries when required, and mark graves with temporary wooden crosses inscribed with the occupants particulars or as "Unknown" for the unidentified. Once in place these crosses were photographed, partly as part of a recording process but also so the next of kin could at least have a photograph of their loved ones grave. This practice also ensured the correct spelling of names etc as next of kin were quick to point out any errors. Sometimes copies of these photographs are found on Casualty P Files. Sadly the presence of these copies often indicates that the next of kin to whom they were sent no long lived at the address held for them by the Casualty Branch. In these cases efforts would be made to trace the next of kin at their new address with the help of the police but these attempts were not always successful. The photographs are often in envelopes marked "gone away" or similar by the Post Office. The temporary makers erected by the GRS were later replaced by the Imperial War Graves Commission with permanent headstones of standard patterns (see the Chapter 16 on *Commemoration*).

In 1948 the decision was taken by the War Office to disband their Graves Concentration Units but many RAF and Dominion Air Force casualties still had to be moved into or around in British Military Cemeteries. This latter requirement resulted from the Air Ministry policy that aircraft crews should lie together, either in collective graves or individual ones placed next to each other. In October 1948 a movement required figure of 3000 to 4000 casualties was given at meeting between the MRES and the Army Graves

Registration Department concerning the GRUs disbandment. Because of the large number of Air Force casualties still to be dealt with the RAF Missing Research Graves Service (MRGS) was established in November 1948. This organisation took over the work that had previously been done by the Army.

The Casualty Branch received lists of burials and a record of each burial was placed on the appropriate casualty file using an Extract from Burial List docket.

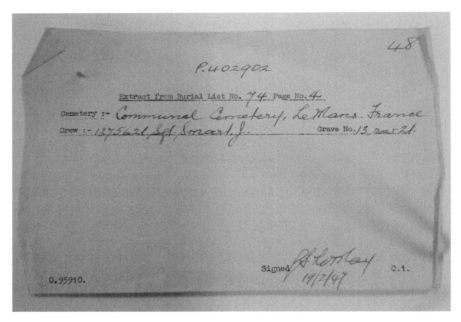

An example of a Casualty Branch "Extract from a Burial List" docket. The origin of the extract is carefully recorded. In this case it came from Burial List No 74, page no 4.

Various other forms were generated by the Army and RAF relating to their work in the registering and/or moving of graves. Some of these can be found on the Casualty P Files. The most common are:

Burial "Tickets"

A common find on Casualty Files are burial "tickets" which record the details of burial and give next of kin details. The Burial slip for Sgt Munn shows that he was presumed dead and his grave is located at Le Mans.

BURIAL DOCUMENTATION

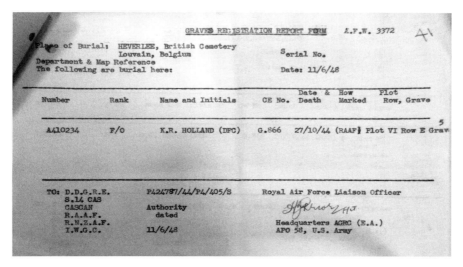

Graves Registration Report Forms

The Graves Registration Reports were either raised by Army GRUs or MRES Units and were submitted on a copy of Form AFW 3372. The MRES usually used locally produced (typed) versions as shown below. Amendments to Grave Registration Reports sent to the Casualty Branch were also submitted on AW3372 and it is not uncommon to find several Grave Registration Reports on a Casualty File.

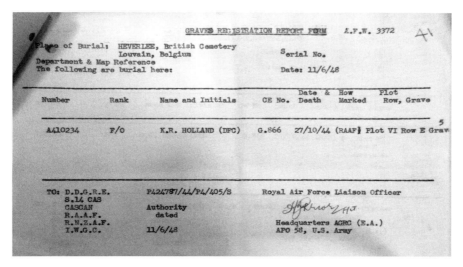

This Graves Registration report above was sent to S14 Cas (the successor to S7 and P4(Cas)) and others in June 1948 by the RAF Liaison Officer with US Army Graves Registration Command in Europe to register the burial of Flying Officer K R Holland of the RAAF.

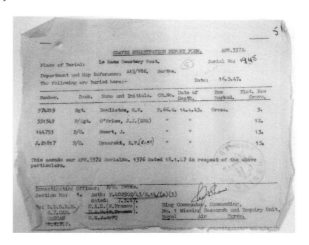

A Final Graves Registration Form produced by the Imperial War Graves Commission in 1956 for 13 graves in the RAF Extension, Reichswald Forest War Cemetery and sent to the Air Ministry as final confirmation of graves at the completion of the War Cemetery.

A Casualty File copy of a Graves Registration Report Form (AFW3372) sent to the Casualty Branch amending a previous Graves Registration Report.

Burial Detail Acceptance Forms

The Burial Detail Acceptance Form (BDA) was introduced by the RAF MRES to inform the Army Graves Concentration Units of the MRES' requirements for cross markings and movements of remains. It was especially important to ensure the correct documentation and cross markings particularly in cases where for Unknowns had been identified. The form was used in conjunction with the Final Graves Registration Report.

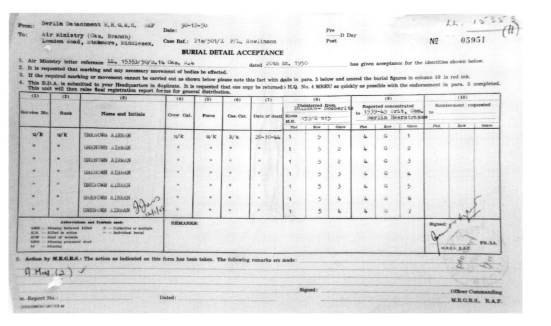

Grave Concentration Reports

These are lists of individuals who have been recovered or exhumed from their original burial location, and moved or concentrated to a particular cemetery. They provide basic details of the individual, but in addition may also include information as to their original location prior to burial.

(1) Serial No.	(2) Regt or Corps	(3) Army No.	(4) Name & Initials	(5) Rank	(6) Date of Death	(7) K.A, D/W or Died	(8) Plot	(9) Row	(10) Grave	(11) Date of Reburial	Previous location of grave	Report Number*
											Place & Map Ref.	
1	RAF		UNKNOWN		14.10.44	N/A	XXX	E	9	1.8.47	OSTERFELD New Cemetery Germany,1/250.000 K.52 A 32	Not registered
2	RAF	1590859	EAYNES R.	SGT	"	"	XXX	E	10	"		"
3	RAF	154079	FORD H.T.	P/O	"	"	XXX	E	11			"
4	RAF		UNKNOWN		"	"	XXX	E	12			"
5	RAAF	Aus/18119	LOUGHAN J.P.	P/O	"	"	XXX	E	13			"
6	RAF	1894389	HUGHES F.A.H.	SGT	"	"	XXX	E	14			"
7												
8												
9												
10												
11												
12												

GRAVES CONCENTRATION REPORT FORM

3 M. S.W. CLEVE

The following has/have been concentrated here:—
Name (Cemetery) REICHSWALD FOREST (OLD) BRITISH CEM. (RAF EXTN)
(Full Map Reference) GSGS 4346 1/250.000 Sht 2A/3A E 858504.

Germany 2 E 1070

Report No.
BAOR/G3/CON/2321

Date 12 April 1948 /IDP

* Where a grave has not already been registered, a Registration Report on A.F.W. 3372 will be prepared, and attached to this FORM.

Signed
Rank & Appointment Lt Col AIGRE

A Graves Concentration Report Form of the Army Directorate of Graves Registration and Enquiry concerning graves moved from Osterfeld New Cemetery to the RAF Extension in Reichswald Forest War Cemetery in 1948.

Chapter 14

Far East Casualty Files

Most Far East Casualty files are woefully lacking in documentation. Although the same paperwork notifying casualties and reporting burials was required from RAF units in the Far East by the Air Ministry Casualty Branch, the Far East Casualty P Files are significantly less informative than those concerning casualties in other theatres (with one or two exceptions). The lack of information stems largely from the paucity of Japanese records and the failure of the Japanese authorities to provide information on casualties or prisoners of war as was required by the Geneva Conventions. Japan had signed the Geneva Conventions but did not ratify them and so was not bound by them. However, in 1942 the Japanese gave an undertaking to abide by the Conventions' terms, an undertaking which they failed to fulfil. Their appalling treatment of combatants and non-combatants alike is well known. Some records about prisoners of the Japanese are held in the British National Archives. Under reference WO367 are registers of Allied prisoners of war and civilians held in Singapore which contain 13,500 names of people captured there. There are also prisoner of war records which can be viewed online through the National Archives collaboration with findmypast.co.uk, a genealogy service.

The attitude of the Japanese towards captured military personnel stemmed from their military code which regarded surrender as a dishonour and a disgrace. Captured records concerning prisoners of war are scant as many were destroyed by the Japanese at the end of the war. However, there are a few Japanese documents on Casualty P Files, some of which are incredibly fragile as they were written on rice paper. The most usual type of document to find on Casualty P Files are prisoner of war index cards.

A Japanese Prisoner of War index card for an Australian soldier. The Japanese gave 4,500 of these PoW records to Australia in 2012.

With the fall of Hong Kong and Singapore and the subsequent loss of Malaya and Burma, thousands of British and Dominion personnel were captured by the Japanese and many were to die as prisoners of war. Those RAF units and personnel who survived the battle for Singapore withdrew to Java and were lost when the Allied Forces in Java surrendered on 12 March 1942; some 5,100 Air Force personnel were taken prisoner of whom some 1,700 died in captivity. The nature of the long fighting retreat down Malaya and the scrambling, last minute evacuation of Singapore by ships and boats which had to run the gauntlet of Japanese aircraft and naval ships which sank many, meant the fate of many personnel listed as 'unaccounted for' was impossible to establish. Some 7,000 Far East RAF personnel were shown as unaccounted for in March 1942.

Further Air Force losses were suffered during the campaigns to retake areas lost to the Japanese. In addition to the threat posed by Japanese aircraft, Allied air crew in the Far East had the forces of nature to contend with. They flew in all weather conditions, contending with monsoon rains, low clouds shrouding hills and mountains, and then, in the heat of the day, clouds rising to 40,000 feet making it difficult to climb above them;

flying in cloud was disorientating and hazardous. Some aircraft were lost to turbulence caused by the mountains and prevalent weather. To make matters worse their aircraft navigational aids were well below the standard of those available in the European Theatre and the crew mostly had to rely on the basic navigation aids of the sky, stars (if they were visible), wind drift (if the sea could be seen) and landmarks that the navigator collected through noticing them during flights and marking them on his map.

The position of an aircraft when it crashed was rarely known. A former Far East Dakota pilot said that once aircraft went down in the jungle they disappeared for ever and were never heard of again: *'The weather conditions out there in the monsoon in these great cu-nims [cumulus nimbus clouds] which would go up to 38-40,000 feet were terrifying; you've never seen anything like them in Europe. You talk about stair rods here, but it is a very different matter there. To hear the hail rattling down on the aircraft as one flew was very frightening and I remember on one occasion flying at about 8,000 feet over the mountains and having to go through a cu-nim because there was no way round it and no way back. I encountered very severe turbulence and at one stage was caught in an up-draught which took me to 14,000 feet from 8,000; I throttled back, stuck my nose down and just hurtled out of the top of this cloud from 14,000 feet. A lot of aeroplanes did break up in those conditions and I think it was a worse hazard than the enemy.'*[1]

When an aircraft crashed, where possible aerial searches were conducted by fellow squadron pilots over the area in which the aircraft had last been seen or where it was believed to have gone down. The nature of the terrain ruled out ground searches, even close to bases, and only occasionally were downed air crew recovered. A commanding officer would mention that searches had taken place in the Circumstantial Report he submitted to the Air Ministry Casualty Branch but other than this very little information about any searches undertaken exists in Casualty P Files. Below is a very rare detailed account of a ground search party which looked for Liberator BZ952 of 357 (Special Duties) Squadron lost on the way to Kunming in China on 5/6th April 1944. The account was sent to the Casualty Branch with a copy of a letter from No 9 Air Transit Section, India, to the commanding officer of 357 Squadron. The search party had been sent out by No 9 Air Transit Section and was led by a RAAF officer. It is a strange case as the Operations Record Book of 357 Squadron states that this Liberator was

---

1. *The RAF and Far East War 1941-1945* Bracknell Paper No 6 dated 24 March 1995 published by the RAF Historical Society. Words of Air Vice Marshal Stanbridge page 82.

carrying fuel as her cargo. However, the aircraft did not catch fire after it crashed into the mountainside as could be expected with a cargo of fuel. The accompanying copy letter says that the aircraft was looted by local Chinese so the true nature of the cargo of this Special Duties Liberator can only be guessed at.

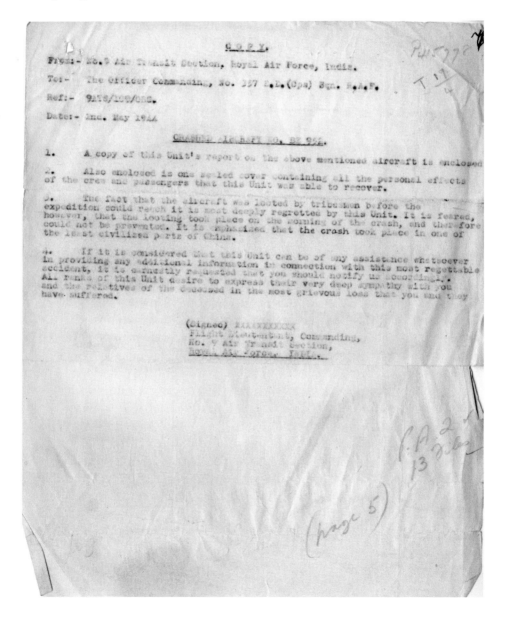

COPY NO. 4.

DISTRIBUTION:

Copy No.1.   Headquarters, Air Command, South East Asia.

Copy No.2.   The Air Attache, H.B.M.Embassy, Chungking, China.

Copy No.3.   Headquarters, No.229 Group, R.A.F.

Copy No.4.   No.357 Special Duties (Operations) Squadron R.A.F.

Copy No.5.   Wing Commander Lord Waleran, R.A.F.L.O., 14th. U.S.A.F.

Copy No.6.   No.9. Air Transit Section, R.A.F. India.

NOTES.

1.   Appendix No.IV., comprising photographs of the crashed aircraft and
     the graves of the crew, is available in one copy only.This has been
     distributed to Headquarters, Air Command, South East Asia, who are
     requested to distribute additional copies to all addressees including
     No. 9 A.T.S.

2.   Appendix No.V., a specimen leaflet, is enclosed to the first three
     addressees only.

3.   The indulgence of all addressees is requested for the unavoidable use
     of Forms 683 as stationery for this report. Supplies of regular
     stationery were exhausted by this report.

4.   No communications have been despatched to the next-of-kin of the
     deceased by this Unit.

                    (Signed)   XXXXXXXXXX
                    Flight Lieutenant, Commanding,
                    No. 9 Air Transit Section,
                    ROYAL AIR FORCE.   INDIA.

(9AT/109/ORG
  2nd. May 1944.

SECRET.

NO. 9 AIR TRANSIT SECTION, R.A.F.
INDIA.

A REPORT

ON AN EXPEDITION INTO THE INTERIOR OF CHINA, UNDERTAKEN

TO ESTABLISH THE CAUSE OF AN ACCIDENT TO LIBERATOR

AIRCRAFT NO. BZ 952, 357 SQDN.

R. A. F.

BY

FLIGHT LIEUTENANT J.A.P. KAINES, R.A.A.F.

C O N T E N T S.

SECRET.   NO. 9 AIR TRANSIT SECTION, R.A.F. INDIA.   Page No.1.

REPORT ON EXPEDITION TO SCENE OF CRASHED LIBERATOR AIRCRAFT NO.
BZ 952 OF NO. 357 (S.D.) OPS. SQUADRON, R.A.F.
BY
Flight Lieutenant J.A.P. Kaines, Commanding
No. 9 Air Transit Section, R.A.F.

OBJECT OF EXPEDITION.

1.   To confirm that an aircraft, reported crashed by the Chinese 5th.
Route Air Force, was in effect a Liberator, No. BZ 952, of No. 357 Sqdn.,
which was reported missing on the night of 5th. - 6th. April, 1944.

2.   In the event of the object above being attained, to

   (i) Establish the cause of the accident,

   (ii) Identify, and if necessary, inter the remains of the deceased,

   (iii) To recover any serviceable equipment, secret documentation, and
         personal equipment of the deceased.

3.   The instructions for the expedition were given by Wing Commander
Lord Waleran, R.A.F. Liaison Officer with the 14th. U.S.A.F.

PERSONNEL OF THE EXPEDITION.

4.   Flight Lieutenant J.A.P. Kaines, 117092, R.A.A.F. (Commanding Officer)

   1240464. Cpl. Massey. H.   (Escort)
   1515489. LAC. Owens, C.J.   (Escort)
             Mr. Tso Chi On.   (Interpreter)
             Chen Ah Dor.   (Driver)

5.   The last two individuals are civilian employees of No. 9 Air Transit
Section.

DISTRICT OVER WHICH THE EXPEDITION OPERATED.

6.   The original report of the crashed aircraft, believed to be British
was received from the 5th. Chinese Route Air Force on the 13th. April
1944, and the report stated that the scene of the crash was in the
District of E-liang, in the province of Yun-nan, China.

7.   The whole territory between Kunming, the base of the expedition, and
E-Liang, is rugged, confused, and mountainous. Roads are few and where
they exist, are little better than mule tracks.

8.   E-liang is distant 685 kilometres (427 miles) from Kunming by road.
The first 620 kilometres (382 miles) of the journey, which terminate in the
town of Chaotung, are passable by truck. The next stage of the journey,
from Chaotung to E-liang is a dangerous and precipitous mountain track
through a district infested with bandits. This track is passable only to
mule and foot transport, but litters may be hired. The final stage of the
journey, from E-liang to the scene of the crash is trackless. It is negot-
iable only by using natural features such as watercourses, and terminates
in an abrupt rise through 1200 feet to the summit of a hill on which the
crashed aircraft rests. This final step was possible only after steps had
been cut in the side of the hill.

PLAN OF THE EXPEDITION.

9.   The prospect of Air Transport was at first considered. The nearest
airfield to the scene of the crash is at Chaotung, 63 kilometres (40
miles) from the scene of the crash. The runway at this airfield is
3,300 feet long, but the airfield is extremely difficult to land in, since
it is surrounded by mountains. The coordinates of Chaotung are 27.20N
103.45E. In view of the extreme difficulty of the journey to E-liang from
Chaotung, and the shortage of aviation gasoline in China, it was decided.

/Contd.

that no advantage would be gained by air transport.

10.   A 15 c.w.t. Ford truck was prepared for the journey. Rations for 12
days for the personnel detailed at para. 4 were loaded, 110 U.S. gallons
of 67 octane gasoline were stowed in addition to the tankage of the truck
(20 U.S. gallons), and for protection against bandits an escort was detailed
armed with two Sten guns. A 12 bore shotgun was also carried primarily in
order to 'shoot for the pot', since the country through which the expedition
passed is plentifully stocked with game.

DAY TO DAY NARRATIVE OF EVENTS.

11.   19th. April 1944.

The morning was occupied with providing the expedition
with the necessary permits and letters of introduction to Chinese authorities
along the route of the expedition. In this connection it is desired to
place on record the assistance given by Colonel Yeng, Commanding the 5th.
Chinese Route Air Force, and his Chief of Staff, Major Moh, who gave every
assistance to the expedition in procuring the necessary documents.
The expedition left Kunming at 1500 hours.   At
1900 hours the town of Kutsing, the first stage of the journey was reached
(160 kilos).   The expedition was accommodated for the night at the hostel
of the Friends Ambulance Unit, a Quaker organisation, at the invitation of
Mr. Bennett, the Superintendant.

12.   20th. April 1944.
The expedition left Kutsing at 0700 hours.   120
kilos out of Kutsing the fuel pump of the truck broke. This was rectified
in one hour. A halt was made at Suanwei at 1200 hours for lunch. Suanwei
was left at 1430 hours, and at 1900 hours, the second stage of the journey
, Weining, was reached (260 kilos, 163 miles). This stage of the journey
is through exceedingly mountainous country, and the road is dangerous. At
Weining, the expedition had been recommended to call on The Rev. Vernon
Stones, the minister of the Methodist Mission at that town. Rev. Stone
immediately asked the expedition to stay at his house for the night. This
offer was gratefully accepted. In the course of a conversation between
the expedition commander and the Rev.Stone, the latter mentioned that an
airman who was a member of a party of escapees from Burma had been accidentally killed there. The Rev. Stone had made all arrangements for the
burial in the churchyard of the Methodist Church, and a headstone had been
erected. The inscription on the headstone reads as follows:-

941960
Cpl. William Richard Swash
R.A.F.
Accidentally Killed
29th. October 1942.

13.   21st. April 1944.
The expedition left Weining at 0700 hours. The next
stage of the journey is through mountainous country, and the road is
extremely narrow and rough. A halt was made at a Chinese inn for food at
1330 hours. A start was made at 1430 hours, and at 1630 hours Chaotung
was reached.   The expedition commander reported to Captain Yue, of the
5th. Chinese Route Air Force, to whom a letter of introduction was carried.
Captain Yue had been warned of the impending arrival of the expedition by
Colonel Yeng, who has been previously mentioned at para.11. Captain Yue
was able to amplify the scanty information with which the expedition had
left Kunming. He stated that the plane had not been destroyed by fire,
and that the delay in notifying the R.A.F. at Kunming was due to the fact
that the aircraft displayed roundels of the new design. Captain Yue had
actually been of the opinion that the aircraft was American until he had
discussed the accident with two American soldiers who were passing through
Chaotung.   These soldiers, whose names are unknown, informed him that
the aircraft was British.   The aircraft had struck the side of a hill
whose summit is about 5500 feet above sea level, and about 1500 feet above
the level of the surrounding countryside. Captain Yue is of the opinion
that the bodies were rifled before his men arrived at the crash. Some of
bodies had very little clothing, and no money, personal jewellery and
trinkets, or any other articles of value were found on the corpses.
Captain Yue arranged for the interment of the bodies. This was carried
out with the authority of the Chief Magistrate of E-liang by the Chinese

/Contd.

Page No. 3.

priest in charge of the Roman Catholic Mission, E-liang. The burial took place of the 13 occupants of the aircraft on the 9th. April, 1944. The bodies were buried in heavy oken coffins of Chinese pattern at a place about 400 feet below the scene of the crash. It was impossible to remove the bodies to the churchyard at E-liang because of the inaccessibility of the aircraft. This may be gauged by the fact that 15 men were required to carry each coffin to the place of burial. The deceased were buried with Christian rites, but since the priest was unable to discover the religions of them, the burial service was non-sectarian.

Captain Yue thoughtfully arranged for a photographer to take the two photographs which form appendices to this report, and of which the negatives are enclosed. He also had all the papers on the bodies packed separately and held in safe custody.

Captain Yue then arranged for the expedition commander to interview Weng Fung Hsui, the local representative of General Lung, Governor of Yunnan. This gentleman advised that an escort of 20 Chinese soldiers be taken of the last stage of the journey, in view of the dangerous nature of the local inhabitants, many of whom are bandits. This number was eventually cut down to six, in view of the unwieldiness of such a large party over such difficult country.

The Reverend Stone, who was mentioned at para. 12, had given the expedition a letter of introduction to the Reverend Charles Steel, of the Methodist Mission at Chaotung. This gentleman, who is a fluent linguist in the local dialects, agreed to accompany the expedition on the last stage of the journey to the crashed aircraft. The Rev. Steel also suggested that since he was well known in the district, everything would be considerably cheaper if the financial arrangements were placed in his hands. This was agreed to, and the sum of $CN 21,000 was handed over to him for the purpose of porter and coolie hire, etc. LAC Owens was detailed in charge of the base detachment of the expedition which was left at Chaotung. This detachment consisted of the interpreter, Mr. Tso, the driver, Chen Ah Dor, and the truck and equipment not required for the final stage of the journey. Arrangements were then concluded for the hire of porters, coolies, and litters; and the advanced detachment of the expedition, consisting of the commander, Cpl. Massey, Mr. Steel, and the porters arranged to leave for the scene of the crash at 0930 hours on the morning of 22nd April 1944.

14. **22nd April 1944.**
The expedition's advanced detachment left Chaotung at 0930 hours. The detachment consisted of 21 persons. At 1700 hours, Hsu Yi village was reached without incident. The detachment stayed the night at a coolie's rest house. This place was verminous in the extreme, and from this point until the return to Chaotung the advanced detachment lived on Chinese food which was not always of the best quality.

15. **23rd April 1944.**
The detachment left Hsu Yi at 0730 hours. The path from Hsu Yi to E-liang is so rough and mountainous that it was impossible to travel in litters, and the detachment proceeded on foot for 12 miles over some of the most difficult country in this part of China. It was necessary to traverse a pass at an altitude of nearly 9000 feet between the mountains whose summits were three thousand feet above the pass, which was covered in dense cloudwhich made going most hazardous. This part of the journey lies in Miao and Lolo country. The Miaos and Lolos are uncivilised tribesmen whose occupations are banditry and opium smuggling. They will kill travellers for their arms and money without scruple. About 12 miles after the pass had been traversed, a tributary of the Yangtsze river was reached and followed for about 7 miles into E-liang, which was reached at 1730 hours. The Deputy Magistrate of E-liang had been warned by runner of the impending arrival of the detachment, which was met at the town gate by the Deputy Magistrate and other civic dignitaries. This deputation, after letters of introduction and the usual courtesies had been exchanged, arranged for the accommodation of the detachment for the night at the courthouse. The early departure of the detachment was also arranged for the next morning. After these arrangements had been concluded, the detachment were invited to a banquet at the house of the Deputy Magistrate, who had arranged it in honour of the Royal Air Force. After the banquet the personal belongings of the deceased members of the aircrew were formally handed over to the Commander of the expedition.

16. **24th April 1944.**
The detachment started for the scene of the crash at
/Cont'd.

Page No. 4.

0730 hours. The crashed aircraft was reached by 1100 hours. The first action xxx taken was to hold a service at which the Reverend Charles Steel officiated. The Service was held in the open air in the English and Chinese languages., and was non-sectarian in nature. Although the uniformed members of the detachment numbered only three, military honours were paid. As will be seen from the photograph which forms an appendix to this report, the Chinese have levelled off a small plot of ground in which the graves are situated, and have planted pine trees around the plot. The graves lie on the side of a lonely peaceful hill, and three mounta nx streams pass close to them. The graves have been marked and numbered, and the following list gives details of the graves and their occupants:-

Grave No.1.   994272 Cpl. Charles Fred Dugdale
                         R.A.F.
                 Killed on Active Service
                         6th. April 1944.

Grave No.2.   1564130 LAC Charles Henry Hutt
                         R.A.F.
                 Killed on Active Service
                         6th April 1944.

Grave No.3.   1810327 AC1 Douglas Morris Leonard
                         R.A.F.
                 Killed on Active Service
                         6th April 1944

* Grave No.4.   James Walton Ridley
                         R.A.F.
                 Killed on Active Service
                         6th April 1944

Grave No.5.   972440 LAC John Alexander Stewart
                         R.A.F.
                 Killed on Active Service
                         6th April 1944.

Grave No.6.   966050 SGT Frederick Joseph Unsworth
                         R.A.F.
                 Killed on Active Service
                         6th April 1944.

Grave No.7.   1439922 Sgt Thomas George Rutter
                         R.A.F.
                 Killed on Active Service
                         6th April 1944.

Grave No.8.   1315521 Sgt Victor A. Graham
                         R.A.F.
                 Killed on Active Service
                         6th April 1944.

Grave No.9.   1158874 Sgt Howard Ross Hughes
                         R.A.F.
                 Killed on Active Service
                         6th April 1944.

Grave No.10.   1087865 Sgt Frederick Sullivan
                         R.A.F.
                 Killed on Active Service
                         6th April 1944.

Grave No.11.   1411516 AC1 Selwyn George Jones
                         R.A.F.
                 Killed on Active Service
                         6th April 1944

Grave No.12.   1030419 Sgt Richard Applegarth Dunn
                         R.A.F.
                 Killed on Active Service
                         6th April 1944.

Grave No.13.   1537040 Sgt R. Vanes
                         R.A.F.   /Cont'd

Page No. 5.

Killed on Active Service
6th April 1944

No papers were found to disclose the rank or personal number of
James Walton Ridley.

It was obvious from an examination of the crash that before any responsible
person had arrived at the crash, tribesmen had rifled the aircraft.   There
was no paper or coined money found except a few Ceylon notes, and the
personal papers of the deceased had obviously been searched for valuables.
Not a single item of personal jewellery was discovered, in spite of the
fact that among thirteen airmen there must have been some such articles.
No small arms were discovered.   The bodies had been stripped of much
clothing, and the only items of flying clothing found were two very badly
torn Irvin jackets.   All the parachutes had been released, but not by the
aircrew.   They were probably released out of curiosity by the Chinese.
The Reverend Charles Steel has offered to write to the next of kin of the
deceased, describing the last rites and the location of the graves.   It is
considered that he should be requested to do this, as it is thought that
such a message would be most comforting to the relatives.   On receipt of
instructions to this effect, the Rev. Steel will be informed accordingly.
It is suggested that the present wooden crosses be replaced by one large
stone to be erected in the centre of the burial site.   Each grave would be
marked with a small stone, numbered to correspond with a suitable inscription
on the large stone.   It must be emphasized that the graves are in a most
inaccessible position on the top of a mountain, and there is therefore a
very definite limitation to the monument that could be erected.   This limit
is about 4 cwt.   It is also suggested that metal plaques could be made under
the arrangements of No. 357 Sqdn., and forwarded to No. 9 Air Transit Section
for onward despatch to the Reverend C. Steel, who has expressed his willing-
ness to undertake any such services.

Details of Crash.
(1) Identification.   The aircraft was definitely identified as a Liberator
with British markings and crew.   The number of the aircraft is
BZ 952.   The Squadron letters are 18 - 2.

(ii) Position.   Approximately 103.45E 27.30N.

(iii) Cause of the Accident.   The aircraft crashed at some time between 0515
and 0530 on 6th April, 1944.   This would be just before dawn.   Local
inhabitants state that the skies were overcast, and that the tops of
the hills were in cloud.   The aircraft appears to have struck the
mountain whilst in a steep bank, which appears to indicate that the
pilot saw the ground just too late to take avoiding action.   Even had
the pilot avoided the hill on which he crashed, he could not have avoided crashing into another hill some 500 feet higher which was just
behind it.   No petrol was found in any of the sound tanks.   It was
impossible to examine any of the port wing tanks, since they were torn
to pieces.   It is not thought that the aircraft had exhausted its fuel
as the airscrews were all in coarse pitch, and were bent in such a
manner to indicate that they were under power when the aircraft struck.
It is also probable that any fuel remaining in the aircraft was stolen
by tribesmen.   The severe damage to the fuselage seen in the photograph of the crash was not caused by the impact, but appears to have
been caused by axes.   Parts of the aircraft were distributed over a
wide area; and one of the engines is over 400 yards away at the bottom
of a watercourse.   The aircraft was off course, and as reported elsewhere by the R.A.F. Liaison Officer, 14th U.S.A.F., was lost only
because the briefing was inaccurate from the signals point of view.
Kunming field heard the aircraft calling on 5550Kc/s., the main guard
frequency, but in spite of switching on a 3 Kilowatt R/T station on
this frequency, could not contact it.   Had this been possible, the
aircraft would have been saved.

(iv) Salvage.   Under the supervision of Cpl. Massey, what little equipment
that remained was dismantled and removed to a farmhouse some 2500 yards
distant, where it is being stored under an armed military guard from
the Chinese Army.   Arrangements are being made with Captain Yue to
have it transported to Chaotung by mule and porter.   Here it will be
stored at the Headquarters of the Chinese Air Force, until instructions
are received for its disposal.   Colonel Clark, the British Military

/Cont'd

231

Page No. 5.

Attache at Kunming has stated that he will provide motor transport for the collection of the equipment from Chaotung. The I.F.F. set was brought to Kunming by the expedition on its return. It is damaged beyond repair and it is requested that permission be given to this Unit to dismantle it for use as radio spares. The detonator did not operate. It is not known what, if any, secret documents were aboard. An empty SYKO case was found, which indicates that the machine and cards have been stolen. No secret documentation other than the colours of the day for the 5th. and 6th. April were discovered. Large numbers of leaflets were discovered, a copy of which forms an appendix to this report. They were collected and destroyed by fire. A list of salvaged equipment forms an appendix to this report and disposal instructions are awaited. It is suggested that the armament of the aircraft be handed over to the 14th. U.S.A.F., who are very short of these items.

17. 25th. April 1944.
At 0700 hours the advanced detachment of the expedition left the scene of the crash for E-lieng. The rest of the day was spent in making the arrangements for the storage of the salvaged equipment and for the return journey to Kunming.

18. 26th. April 1944.
At 0700 hours the advanced detachment departed for Chaotung. Once again the civic dignitaries put in an appearance, together with practically the whole population of the town, who gave the detachment a most cordial send-off and refreshments prior to the journey. Hsu Yi village was reached at 1900 hours without incident.

19. 27th. April 1944.
Departed from Hsu Yi 0700 hours. After a most difficult march through thick cloud and continuous rain, the advanced detachment arrived at Chaotung at 1630 hours. The base detachment, in the absence of the remainder of the expedition, had made arrangements for the advanced detachment on its return to be billetted on various European families in the town in order that they might clean up after the arduous journey back from E-lieng. The families who showed these kindnesses were:-
The Reverend Charles Steel, Missionary Hospital, Chaotung.

Mr. and Mrs. Harrison, The Educationalist, Chaotung.

Dr. and Mrs. Lyth, Missionary Surgeon, Chaotung.

It was decided to delay the departure from Chaotung for one day in order that courtesy visits might be paid to the Chinese Civil, Military and Air Force Authorities. An audience was granted to the Commander by the Governor of Chaotung District, and an account was rendered to him of the work accomplished. Throughout the whole time during which the expedition was in his territory, Governor Wong Fung Hsui took a real interest in its work, and was instrumental in procuring every kind of assistance and cooperation from his subordinates. By way of a small token of appreciation of the assistance given, the Commander of the expedition gave a luncheon party which was attended by a representative gathering of Civil, Military and Air Force dignitaries. The afternoon was spent in preparing notes and accounts relating to the expedition. In the evening a singsong was held in honour of the expedition by the Rev. Steel.

20. 29th. April 1944.
The expedition departed from Chaotung at 0700 hours after a certain amount of trouble with the truck had been overcome. Weining was reached without further incident at 1830 hours. Once again the Rev. Vernon Stone was kind enough to accommodate the expedition for the night.

21. 30th. April 1944.
The expedition departed from Weining at 0730 hours. A stop was made at Shuenwei for lunch, and the opportunity was taken to purchase some of the hams for which this town is renowned. Kutsing was reached without incident at 1900 hours after a journey through a violent thunderstorm. Mr. Bennett of the Friends Ambulance Unit was once again good enough to accommodate the expedition for the night.

22. 1st. May 1944.
The expedition left Kutsing at 0830 hours. Three pass-

Page No. 7.

engers were taken to Kunming for the F.A.U., and Kunming was reached at 1230 hours.

CONCLUSION.

23.   All necessary arrangements have been made for the removal, storage, and transport to Kunming of the salvaged equipment.

24.   The interment, marking of graves, and disposal of effects of the casualties had been accomplished.

25.   Sufficient evidence has been gathered to establish the cause of the accident as a combination of inexperience of the country on the part of the aircrew, who were hopelessly lost; bad briefing; and adverse weather conditions.   It is imperative that aircrew who are detailed to overfly unmapped and unsurveyed territory be given all assistance by those responsible for Briefing, particularly of Signals facilities. It is also desirable that all aircraft flying over such territory be accompanied by a pilot and wireless operator experienced in flying over China until such time as they are competent to make such flights alone.

26.   Invaluable assistance was rendered by the Chinese Civil and Military authorities mentioned elsewhere in this report. It is recommended that they be given some official token of appreciation by Higher Authority. The unsparing efforts of the missionaries deserve some more practical recognition.   These folks are stationed in most isolated locations, and are completely cut off from their countrymen. They live in many cases under conditions what border on those of extreme poverty. A letter, which is appended to this report, from the Reverend Charles Steel will give some idea of their situation.   It is strongly recommended that recognition of the services performed by them should take the shape of the allotment of a small amount of space on the Calcutta-Kunming air service. This need not exceed 10 pounds or so per aircraft. The first consignments might well be donated by the Royal Air Force in recognition of their many kindnesses. In can be stated with confidence that such recognition would be enthusiastically received, without any embarrassment on the part of the recipients.

LESSONS LEARNED FROM THE EXPEDITION.

27.   It is imperative that any expedition of this nature be accompanied by an interpreter, who may well be one of the missionaries, since these people generally speak local dialects, of which there are many in China.

28.   It is imperative that any expedition of this nature into the interior of China should provide itself with credentials in both English and Chinese, as a thorough examination of all travellers is made at every town.

29.   Any expedition of this nature must be provided with an armed escort, and it is worth while to carry a sporting gun in order to augment the rations carried.

30.   It is now established that Chinese food, prepared in the Chinese manner, is nutritious, appetising, and sustaining, and may be eaten with safety.

(sgd) J. A. F. Kaines.

Flight Lieutenant, Commanding,
No. 9 Air Transit Section,
Royal Air Force,   INDIA.

Kunming, 2nd. May 1944.

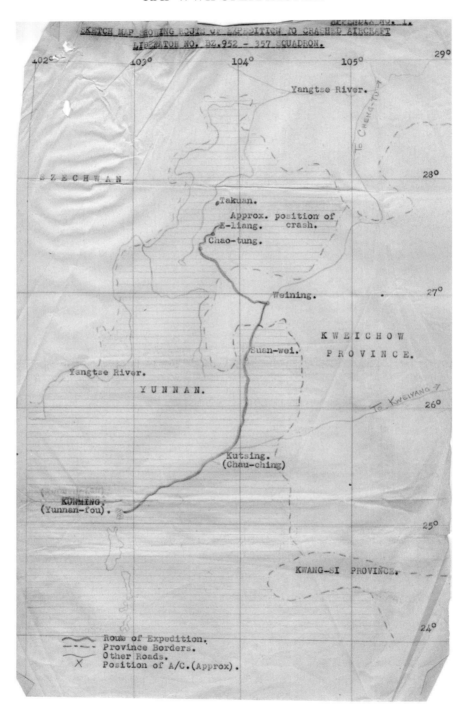

SKETCH MAP SHOWING ROUTE OF EXPEDITION TO CRASHED AIRCRAFT
LIBERATOR NO. BZ.952 - 357 SQUADRON.

Yangtse River.

S Z E C H W A N

Takuan.

Approx. position of
E-liang.   crash.

Chao-tung.

Weining.

K W E I C H O W

P R O V I N C E.

Suan-wei.

Yangtse River.

Y U N N A N.

To Kweiyang

Kutsing.
(Chau-ching)

KUNMING.
(Yunnan-fou).

KWANG-SI PROVINCE.

Route of Expedition.
Province Borders.
Other Roads.
X   Position of A/C.(Approx).

The Missing in the Far East

IN HONOURED REMEMBRANCE OF THE FORTITUDE AND
SACRIFICE OF THAT VALIANT COMPANY WHO PERISHED
WHILE BUILDING THE RAILWAY FROM THAILAND TO BURMA
DURING THEIR LONG CAPTIVITY
THOSE WHO HAVE NO KNOWN GRAVE ARE COMMEMORATED
BY NAME AT RANGOON SINGAPORE AND HONG KONG AND
THEIR COMRADES REST IN THE THREE WAR CEMETERIES
OF KANCHANABURI CHUNGKAI AND THANBYUZAYAT

*I will make you a name and a praise among all people of the earth
when I turn back your captivity before your eyes, saith the LORD*

The Memorial Plaque at Kanchanaburi War Cemetery.

If Japanese records about prisoners of war are scant, those about casualties are virtually non-existent. The Japanese provided no information on Allied casualties to the International Red Cross and therefore, during the war years, little information was available to the Air Ministry Casualty Branch. Not much other than that the person was missing could be added to the Casualty P Files unless an aircraft was actually seen to go down by other aircraft or troops on the ground. Many Far East Casualty Files contained nothing other than the initial information until more information became available at the end of the war. Then at least it was possible to establish whether the casualties were dead or alive.

Initially, the Air Ministry, in the hope that the Japanese would provide an equivalent to the German *Totenlisten*, held off notifying the next of kin about Far East casualties. When nothing was heard from the Japanese authorities, the War Office decided to list army personnel as 'Unaccounted For' rather than the usual 'Missing'. The Air Ministry followed the army's lead but this new casualty 'category' did not fit the regulations governing casualty handling procedures. Its use prevented next of kin receiving allowances and other benefits. The Far East casualties were in limbo. Growing public pressure, together with representations from the Australian government on behalf of the 'Unaccounted For' Royal Australian Air Force (RAAF) personnel, made the Air Ministry rethink its position, and finally, in February 1943, RAF and Dominion Air Force personnel listed as 'Unaccounted For' were reclassified as 'Missing' and entered the established casualty handling process. However, whereas those listed as Missing in the European Theatre could be presumed dead (for official purposes) after six months from the date they went missing, this was not the case for Far East casualties.

In the view of the Air Ministry, the dearth of information about Far East prisoners of war and casualties made any Presumption of Death unsafe. In April 1942 the Director, Personnel Section (RAF), agreed to a proposal put forward by the Casualty Branch that action to presume death in respect of Far East casualties which had occurred after the entry of Japan into the war (7 December 1941) should be deferred until satisfactory reporting of prisoners by the Japanese authorities. The initial proposal was that the period of six months usually waited before death was presumed would be extended initially to twelve months or longer in 'no news' cases.[2] The RAF policy on Presumption of Death in Far East cases was not popular with the RAAF. Their Overseas Headquarters in London consistently applied pressure to the Air Ministry to take Presumption action on a number of RAAF cases. The Air Ministry Casualty Branch resented the constant pressure applied by the Australians and complained to DPS that '*If these tactics are allowed to go on, premature presumption in Australian cases will speedily take away whatever virtue there may be in the Death Presumption action taken by the Air Ministry, as it will be impossible to separate RAF from RAAF presumptions in similar circumstances: the Air Board [RAAF] do not mind how far the Air Ministry commits itself, provided they can please their public, and if, on the motion of the [Australian] Air Board, the Air Ministry should make a wrong presumption, it will be advertised as the Air Ministry's fault.*'[3] The Air Ministry did not give way to the Australian demands; in the case of the great majority of Far East cases Death Presumption action was not taken until after the war. Many next of kin of Far East casualties had to wait for four years for death to be officially presumed.

When the war in the Far East ended in August 1945 and the prison camps were liberated, senior officers and other former prisoners brought out with them lists of personnel who had died while prisoners of the Japanese and, sometimes, of those who had died fighting during the Japanese advance or while attempting to escape capture after the fall of Hong Kong, Malaya, Singapore and other Far East countries. This information was speedily

---

2. National Archives AIR2/942 Air Ministry File A441170/42 Minutes 1 and 2.
3. National Archives AIR2/942 Air Ministry File A441170/42 Minute 4.

collated and in September/October 1945 a War Graves Registration team consisting of British, Australian and Dutch personnel together with some ex-prisoners of war went to the Burma railway and located the graves of some 10,500 Allied prisoners who had died during its construction and who were buried in cemeteries and isolated graves along its length.[4] All the graves found were registered. News of the missing also came through an organisation called 'Recovery of Allied Prisoners of War and Internees', known as RAPWI, which had been set up in February 1945 at the Headquarters of South East Asia Command. RAPWI was responsible for the finding, treatment, and evacuation of Far East PoWs and civilian internees. Their work began in earnest in August 1945 with the surrender of Japan on the 15th of that month. By the end of November 1945 all the Japanese prisoner of war and internment camps had been located and cleared and the fate of some of the missing RAF personnel was established.

In addition to RAPWI, the first teams on the ground in the Far East were the War Crimes Investigations teams and the Army Grave Concentration Units. These gathered any information available and passed it to a central clearing house for forwarding to the appropriate departments of the British and Dominion Armed Forces. By November 1945, the work of these teams together with the information gained from released PoWs and captured Japanese personnel enabled the Air Ministry to identify the number of personnel about whom there was still no news. At the end of 1945, Headquarters, Air Command South East Asia, estimated that about 300 aircraft and crews had disappeared in Burma, which meant about 1,000 air crew were missing.[5] In February 1946 the Air Ministry gave a lower figure of 894 personnel missing in South East Asia. The decision was made to form a number of search teams, similar to those operating in Europe, to try to establish the fate of those still missing. In addition to these RAF Missing Research and Enquiry Service Searcher Teams the RAAF operated their own Search Teams amongst the islands of the South West Pacific where many Australians had fought. In a reciprocal agreement with the Air Ministry these RAAF search teams also conducted searches for missing RAF personnel.

---

4. Diary of Chaplain H.C. Babb held in the Private Papers of Reverend H.C. Babb. Imperial War Museum Documents Dept.
5. National Archives reference AIR40/2500 *Air Command Far East Monthly Intelligence Summaries* Summary for January 1948 Section II page 3 Missing Research South East Asia.

The Far East MRE search teams had several problems to overcome: First, a large number of the missing aircraft had simply failed to return to base, there was no information as to where they had come down. Second was the inhospitable terrain, for example much of Burma was covered by impenetrable jungle and mountainous areas only reachable by almost inaccessible mountain tracks. In the watery Burmese Arakan Peninsula, where there had been heavy fighting, the RAF searcher team had to travel by boat and then wade through the mangrove swamps surrounding the waterways to reach aircraft crash sites. Third was the weather: the torrential rain of the monsoon season which lasts from May to September turned rivers and streams into raging torrents, and the plains of Central and Southern Burma became covered in vast tracts of water making roads impassable and destroying evidence of aircraft wreckage and burial sites. An officer who served in the Far East said, *'I think that unless you have seen the Burmese jungle in the monsoon it is almost impossible to believe that anything can be quite so horrible.'*[6] Fourth was both the lack of information about crash site locations and of physical evidence at crash sites when they were reached. Not only had aircraft wreckage succumbed to the eroding effects of the climate and jungle but the indigenous peoples stripped aircraft wreckage for their own use. Fifth, the fierce fighting and heavy air and ground attacks during the recapture of Burma had severely damaged the country's infrastructure. Such roads and bridges as had existed had been destroyed or badly damaged and, again, evidence of aircraft wreckage etc obliterated. Sixth, it was difficult to obtain information from indigenous people for a variety of reasons. Seventh, there were security concerns, both in Burma and other parts of South East Asia nationalist/anti-colonial feelings were growing, and fighting was occurring in many areas. Rebellions broke out in Malaya and in the Dutch East Indies on Sumatra and Java. These latter areas were deemed too dangerous to search at all and the search of Malaya was delayed until June 1947. In addition to rebels, roaming bands of Dacoits (bandits) also made areas dangerous to enter; although the RAF search teams were armed, some local army commanders refused to let them enter dangerous areas.

Despite the recognised problems a number of MRE searcher teams were established in February 1946 and began to search Burma, Thailand and French Indo-China (Vietnam). Although hampered by the difficulties, MRE searcher teams were able to locate a good number of the missing aircraft and, where it was possible to do so, recovered the remains of crews for burial in cemeteries.

---

6. Sir Denis Spotswood.

Burials in the Far East

Captured air crew who died while prisoners of the Japanese were, in most instances, buried by their fellow prisoners. Efforts were made to record where these burials had taken place. Along the Burma railway there were graves in major cemeteries near former prison camps and also isolated graves scattered the length of the railway.[7] These graves were exhumed and the remains concentrated into British military cemeteries where they were reburied with military honours and the graves marked with headstones which can vary in type. Some are of the usual pattern but others are in the form of a small pedestal with an inscribed tablet attached. Local conditions normally determined what type was used. These graves are now maintained by the Commonwealth War Graves Commission who took over the care of British military cemeteries.

The Commonwealth War Graves Commission Cemetery at Kanchanaburi on the banks of the River Kwai in Thailand. It contains the graves of 6,982 servicemen who died building the infamous railway. Included amongst them are 136 Air Forces personnel. The graves are marked by inscribed pedestal grave markers. (Copyright CWGC)

---

7. Diary of Chaplain H.C. Babb held in the Private Papers of Reverend H.C. Babb. Imperial War Museum Documents Dept.

The graves of those killed in the battle for Singapore and of Service personnel who died in captivity in Changi and other prisoner of war camps on Singapore are in the Kranji War Cemetery. Kranji Cemetery was originally the burial ground for those who died in the Kranji PoW camp and was enlarged into a War Cemetery in 1946. It contains 169 Air Forces graves. Other war graves on Singapore Island were concentrated into this cemetery together with remains recovered from Saigon. In Hong Kong, Sai Wan War Cemetery contains a number of Air Force graves including those of two air crew whose remains were brought there from Phu Phoc Cemetery, Hanoi.

Other air crew, missing during the Japanese advance or from the battles to regain the captured territories, still had to be located. The RAF Missing Research and Enquiry Service, as they had done in Europe, worked in conjunction with Army Graves Units. Although every effort was made to recover remains from isolated graves and crash sites for burial in military cemeteries, local conditions, dense jungle and mountainous terrain at times left no option but to bury the crew where they had died. In these cases the crew were usually buried in the vicinity of their aircraft by the RAF searcher party who had located them. Prayers would be said at the graveside, the location of the burials carefully recorded by the search team, and the details provided to the Air Ministry Casualty Branch who added them to the appropriate Casualty P File. These isolated burial sites remain the official burial place of the crew and it is the wish of the Ministry of Defence that these war graves remain undisturbed. However, a number of groups of aviation enthusiasts have disturbed such burial sites when searching for aircraft wreckage. Remains found this way are required to be handed to the British authorities or to the Commonwealth War Graves Commission. The Ministry of Defence then arranges for them to be identified, traces living next of kin, and then the remains are buried with full military honours in the appropriate Commonwealth War Graves Commission Cemetery.

Any further information about crash locations and burial sites found either during the MRS search teams' operations or later was placed by the Casualty Branch on the appropriate Casualty P File. However, despite the best efforts of the MRE search officers, of the 4,858 RAF personnel listed as Killed or Missing while fighting the Japanese, or who died later in captivity, only 1,868 now lie in known graves.[8] Those who have no known grave are commemorated on Commonwealth War Graves Commission memorials in the Far East.

---

8. *The Forgotten Air Force* by Air Cdre Henry Probert.

Part 3

Correspondence With Next of Kin & Civilian Organizations Held on Casualty Branch P Files

Chapter 15

Correspondence with Next of Kin

The RAF Casualty Branch operated an 'open door' policy and welcomed visits from next of kin and friends of casualties who were seeking information in person. Each visitor was seen by one of the RAF or WAAF officers in the Casualty Branch and a record of the visit was kept. Notes, which give the name of the visitor and some detail of their enquiry, can be found on the relevant Casualty files.

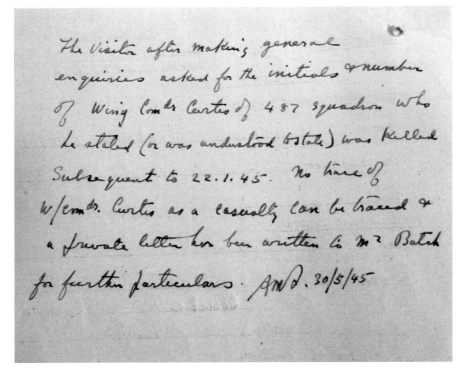

A note of an enquiry made in person to the Casualty Branch. It is written on the back of the in house Casualty Branch form used to record the details of the enquirer.

However, most communications between the Casualty Branch, next of kin and other interested parties were by telegram or letter. Correspondence to and from next of kin, other family, friends and other interested parties before 1948 can be found on the relevant Casualty File. Correspondence received by the Casualty Branch from private individuals after 1948 is removed by the Ministry of Defence for Data Protection compliance reasons before the release of the Casualty P Files into the National Archives.

Ongoing contact was maintained with next of kin by the Casualty Branch which was concerned that relatives and friends should receive accurate information. They updated next of kin when verified news about the casualty was received or any new action was taken. Copies of these letters and replies to them form the bulk of the correspondence on many of the Casualty Files. Letters from commanding officers in the UK to next of kin are not usually found on Casualty Files. In the rare instances one is found it is usually in the form of a copy of the correspondence which was sent to the Casualty Branch for their information.

The Casualty Branch did not discourage any officer or airman from writing to the next of kin of a casualty but were concerned that any information sent was based on fact not rumour and that the information they intended to send had already been passed through official channels. The Casualty P Files contain a few examples of letters sent by fellow squadron members giving information about the circumstances surrounding the loss of the casualty. Some of these were sent directly to the Casualty Branch; others were sent originally to next of kin and forwarded by them to the Air Ministry. Not all the information in these well-meaning letters was correct and problems were caused. The Casualty Branch made its position clear in an Air Ministry Order '*The Air Ministry has a responsibility to discharge to the relatives of officers and airmen who become casualties, and if information not in the possession of the Department is conveyed to them through unofficial channels, not only is the Department placed in an embarrassing position, but the next of kin may be misled as to the true facts.*'[1]

However, anxious relatives frequently contact the squadron and friends of their missing loved one directly and vice versa. Answers sent by squadron comrades in response to these enquiries could also difficulties for the Casualty Branch; as illustrated in an Air Ministry Order '*In a case recently brought to notice, the relatives of a deceased officer were informed direct by a fellow officer of important details regarding his fate which had not been brought to the official knowledge of either his unit or the Air Ministry...*'

---

1. Air Ministry Order A299/45. Communications with Next of Kin of Casualties.

and RAF units were advised to forward the enquiries they received from next of kin to the Casualty Branch and leave them to send a response.

Some of the correspondence on the Casualty Files is deeply personal and much is moving. There are many very sad letters begging for news of missing husbands, sons, brothers, fiancés and boyfriends. The filed correspondence includes copies of the initial telegrams notifying the next of kin of the casualty, updates of news received, letters from relatives concerning financial matters, and some more intimate family affairs. There are letters from girlfriends of casualties sent either directly to the Casualty Branch or forwarded by the unit. Neither fiancées nor girlfriends had any right to be notified officially of a casualty by the RAF unless they were nominated by the officer or airman as a 'person to be informed'. The Casualty Branch staff could find themselves in tricky situations: the contents of some Casualty Files make it clear that the casualty had several girlfriends and, in some cases, a wife and a girlfriend. Sometimes correspondence shows the casualty had an illegitimate child that his family knew nothing about. Such situations required tactful handing by the Casualty Branch personnel; the Casualty Branch was not judgemental and did its best to provide such information as it was permitted in these circumstances.

Some of the saddest and most moving letters on file are those from next of kin who could not accept that their son or husband was dead. Many clung to the hope that their missing loved one would be amongst the prisoners of war repatriated at the end of the war. Others were convinced that their relative was suffering from loss of memory and was wandering somewhere in Europe. These letters continued to come into the Casualty Branch for several years after the end of the war. The desperation of the relatives is all too clear in their letters, which the Casualty Branch endeavoured to answer with tact and sympathy.

In addition to writing to the Casualty Branch, next of kin often wrote to Members of Parliament and to any other notable figures they thought could help them. These people then made enquiries on behalf of the next of kin and the P Files contain the answers the Casualty Branch sent in response to these third parties. In a similar vein, next of kin wrote to the British Red Cross Prisoner of War Section who made enquiries on their behalf with the International Red Cross based in Geneva, and copies of the Red Cross responses to the next of kin are also sometimes found in Casualty P Files.

Copies of letters of condolence from overseas units are found on Casualty Files as overseas units were instructed to send copies of the Commanding Officer's letter of condolence to P(4) Cas. Letters from chaplains to next of kin were also sometimes copied to the Casualty Branch. Where a funeral had been held a description of it was to be included in the letter to the next of kin with details of who had attended and the wreaths sent. Such letters were placed on the relevant Casualty P File. However, there are very few copies of such letters sent from Far East units in the chaos which ensued during the Japanese advance in 1941/42.

The Casualty P Files contain some copies of letters or messages sent from prisoners of war to their families and forwarded to the Air Ministry. Some of these contain information about other crew members while others concern requests for the release (from the RAF Central Depository, Colnbrook) of items of uniform such as the warm uniform 'great coats' to next of kin so that they could forward the clothing on to the prisoner.

Correspondence with non-relatives on personal matters

Some Casualty P Files contain letters from next of kin sent in response to requests from the Air Ministry for assistance in identifying personal effects found with casualties. In some instances the Casualty Branch lost contact with next of kin (parents died, widows remarried or people moved away) and letters sent to them were returned 'gone away'. These returned letters, some still in their original envelopes, can be found on some Casualty P Files. With these returned letters are often filed copies of letters to local civilian police stations and other organizations which the Casualty Branch had approached in their efforts to locate the new address of the next of kin.

As well as correspondence with next of kin, there are some instances of letters from friends and fellow airmen making enquiries about casualties or providing information and the replies sent to them by the Casualty Branch. The Casualty P Files also contain correspondence from companies or organisations connected with the casualty. Some letters concerned private matters and were often sent directly to RAF units who then forwarded them to the Casualty Branch for response. Amongst these are instances of letters from people chasing unpaid bills who were unaware that the creditor was dead or a prisoner of war. In this way letters from garages about unpaid bills, or uncollected vehicles, or from tailors owed for uniforms, have found their way onto Casualty Files. There is also official correspondence between the Air Ministry (usually the Casualty Branch itself) and others, such as the Imperial War Graves Commission, regarding specific casualties and matters concerning them on the relevant Casualty Files. These letters are primarily from the post-war period.

Correspondence concerning identification and concentration of the dead

The Casualty Branch did their best to keep next of kin informed of the efforts being made to establish the fate of their lost relative. However, owing to the large numbers of air crew listed as Missing, relatives often had to wait many months to hear definite news. In addition, the Casualty Branch was anxious that the news they passed on was accurate and there were often long waits before any confirmation of the accuracy of that information was received. Anxious relatives wrote frequently for news and it was with regret that the Casualty Branch had to reply that there was no news as yet. Not all relatives were happy with the news they received.

One case in point was news about the crews of the Lancasters which were the subject of Flt Lt Dawes' Search Report reproduced in Chapter 12. The aircraft had been lost on 16 July 1944; in January 1946 a Casualty Enquiry about the lost crews was sent from the Casualty Branch to the MRES in France. The MRES reported back to the Casualty Branch in June 1946 but they asked the MRES to investigate further. The MRES officer tasked to do so (Flt Lt Dawes), having studied the existing information, concluded that there was a case for exhuming the remains, believed to be those of the crews, for identification and was given permission to do so. Out of the fifteen bodies exhumed, thirteen were individually identified. Flight Officer Leach WAAF of the Casualty Branch tactfully wrote to the relatives to inform them of the new development:

'I hesitate to re-open a painful subject by referring again to the loss of your son [or husband where she was writing to a wife] but I think you would wish to know about some further information which has now reached us.

'An officer of the Royal Air Force Missing Research and Enquiry Service, after reading all the papers concerning the two crews buried at Lignières, considered that it might be possible to obtain separate identities for at least some of the men by exhumation. The graves were accordingly opened, and the results forwarded here, and I am glad to say that we have succeeded in identifying most of the men who lie there.'

Where she was writing to the next of kin of one of those identified, Flt Off Leach went on to provide the information that their son or husband had been identified and gave details of the grave.

In her letter to the father of one of the airmen who was not individually identified she continued:

'I grieve to say that it was not possible to prove the identity of either your son or Sergeant Fellows, but as all the other members of both crews have been accounted for, there is no doubt that it is they who lie together in Row B, Grave 2. We are arranging for this grave to be marked with their names.'

Flight Officer Leach's letters to the relatives of the crews elicited a varied response. The father of one of the unidentified replied:

'Dear Flight Officer Leach
I should be ungrateful if my reply to your extremely sympathetic and informative letter of the 28ᵗʰ instant was not immediate, and although your hesitancy to reopen an incident of (to us) painful and distressing circumstances is appreciated, yet the news contained in your communication confirms that the last resting place of our dear lad is now known and will be cared for. It is a consoling factor to learn too, that although identification under the circumstances was attended with difficulty, no effort seems to have been spared to establish this and for this we feel we owe the Air Ministry a deep debt of gratitude, and if this can be conveyed, I should be glad.

Thanking you again, for the kindness and sympathy expressed so often in your communications to me.'

On the other hand her efforts and those of the Air Ministry Casualty Branch were not always appreciated. The parent of another crew member wrote:

'Madam
Your communication of the 28ᵗʰ November [1947] to hand. I need hardly say that the reopening of this subject not only re-opens a wound which time alone can heal but also, in my opinion, reflects very gravely upon the administration of the Royal Air Force. This matter, as far as the Air Ministry is concerned, has been treated in a very light hearted manner and all information supplied by them to the relatives based solely upon assumption.

Some three and a half years have elapsed since it was known that from the operation in which my Son took part two planes only failed to return, and accordingly it was reported that my Son was among the victims. However, the only definite news obtained was through the combined efforts of the Parents of these boys, assisted in no small way by the Curé and Local Representatives of Lignières. As I understand it, a decent burial was afforded all victims and suitable memorials erected by the People of Lignières, photographic evidence of the latter having been taken on the 16th July, 1947, the third anniversary, by the Curé and forwarded to the Parents and Relatives in England.

To have carried out the exhumation without the prior consent of the Parents appears to me to be particularly high handed but is, no doubt, typical of the Department concerned, and I can only place on record my complete disapproval of such action.

...I feel that the re-opening of this case has, without doubt, incurred considerable expenditure which may well have been put to better purpose in compensating in some small way those who were, maybe, solely dependent upon the men they lost.'

Stung, Flt Off Leach's senior officer replied:

'Sir
I am directed to refer to your letter dated 3rd December 1947, and to say how much the Department regrets that the efforts of the Royal Air Force Missing Research and Enquiry Service to identify the remains of your son and his companions should meet with your disapprobation.

It is the policy of the above-mentioned Service and the Graves Registration Service of the War Office [Army] to see that our fallen do not remain buried in communal or unidentified graves, if there is any possibility that the individual identities can be established, and the many letters of thanks from wives and parents received in the Department fully justify the policy which has been adopted.

In view of the fact that the exhumation of the fifteen officers and airmen buried at Lignières resulted in establishing the individual identities of all but two, it is considered that the financial considerations involved are very small in comparison with the result achieved and the satisfaction given to the next of kin in knowing that their loved ones now lie in separate graves.

It is hoped that you will, on reflection, realise that the action to which you have taken exception was undertaken with the best possible motives, namely that the deceased crew members should be adequately honoured in their last resting place, and for the peace of mind of their next of kin.'

Chapter 16

Concerning Commemoration
of the Dead

Letters about type of official commemoration

The British government, through the three Services and the Imperial War Graves Commission, was responsible for the commemoration of war dead. The Air Ministry held responsibility for informing next of kin of Air Force casualties of how their relative would be commemorated and copies of letters providing this information are on Casualty P Files. Where the casualty was buried in a graveyard in France or the Netherlands (and it had been agreed by the Air Ministry and the IWGC that the grave could remain in situ) information about the siting of the grave and graveyard (or cemetery) and a photograph of any headstone that had been erected were sent to the next of kin by the Casualty Branch. Next of kin of casualties with known graves waiting for action by Imperial War Graves Commission were sent a photograph of the grave showing the temporary wooden cross marker and informed that the IWGC would later replace these with permanent headstones. Some Casualty Files contain correspondence with the next of kin about these temporary wooden crosses whose erection was the responsibility of the Directorate of Army Graves Registration Graves Units and later, when these units ceased work in Europe, of the RAF Grave Service. This correspondence is mostly about corrections to birth dates or the spelling of names. Some Casualty P Files contain letters informing next of kin about the concentration (i.e. the moving of remains) of their relative to a British military cemetery. This correspondence gives information as to the new place of burial.

Casualty P Files also contain copies of letters sent to the next of kin of the casualties who had No Known Grave. Those classed as such might actually have a grave marked for an 'Unknown Airman' as they were unidentified. The letters informed them that their relative would be commemorated on an appropriate official Memorial to the Missing when these were erected. The Casualty Branch were unable to provide further information about these memorials as the sites and form they would take had not yet been decided. Copies of these letters were placed on the Casualty P Files. There the Air Ministry Casualty Branch's direct involvement with commemoration of the dead ended and it became a matter for the Imperial War Graves Commission.[1]

Role of the Commonwealth (formerly Imperial) War Graves Commission

Any person serving in the British and Imperial Armed Forces during the Second World War who died between 3 September 1939 and 31 December 1947, regardless of the cause of their death, their rank, race or creed, is entitled to be commemorated by name on a permanent headstone or memorial provided by the Commonwealth War Graves Commission. The extended date allows for those who died of wounds or other Service-related causes to be included. Although the Commission's headquarters are in England, the UK is only one of the partner nations of the Commission, a position which is sometimes forgotten. The Commission's member states are the United Kingdom, Australia, Canada, India, New Zealand and South Africa. All policy decisions made by the Commission are agreed by the member countries and the Commission undertakes the work of commemoration of the war dead from the two world wars on behalf of all of them.

One of the policies of the member countries is that an individual is only officially commemorated by name once, either at the grave or cemetery, or, if the individual has no known grave, on the appropriate memorial. When remains of service personnel previously classified as having No Known Grave are discovered and identified their name will be removed from the memorial and their new grave is marked with their details instead. Today, when remains belonging to members of Dominion Air Forces are discovered, the Commission consults the appropriate country as to their requirements for identification and burial of the remains and each member country can have its own variations in accordance with religious or other requirements. The UK Ministry of Defence can be asked to assist but does not have any direct responsibility for the disposal of remains other than those of British Service personnel.

---

1. The Imperial War Graves Commission was renamed the Commonwealth War Graves Commission in 1960.

The Commission has the responsibility for the upkeep of former British military cemeteries (such as that in Berlin) which were handed over to them, as well as the cemeteries the Commission has created itself. It is also responsible for all the First and Second World War graves which lie in churchyards, graveyards and civil cemeteries in the UK and overseas (other than those of individuals for whom the next of kin chose a private burial) and for the official war memorials commemorating those who have No Known Grave. The funds for this work come from the governments of the member countries of the Commission. The amount each country contributes is based on the number of their graves; the UK is the major contributor with an annual donation of some £45 million for the care and maintenance of British war graves (they include the graves of Polish and Czech nationals who died fighting in the British armed forces.) and the Commission's war memorials.

Marking of Air Force Graves

Unless a private family burial had taken place, it was the responsibility of the Director General Graves Registration and Enquiries (part of the War Office known as AG13) to erect a temporary wooden marker on the war grave if it did not already have a marker. In Europe each Air Force grave had to be visited and verified in person by a MRES search officer who vouched for the accuracy of the information contained in the Graves Registration Report sent to the Army Graves Registration. Once this had been done the temporary wooden marker, usually in the form of crosses, was placed on the grave. These wooden markers remained in place until permanent headstones were erected by the Commission.

The permanent headstones put in place by the Commission were of uniform patterns for Commonwealth casualties. The most usual type of headstone is made of Portland stone and is erected at the head of the grave. In Malta, because of the rocky nature of the island, collective crypt burials were used for the Air Force dead; these have recumbent headstones incorporating a number of names. Headstones in the Far East vary according to ground conditions. Where possible, the normal upright Commonwealth War Graves Commission pattern headstone is installed, as in Kanji War Cemetery, but where ground conditions make these unsuitable a pedestal grave marker is used. The pedestal type of marker can be seen in the picture of Kanchanaburi War Cemetery. In both cases the next of kin were invited to add a personal inscription at the bottom of the grave marker.

Flight Lieutenant Noel Archer recording details of the graves of Flying Officer James Battle RAAF and Flying Officer Alfred Briant RAAF, both of 151 Squadron, who were killed on 23 June 1944 when their Mosquito was shot down near Saumur while on a day intruder operation from RAF Predannack. They are buried in La Fleche Communal Cemetery.

Unlike the War Office which chose to use to use regimental badges on Army headstones the Air Ministry chose to use the RAF Crest rather than squadron badges. Squadron badges were not granted by the Monarch until 1936 and not all squadrons met the required criteria for a squadron badge or applied for one. Instead, the Air Ministry chose to use the RAF Crest and the Dominion Air Forces followed suit so all headstones of Air Force personnel have the crest of the appropriate Air Force (RAF, RAAF, RCAF, RIAF RNZAF and SAAF). Some headstones for collective graves show more than one crest where the crews came from different air forces. The appropriate religious symbol is also inscribed on the headstone however; the wording of inscriptions and placing of headstones vary according to the circumstances.

It was Air Force policy that the lost crews lay together in death. To ensure this was the case the Canadians issued an instruction that RCAF personnel flying with a crew from other nations were not be exhumed and concentrated to Canadian War Cemeteries but were to be buried with the members of their crews.[2] The Imperial War Graves Commission caused some

2. Order issued by Director of Directorate Graves Registration Europe dated 20 May 1946.

CWGC headstones made of Portland stone and inscribed with the Air Force crests at Hannover War Cemetery. (Copyright CWGC)

consternation when the Commission ruled that graves which were already in established war cemeteries could not be moved again. These graves remain the exception to the Air Force policy of crews lying together. The policy followed by the Commission when marking Air Force graves was adopted after discussions with the Dominion authorities and accepted by the Air Ministry which announced it in Air Ministry Order 682 of 1945. The main elements were:

- When all the bodies of a crew were recovered and identified, each grave had an individual headstone inscribed with the service number, rank (held at the time of death and not reflecting posthumous promotions), name, military decorations (DFC, DFM etc), date of death and age at death.
- In cases where all the bodies of the crew were recovered but not all were identified: for those identified, individual headstones were

erected with inscriptions. Headstones for the crew whose remains were unidentified were placed next to these in alphabetical order with the usual inscription.

- In cases where all the separate bodies of a crew were recovered but they were not identified, individually inscribed headstones were erected in alphabetical order.
- Where all the remains of all the crew were recovered but not individually identified, close grouped headstones were erected and crew members listed individually in alphabetical order with the usual inscriptions. Collective graves are also marked in this way.
- Graves of unidentified airmen to have individual headstones, inscribed with the Crest of their Air Force if this is known (and plain if not) and the wording 'An Airman of the 1939-1945 War' with the inscription 'Known Unto God' at the foot of the headstone.
- Where only some members known to belong to a specific crew were recovered but not identified, the Air Ministry policy was that the graves were to be marked as being of an Unknown Airman or Airmen. The headstone was to be inscribed with the appropriate Air Force crest and usually the date of death. In 2014 the RAF amended this policy and now such unidentified remains are to be marked as belonging to the known crew and are acknowledged as such by the inclusion of their aircraft's serial number on the grave stone. In 2015 the first grave to benefit from this official change in policy was that of some members of the crew of a Halifax lost at Besançon. Their headstone now records that the grave contains 'Members of the Crew of Halifax JD211'.
- Lastly there are memorial headstones. These usually are inscribed 'Believed to have been buried in this Cemetery', or 'Buried near this spot' (used when there was uncertainty as to which body was in which grave) or 'Believed to be in Grave' (used by the Commission in cases of reasonable but not certain identification). There are also memorial headstones for the graves of those individuals originally buried in a known cemetery but whose graves were later lost. These are often known as Kipling Memorials after the epitaph 'Their Glory Shall Not Be Blotted Out' specially composed by Rudyard Kipling which is inscribed on them. These Kipling Memorials are inscribed 'In Memory of' followed by the crest and personal inscription with an explanation at the bottom of the headstone. An example of

this memorial headstone is that of Fg Off C.C. Gibson RAAF of 605 Squadron, lost when Mosquito PZ390 crashed at Terheeg on 18 January 1945. He is commemorated in Rheinberg War Cemetery with a Kipling Memorial, at the bottom of which are the words 'known to have been buried at the time in Erkelenz Town Cemetery, but whose grave is now lost.' Also inscribed is the epitaph by Rudyard Kipling.

Where the Commission was able to contact the official next of kin they were invited to add a personal inscription at the bottom of the headstone. The length was limited to a maximum of four lines of not more than twenty-five letters. The Commission upholds the original wishes of next of kin regarding an inscription and does not permit their choice to be altered; for example at the time not all official next of kin chose to include a personal inscription but now some family members might ask for and inscription to be included. However, where the original next of kin were not traced the Commission does permit newly traced next of kin to add an inscription.

As the Air Ministry was not involved in the correspondence between the Commission and the next of kin about the personal inscription, the Casualty P Files do not normally contain information about the inscriptions. However, they are recorded on verification forms and headstone schedules held by the Commonwealth War Graves Commission.

The Commemoration of those with No Known Graves

The principal Air Force Memorial for those with no known grave is at Runnymede near Windsor. Administered by the CWGC, it was opened in October 1953 by HM Queen Elizabeth II in the presence of the relatives of the fallen. The memorial commemorates the men and women of the Commonwealth Air Forces who were lost from bases in the UK and North and Western Europe and who have no known graves. They include individuals lost in both air and ground operations, and amongst their number are remembered two members of the WAAF who were captured and killed on operations with the Special Operations Executive, Section Officer Diana Rowden and Section Officer Noor Inayat-Khan. Over 20,000 names, listed by year and air force, rank and name, are inscribed on panels lining the walls of the memorial.

*The Air Forces
Memorial at Coopers
Hill, Runnymede near
Windsor.*

*HM Queen Elizabeth II, followed by the Duke of Edinburgh, walks through the
crowds of relatives of airmen lost in the UK and North West Europe and who have
no known grave as she arrives to open the Runnymede Air Forces Memorial on
17 October 1953.*

In addition to the Runnymede Memorial there are the following CWGC memorials which record Air Force personnel with no known graves:

Malta: The Air Force Memorial at Floriana in Malta commemorates airmen who 'fell in raid or sortie' flying from bases in Malta, Gibraltar, Sicily and other islands of the Mediterranean and Adriatic, Tunisia, Algeria, West Africa, the former Yugoslavia, and Austria and who have no known grave. The memorial was unveiled by Queen Elizabeth in May 1954.

The Air Forces Memorial at Floriana, Malta.

Egypt: The memorial at El Alamein War Cemetery includes the names of over 3,000 airmen with no known graves lost in the campaigns in the Western Desert, Syria, Lebanon, Iraq, Greece, Crete and the Aegean, Ethiopia, Eritrea, Somaliland, Sudan, East Africa, Aden and Madagascar. The names include instructors and trainees of the Rhodesian and South African Air Training Schools who have no known graves. The memorial was unveiled in 1954 by Field Marshal Viscount Montgomery of Alamein.

The Egypt Memorial at El Alamein War Cemetery.

Memorials in the Far East
Air Forces personnel with no known grave who died during operations over Southern and Eastern Asia and the surrounding seas are commemorated on the Air Forces Memorial in the Far East which is part of The Singapore Memorial which is situated in the Kranji War Cemetery, Singapore. Seen from the air the Memorial has the shape of an aircraft tail. The Memorial is inscribed with the names of 24,317 Commonwealth Armed Forces personnel who have no known graves.

The Singapore Memorial in Kranji War Cemetery. Note the similarity to the tail of an aircraft. (Copyright CWGC)

Private Memorials

Post-war, both military and civil organizations (such as town councils, universities and schools) wanted to be involved in the commemoration of the dead. While the RAF and Dominion Missing Research Enquiry Service did their utmost to ensure that all Air Force burials were found, registered and marked, the Air Ministry also formed an Air Council Committee to consider the subject of RAF war memorials. All ranks were encouraged to send in their suggestions or ideas on the subject.[3] By July 1945 a number of ideas for unit and formation war memorials, some of which were already underway, had been sent to the Committee which became worried at the number of memorials proposed. An Air Ministry Order[4] was issued which said, 'The Air Council Committee do not wish to discourage war memorials of this nature. They are, however, anxious that all COs should be aware that the Imperial War Graves Commission will commemorate by name all the fallen, either in cemeteries where graves are known or, in the case of the missing where no known graves exist, by other suitable memorials.'

The main worry for the Committee was the costs of the care and maintenance of all the proposed unit and formation memorials. They were concerned about the memorials falling into disrepair as the inevitable post-war shrinkage of the RAF brought about the closure of bases and the disbandment of squadrons and other formations. Air Ministry Order

---

3. Air Ministry Order A.657/45 Air Council Committee on RAF Memorials.
4. Air Ministry Order A.764/45 RAF Unit and Formation War Memorials.

A764/45 clearly stated, 'Neither the Air Ministry nor the Imperial War Graves Commission can undertake financial or other responsibility in connection with memorials erected by units or formations on their own initiative.' The units were also instructed to refer to the Air Ministry any approaches from local bodies or civic authorities to participate in local war memorial projects or appeals for funding for RAF connected projects. It was felt that 'such local schemes may run counter to, or prejudice the success of the more general plan for commemorating those who have fallen in the course of the war.'[5]

This approach remains the same today within the Ministry of Defence. The long-standing policy of successive UK governments is that the cost of erecting memorials and associated projects, other than those of the CWGC, is not usually met from public funds but from private donations or public subscriptions. The Ministry of Defence, in line with this policy, does not make financial contributions to memorials other than those of the Commonwealth War Graves Commission. The Ministry of Defence does, however, sometimes facilitate the erection of memorials by civilian organizations, for example the Bomber Command Memorial in Green Park, which was financed by public subscription but also received advice and support from the RAF such as that provided by the Air Historical Branch. The only RAF memorial other than those of the CWGC which is supported by public funds is the RAF's unique Battle of Britain Memorial Flight.

In addition to official memorials a large number of memorials to the dead, funded by public subscription, were put up. Town and parish councils' war memorials had new names added and companies and organizations such as railway companies, police authorities, the General Post Office and water companies, raised memorials to honour former employees. State and private schools, universities and colleges also raised memorials to honour old boys. The Air Ministry supplied appropriate information to the organizers of these memorials on request but did not contribute financially towards them. Memorials raised by squadrons or other RAF units and formations were financed by donations from personnel serving with the unit or former members, not by the Air Ministry.

In the last thirty years a number of new memorials to air crew of the Second World War have been set up through public donations, such as the Battle of Britain memorials on the Embankment in London and at Capel le Ferne in Kent, the Bomber Command Memorial in Green Park and the Coastal Command Memorial in Westminster Abbey. Others have been

---

5. Ibid Paragraph 5.

erected by squadron associations, local councils, and private individuals at home and overseas. As has been explained, the Ministry of Defence does not contribute to the costs of these. Instead it honours its commemoration obligation through the annual £45 million a year given to the Commonwealth War Graves Commission to maintain the graves and official memorials in the care of the Commission.

The unveiling of a private memorial to Flight Sergeant George Thomson VC at his old school, the Kinross Higher Grades School.

On 1 January 1945 Flt Sgt Thomson was the Wireless Operator/Air Gunner on Lancaster PD377 which caught fire after being hit by Flak. Flt Sgt Thomson pulled two of his fellow crew from the flames despite being very badly burnt himself in the process. The pilot got the aircraft down and the crew got out. One of two air gunners Thomson had pulled from their turrets died in hospital the next day and Flt Sgt Thomson died of his injuries complicated by pneumonia on 23 January 1945.

Chapter 17

Concerning Disposal of Personal Effects

When a person was killed, listed as Missing, or captured, the belongings they left at their unit had to be dealt with. There was a well-established system for the handling of the property and personal possessions of military casualties. At the outbreak of the Second World War in 1939, a 'Standing Committee of Adjustment' was formed under the provisions of the Regimental Debts Act 1893 at the RAF Record Office in Gloucester. This Standing Committee later moved to the RAF's Central Depository[1] at Colnbrook near Slough. The job of the Standing Committee was to deal with the belongings left behind by officers and other ranks serving with home-based units who became casualties (and also those absent without leave or declared insane) in a process known as 'the disposal of effects'. Standing Committees of Adjustment were also formed to deal with the disposal of effects belonging to individuals serving overseas; these were usually based at the various overseas Air Command Headquarters. The Casualty Branch was not directly involved with the disposal process but some Casualty P Files contain some documents relating to it. These are usually in the form of correspondence with next of kin enquiring about personal items and/or lists of the personnel effects copied by units to the Casualty Branch.

The disposal process to be followed by units was described in Air Publication 1922 *Notes on Casualty Procedure in War.* All items belonging to the casualty that were at their base, billet (or, where death occurred in hospital, had with them there), were gathered together by a nominated officer known as the Effects Officer. This officer was required to follow detailed instructions for the handling of the items which included making an inventory of all items before the division of the items into public and private property. Public items were those which had been issued to the casualty by the RAF and were to be retained. This included any official publications and records in the possession of the individual, flying clothing

---

1. Sometimes also called the RAF Central Repository.

and items of uniform issued to airmen (officers bought their own with an allowance). The Effects Officer was to remove an example of the air crew badge the casualty was entitled to wear from their uniform and add it to the personal possessions to be sent to the next of kin.

Amongst the official documents issued to the casualty which were set aside by the Effects Officer to be retained by the RAF were Flying Log Books (RAF Forms 414 and 1767). Before the Second World War flying log books of deceased officers and airmen were forwarded to next of kin when no longer required for official purposes such as investigations into aircraft accidents. However, when the war started this practice was discontinued for the 'duration of hostilities'. The flying log books of missing or deceased aircrew were instead to be sent from home units to the RAF Central Depository at Colnbrook where they were recorded and kept in safe custody. Overseas units sent the flying log book to their command headquarters for safe-keeping. A similar practice was observed for the flying log books of personnel who were declared to be prisoners of war.

In January 1946 authority was given by the Air Ministry for the release of the Flying Log Books of air crew who had either been discharged or released from the service, who had died, or who been withdrawn from air crew duties. Next of kin of deceased air crew were invited to apply for the Flying Log Book through newspaper advertisements and by radio announcements. Following this some next of kin wrote to the Casualty Branch about the Flying Log Books of their relatives and these letters, and the responses to them, were placed on the on the relevant Casualty Files. Unclaimed Flying Log Books were kept at the RAF Central Depository until 1960 when it was again publically advertised that Flying Log Books still held by the RAF could be claimed by air crew or, where deceased, their next-of- kin. Of those still left unclaimed after this second announcement a small number were preserved as examples and are now held at the National Archives in the Air 4 Series. The remainder were destroyed in late 1960.

Disposal of Effects of Prisoners of War

Where a casualty was listed as a prisoner of war his personal effects were sent to the RAF Central Depository at Colnbrook to await his return. Access to these items required the prisoner's authorisation. However, items from those held in the Central Depository could be sent to a prisoner at his written request. Usually these items were clothing; PoWs held in Germany often requested their warm winter uniform coats, (known as great coats) to be sent to them to help combat the cold winters of eastern Germany where many PoW camps were sited. Such requests were sent to their next of kin who then contacted the Air Ministry. Some of the letters requesting items are found on the Casualty Files, sent by relatives who misdirected them there rather than correctly to the Standing Committee at Colnbrook. The requested item was sent from the Central Depository to the next of kin who forwarded the item to the prisoner.

Disposal of Effects Process – The Deceased and those Presumed Dead

Where a casualty was known to be dead or Presumption of Death action had been taken, the private effects of the casualty were inventoried by the Effects Officer who was also instructed to make a careful search for any will. If one was found it was to be sent to the Air Ministry Director of Accounts where a department called 'Accounts 13' dealt with any money belonging or owed to casualties. The contents of the will were not to be disclosed to anyone. Any other valuable documents such as savings books and certificates, insurance policy documents, War Bonds, or cheque books were also to be sent to Air Ministry Accounts. Any cash found was paid into the Station Accounts Section and, after any RAF related debts were settled, paid to the deceased's next of kin. In the case of prisoners of war the money would be held for them until their return. Personal non-public items were packed up and sent to the Standing Committee of Adjustment at The RAF's Central Depository, Colnbrook, together with an inventory. The RAF only took responsibility for belongings of the casualty which were on RAF property. If a car was away in a garage being mended the Air Ministry took no responsibility for its recovery or for any bill owing. There are several instances of letters from garages, tailors etc on the P Files who wrote to the Air Ministry requesting their assistance in getting a bill paid not realising the person owing them was dead or missing. The Casualty Branch would reply explaining what had happened and giving the address of Accounts 13 as the department of the Air Ministry to contact.

Air Ministry Accounts 13 was also responsible for identifying the person legally entitled to receive the personal effects and money of the deceased. When this had been done the Standing Committee of Adjustment would arrange for the sending of the items they held to that person. The Standing

Committee also gave authority to the station at which the deceased was serving to release any items such as cars and bicycles which they held. These were kept at the RAF station until the next of kin could arrange for their collection or disposal. Next of kin could request that their relative's belongings were put up for sale at the unit (a well-established traditional military method of disposal of effects dating back to before the Napoleonic Wars) but this sale could not take place without the authority of the Standing Committee. Money made from the sale was forwarded to the next of kin through Accounts 13.

Disposal of Effects of those based Overseas

The personal possessions of casualties based overseas were held by the Standing Committee of Adjustment for the area in which the casualty was based. They were returned to the next of kin when it became possible to do so. Sales of personal belongings on the authority of the Standing Committee were frequently held, with the money they raised sent to the next of kin through Accounts 13. Sales were often the most practical way of dealing with the disposal of items belonging to overseas casualties.

Personal Belongings recovered Post-war

Some personal belongings were recovered post-war when they were handed in by local inhabitants to RAF units in Europe, found amongst captured German material or found by the RAF Missing Research Enquiry Service. These were normally small items such as cigarette lighters and cases, pens, watches, mascots, bibles, rosaries, and personal photographs which had been taken from the bodies of casualties, either at the time they were buried or later on exhumation. These items made their way to the Casualty Branch.

As previously explained, personal items retrieved from bodies at exhumation could be valuable aids to identification, and many would have sentimental value to next of kin. The items recovered were reviewed by the Missing Research and Enquiry Service units. Many were in a poor condition through prolonged burial or were badly burnt and these were retained by the MRES units. Where the items were in reasonable condition and would help identification and/or be of value or treasured by next of kin, they were carefully bagged and labelled before being forwarded to the Casualty Branch. When ownership was not established the items were retained by the Air Ministry Casualty Branch. A number of the retained personal items have found their way onto Casualty P Files. One example is Casualty P File 352449/40[2] which concerns the crew of Blenheim L8735 lost on 27 May 1940 near Lille. A gold ring belonging to a crew member was recovered and was placed on the P File.

A common find on Casualty P Files are RAF or Dominion Air Forces identity cards which include a photograph of the serviceman. These were often taken from the dead by German authorities who also tended to remove issued identity discs. The Germans included these items in the KE Files they opened on crashed aircraft and, when these files were captured in 1945, the items were transferred on to the appropriate Casualty P File. Other personal papers such as pay books and the small passport-type photographs carried by crews to be used on faked documents during escape or evasion are also found on P Files. Again these have either been removed from captured German files or recovered from bodies before burial or on exhumation. A note of caution should be sounded here: a considerable number of such documents are stained, as can only be expected bearing in mind where they were found. Personal items which were in a fit state to be returned and whose ownership could be proved were sent to the next of kin by the Air Ministry Casualty Branch.

Some P Files contain letters to and from next of kin who had been asked to identify items which had been recovered; in some instances the next of kin of a number of the crew had to be contacted before the right owner was identified. Sometimes personal items were left with the remains such as the rosary which a French woman had insisted a German officer return her and which she placed on the casualty before burial (see Search Report and Exhumation Report 29c). On exhumation the rosary helped identity Flight Sergeant Cantwell, but it was left with his remains when he was reburied. When an item was not removed and remained with the deceased a note was made on the Exhumation Report to account for its whereabouts. The Casualty Branch was meticulous in recording and placing on file a note of what happened to the items they received. Lists of effects were marked as being sent to the RAF Central Depository, Colnbrook, or as having been destroyed, or (where personal items were in a fit state) as being sent to next of kin.

---

2. The National Archives Reference is AIR81/605 for the P File and AIR81/605/1 for the ring.

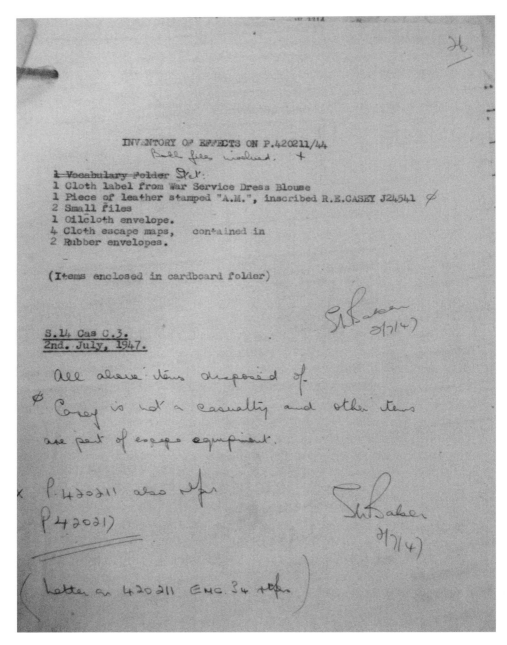

INVENTORY OF EFFECTS ON P.420211/44

~~1 Vocabulary Folder~~ Str:
1 Cloth label from War Service Dress Blouse
1 Piece of leather stamped "A.M.", inscribed R.E.CASEY J24541
2 Small files
1 Oilcloth envelope.
4 Cloth escape maps, contained in
2 Rubber envelopes.

(Items enclosed in cardboard folder)

S.14 Cas C.3.
2nd. July, 1947.

Notes on an inventory of items held on Casualty File P420411/44 saying that the listed items have been disposed of.

Chapter 18

Financial Matters

Correspondence with Next of Kin

Where casualties occurred in the UK the Casualty P File usually contains correspondence concerning funeral expenses. However many next of kin had a financial concern that arose regardless of whether the casualty had occurred at home or overseas. They were anxious about the cessation of monies they had previously received from the casualty to help with their day to day expenses and wrote to the Casualty Branch for help. The Welfare State was not introduced until after the end of the war and many single men lived at home until they married and contributed to the household finances of their parents. Conscription increased the number of married men with families serving in the RAF. There are many letters on Casualty P Files from both wives and parents concerned with financial problems stemming from the loss of the relative who had supported them financially whilst alive. Such matters were not the concern of the Casualty Branch which told next of kin to contact Accounts 13 at Gloucester or the Senior Account Officer at the Air Ministry's War Casualties Non Effective Accounts Department. However the Casualty Branch did place the letters they received about financial matters on Casualty Files and so an explanation of some of the matters raised by the correspondents in these letters is required. Below is a brief summary of the main state-paid allowances and pensions which are mentioned in the correspondence from next of kin.

Pay and Allowances

The rates of pay and allowances of members of the armed forces during the Second World War were laid down in the Royal Warrant for Pay 1940. This document listed the hundreds of differing pay scales applied to the various ranks, trades and specialisations of the Army and RAF. Ministry of Labour data gives the average civilian industrial earnings in July 1943 as being £6 1s 3d per week. Amongst the highest paid civilian workers were munitions workers, engineers and shipbuilders. Service personnel were paid considerably less but the Treasury argued that when the allowances that service personnel could claim for meals, clothing, accommodation etc together with the Family or Dependants' Allowances available to eligible servicemen, and free medical provision were added military wages were on a par with those of civilians. This is debateable and the disposable income of many families of serving personnel was low. However, the armed forces did benefit from favourable tax arrangements regarding income tax and death duties: the latter was not paid on the estate of a War Casualty.

While members of the RAF were better paid than men in the British Army, they were still paid less than their Dominion Air Forces counterparts. Air crew, both officers and airmen, also received an allowance called Flying Pay and all RAF personnel serving abroad got a Foreign Service Grant after six months overseas. Officers' pay was dependent on rank and junior officers often had to exist on very little once their Service obligations such as mess bills had been met. This was recognised as a problem and in 1942 an effort was made to alleviate the situation when the time which had to be served between Pilot Officer, the lowest paid commissioned rank, to Flying Officer, the next higher paid rank, was reduced from 12 to 6 months.[1] Officers had their pay, and any allowances they were eligible for, paid directly into their bank accounts. The officer was expected to make his own arrangements to allocate funds to maintain his wife and family or dependent parents by sending a letter to Air Ministry Accounts for forwarding to his bank manager. When an officer failed to make these arrangements and his family suffered financial hardship as a result, the Air Council had the power to order that the whole or part of the officer's pay and allowances was paid to his wife or other dependant. However, in such cases the dependant had to show that the officer had previously contributed to their upkeep or that he would have contributed had he been aware of their circumstances.

Non Commissioned flying specialisations had separate higher pay scales from the ground personnel who were split into Trade Groups; the highest paid ground trade was Trade Group 1. In addition to basic pay a special payment called War Pay (6d a day) was paid from 31 August 1940;[2] on 1 October 1942 this War Pay was doubled to one shilling.[3] Other ranks were paid in cash at the weekly Pay Parades held at their units.

---

1. Hansard Vol 383 cc 337 House of Commons Sir S Cripps in Debate on Service Pay & Allowances 10 Sept 1942.
2. Air Ministry Order A672/1940.
3. Air Ministry Order A1114/1942.

FINANCIAL MATTERS

Allotments

The system of conscription that existed during the Second World War meant that men with financial responsibilities for wives and children or impecunious parents were called up. Many volunteers also had similar responsibilities. The government recognised that provision had to be made to permit these financial obligations towards dependants met in civilian life to continue when a person volunteered to serve or was conscripted. A system of 'allotment' was established to cater for this. An allotment was a sum of money deducted from the pay of service personnel with dependent family. Allotments were voluntary for officers (unless they were commissioned from the ranks) but compulsory for other ranks. In the RAF the allotment was linked to rates of pay and increased as a man's pay increased. The amount taken in allotment was not large: an airman paid 9 shillings a day had 1 shilling and 6 pence a day taken as his compulsory allotment. The airman could choose to add a further sum to the compulsory allotment by making an additional voluntary allotment which he could vary at will. The money taken for allotment from the airman's pay was paid to the dependent wife or parent through the Post Office.

When an airman was known to have been killed, any allotment paid to his dependants ceased but the Air Ministry paid a temporary allowance for thirteen weeks which gave a widow time to apply for her pension. If an airman was posted as missing the allotment and family allowance was paid for seventeen weeks after the date they were reported missing and then ceased, but resumed if the casualty was found to be alive (e.g. as a prisoner of war) and any necessary back payments were made. When the Air Ministry officially presumed an airman to be dead, his widow (or dependent parent if eligible) could apply for a pension. The families and dependants of prisoners of war were entitled to the prisoner's pay and allowances.

An allotment had to be made before a serviceman had access to the other allowances available to assist his dependants. This encouraged officers to make voluntary allotments of pay. Such allowances were paid at a flat rate and did not involve a means test. They were not generous but were tax free.

Family Allowance

The family allowance could be claimed by married men who had made an allotment and was paid directly to their wife. Included in it, when appropriate, was a Children's Allowance, payable until the child was at school leaving age. In 1940 junior officers (Pilot Officer, Flying Officer and Flight Lieutenant) received an allowance of 6 shillings for a wife and one child, 7 shillings and 6 pence for a wife and two children, 8 shillings and 6 pence for a wife and three children and an additional one shilling for every child beyond three. This was raised by 1 shilling in 1942. Non-commissioned ranks received slightly more; until 1944 the children's allowance was staged according to the number of children: in 1940 the amounts were 8/6 for the 1st child, 6/6 for the second child and 5/- for the third. In 1942 these payments were raised by a shilling each and in 1944 the allowance was set at 12/6 for each child.

Sometimes letters on the Casualty Files indicate that the family situation of the deceased was not straightforward. The case below was one raised in Parliament but is not dissimilar from some of those appearing in letters on Casualty P Files.

A Flight Lieutenant who was a bomber pilot married secretly, he did not wish his family to know about his marriage. Just before his last mission from which he failed to return, the Flight Lieutenant tried to make arrangements for his wife to have an allotment but for nearly two years previously he had not officially allotted her any money but did maintain her. A son was born but when the Flight Lieutenant was killed the RAF had not recognised her as a wife so the Ministry of Pensions could not recognise her as a widow.[4]

Dependant's Allowance

For some single RAF personnel the Dependant's grant was as important to them as the family allowance was to married men. In the 1930s it was common practice for single men to remain at their parents' home and contribute towards the household costs. Many of those conscripted into the armed forces (both men and women) had supplied additional income for their parents. This was recognised by the government who provided a Dependant's Allowance which could be claimed by single Service personnel who had contributed to their parents' finances. However, applications for this allowance were subject to the scrutiny of the Unemployment Assistance Board who investigated the circumstances of the applicant. If a son made an allotment to his parents and their means were above a certain level they got nothing further from the State.

War Service Grants

Some of the letters on Casualty Files refer to the War Service Grant which was a means-tested grant paid by the Ministry of Pensions to provide a

---

4. Hansard Vol 383 cc 1898 House of Commons Debate on Armed Forces (Pensions and Grants) 20 October 1942 Mr Evelyn Walkden MP for Doncaster

certain minimum standard of living to the families of servicemen. A War Service Grant could only be paid when a serviceman could not meet his pre-war level of financial commitment to his dependent family as a result of his war service. The qualification was whether a man's ability to provide for his dependants (which he had to have been doing in civilian life) had been lessened by his war service. The War Service Grant was not available to dependants of service personnel who had joined the armed forces before 3 September 1939. The dependants of these men had to apply for Poor Law Relief.

In 1941 the minimum amount for a family to live on (after paying rent and other standing charges) was set at 16 shillings a week for each adult member of a household (two children were rated as being equivalent to one adult). If the family standard of living had been higher than this when the serviceman joined up, the War Service Grant assessment could take this into account and pay up to a maximum of £3 a week.[5] The basic War Service Grant was 18/- a week which was raised to 22/- in 1944. The War Service Grants Advisory Committee could make additional special grants in cases of special hardship.

Pensions

Widow's Pension
Pensions were payable to the widows of servicemen killed during the war (or whose deaths were attributable to war service). However, the widow lost the pension if she remarried. A stop-gap was provided for widows of men below the rank of Warrant Officer who could be granted a one-off gratuity equal to one year's pension if they decided to remarry.

Parent's Pension
Many parents of unmarried service personnel who were killed felt they should get something from the state in recognition of their loss. However, their ability to do so was limited. Parents, usually widowed mothers, were sometimes eligible for a pension but had to have been previously in receipt of an allotment. The criteria a parent had to meet were strict: women had to be over 60, men over 65 and be in financial need.[6] Any pension claim

5. Hansard House of Commons Debate on Service Pay and Allowances 10 September 1942 vol 383 cc456 Sir J. Grigg Secretary of State for War.
6. Article 49 of the Royal Warrant on pay of the Armed Forces gave the conditions under which a parent could receive a pension.

received from a parent was subject to a means test; thousands of parents got nothing because their means were above the prescribed level which was low. They were informed that no state help was available unless their means fell to the level where they could apply for financial assistance.

War Gratuity

At the end of the First World War a War Gratuity had been paid to all servicemen. In 1944 the government announced that a similar War Gratuity would be payable to all service personnel who had served for more than six months between 3 September 1939 and 15 August 1946. In cases where the serviceman or woman had been killed during their war service, providing they met the six month criteria, the War Gratuity would be paid to their heirs according to the provisions of the deceased's Will. All ranks were eligible for the War Gratuity, which was based on rates of pay. The basic rate War Gratuity for Other Ranks was 10 shillings for each completed month of service and 25 shillings for Pilot Officers, (higher ranks received more). When a person had served in both non-commissioned and commissioned ranks the Gratuity was calculated separately for each. The War Gratuity was applied for by service personnel and from 31 October 1946 was paid through an account opened by the government in the individual's name with the Post Office Savings Bank. The applicant was sent a Post Office Bank Book which gave them access to their account.

Post War Credits

Towards the end of the war it was announced that non-commissioned personnel would be eligible for a government grant in addition to the War Gratuity. This grant was called a Post War Credit. It was calculated on a sum of 6d for each day of service (servicewomen got 4d) and was paid post-war as a lump sum deposited in the Post Office Savings Bank together with the War Gratuity.

Far East Casualties

Allowances paid to families and dependants were another area in which the Far East casualties had to be treated as a special case. As I have said above, when a man was reported missing, allowances would normally continue to be paid for seventeen weeks and then a lower rate of pension would be paid until their fate was determined. In November 1942 the War Office, supported by the Air Ministry and the Admiralty, persuaded the Treasury that, owing to the lack of information about the status of casualties in the Far East, the 17-week period during which temporary allowances were paid to dependants should be extended to 26 weeks. Further 26-week extensions continued to be made until, in November 1945, the Air Ministry informed the dependants of the 568 airmen still listed as missing that on 1 February 1946 the allowances received under the extensions would cease and temporary allowances at pension rates would come into effect.

Monies from Previous Employers

During the First World War many large employers and local authorities had ensured that the wives and families of the men who volunteered or were conscripted into the armed forces did not suffer as a result of a drop in income caused by low rates of Service pay by making up the difference between their civilian and military pay. This precedent was followed in the Second World War by many large employers, local authorities and the government (for public service workers who joined the armed forces). These payments made to their former employees were known as 'Balance of Civil Pay' (BCP) payments. The BCP ceased on the death of the individual to whom they were paid but their dependants were often then eligible to receive a pension from the previous employer which the deceased serviceman would have received. For example, if the deceased serviceman had been a policeman before enlisting, the dependants could qualify for a police pension. Casualty P Files contain letters from previous employers requesting Air Ministry confirmation of the status of a casualty (deceased, presumed dead, missing, or prisoner of war) to whom they had made a financial payment or whose dependants wished to claim a company pension.

Chapter 19

Remains Recovered Post-1952

The burial of three Canadian crew from Hampden AE436 of 144 Squadron which was lost on 5 September 1942 on its way from Sumburgh in the Shetlands to a new base in north Russia called Afrikanda. The burial took place at Kviberg Cemetery, Gothenburg, on 24 September 1976. The remains of their aircraft had been found on the Tsatsa mountain in the Sarek National Park in August that year.

With the disbandment of the last unit of the Royal Air Force Grave and Missing Research and Enquiry Service in February 1952 the Air Ministry ended its search for the remains of RAF, Dominion and Allied Air Forces personnel. The UK Ministry of Defence (the successor of the Air Ministry), unlike the US and Australian governments, does not actively conduct searches for historic missing service personnel nor do they encourage others to do so. However, remains continue to be discovered. In cases where the recovered remains are found to be those of RAAF, RCAF, RNZAF or SAAF personnel rather than RAF, the Joint Casualty and Compassionate Centre (JCCC) informs their equivalent organization in the appropriate country which then assumes responsibility for the identification and burial of the remains. However, when any British military remains are found anywhere in the world, the Ministry of Defence, through the JCCC, is the responsible authority for the identification of the remains (although it is not always possible to establish individual identification) and is the authority which makes the final decision as to identity.

The task of identification of the remains of newly recovered RAF personnel from the Second World War is undertaken by the JCCC in conjunction with the RAF's Air Historical Branch which investigates identity cases on behalf of the JCCC and advises them of their findings. The information held in the Casualty P Files, together with other contemporaneous documentation, provides part of the material used in the Air Historical Branch's rigorous investigation. The final decision on identity rests with the JCCC who is the Ministry of Defence Authority for such matters. When they decide to accept identification, JCCC will endeavour to trace next of kin and family members and also liaise with the Commonwealth War Graves Commission regarding the burial. Where it is warranted, the JCCC will use DNA testing to confirm an identity. This method will only be used with recovered remains. Existing graves will not be exhumed in order to DNA test remains. This is in accordance with the policy of the Commonwealth War Graves Commission on DNA testing with which the Ministry of Defence concurs.

The remains of those who died in the First and Second World Wars are not repatriated in accordance with decisions made by the UK and Dominion governments at the time. The repatriation of remains of British service men and women did not begin until the 1960s (1963 for North West Europe and 1967 for the rest of the world). The burial of recovered remains is done at public expense. The Ministry of Defence JCCC arranges a military funeral but, where the remains are individually identified, consults the nominated next of kin or immediate family as to the level of military participation and also pays for 2 relatives (who meet the required level of relationship) to attend the funeral/burial. The remains are then buried, by arrangement with the Commonwealth War Graves

Commission in their nearest appropriate Cemetery or a suitable military/ civil cemetery in the country where the remains were discovered. Very occasionally, due political or other similar circumstances, burial takes place in a neighbouring country.

Identity investigations of 'Unknowns'

Cases raising questions as to the identity of deceased service personnel from the First and Second World Wars are sent to the JCCC by the Commonwealth War Graves Commission and by members of the public. The JCCC is responsible for decisions regarding the identification of British service personnel formerly buried as 'Unknowns'. This task was previously undertaken by the Commonwealth War Graves Commission who conducted in-house investigations of cases sent to them. However, in the 1990s the Ministry of Defence took back this responsibility and now makes (through their nominated authority, JCCC) final decisions regarding identity in such cases, and the Commonwealth War Graves Commission acts on the decision taken. Identity cases relating to members of the armed forces of Commonwealth countries are referred to their appropriate national authority.

When a grave is marked as that of an 'Unknown Airman/Airmen' but the possibility exists that identity can be now be established, the RAF's Air Historical Branch conducts an investigation on behalf of JCCC and provides recommendations to the JCCC who are the authority which makes the final decision. If it is decided that the identity of the remains formerly marked as an 'Unknown' has been satisfactorily established the JCCC arranges for the Commonwealth War Graves Commission to provide a new headstone to record the newly established identity and a rededication service is held at which members of the deceased airman's family are invited to be present. Again the Ministry of Defence, through the JCCC, arranges for the attendance of two relatives at public expense.

Since 2014, following a change of RAF policy, where the investigation of an 'Unknown Airman' identity case cannot confirm the identity of a crew member or members (and not all the crew were recovered) but does establish the identity of the aircraft from which the remains came, JCCC arranges for a new headstone or inscription to be provided by the Commonwealth War Graves Commission. This records that the grave is that of a member or members of the crew of the identified aircraft. An example of a new inscription is that on the grave of two members of the crew of Halifax JD211. The inscription was added in June 2015 following the Air Historical Branch investigation of an identification case raised by a relative of a crew member. The headstone now records 'Two Airmen of the 1939-1945 War 16ᵗʰ July 1943 Members of the Crew of Halifax JD211 Royal Air Force'.

Military Aircraft Excavations

The wreckage of aircraft which crashed in military service in the UK, and its territorial or international waters, are subject to the Protection of Military Remains Act. Under this Act a licence must be granted before aviation archaeologists or other interested parties can excavate the site of the crash. The consent of the landowner must also be obtained. Licence applications are sent to the JCCC and if approved a licence is issued by the JCCC valid for one year. Where it is suspected that human remains may be present the licence application will not be granted. Inevitably there are cases where, although the crew are recorded as being recovered not all the remains were in fact found. When these are found at an aircraft excavation the licence requires that the JCCC and the local police are notified straightaway. The JCCC arranges for the appropriate burial of the recovered remains and the tracing and notification of next of kin.

The aircraft wreckage and service equipment remains the property of the Crown and the Ministry of Defence decides on their disposal. Any personal property discovered at the crash site by the licensee remains the property of the original owner and under the terms of the licence must be sent to the JCCC for return to the crew member or his family.

Overseas aircraft crash sites

The crash sites of RAF aircraft overseas are not covered by the British Protection of Military Remains Act. They are subject to the local regulations and permissions of the country in which the aircraft came down. In Europe and the Far East there are groups of aviation enthusiasts and others who search for crashed aircraft. Not all are scrupulous about what they are doing and recover wreckage and items to sell. Other groups have the good intention of recovering remains from crash sites to return to families. Notification of the discovery of British or Dominion remains should be made to the Commonwealth War Graves Commission and the appropriate embassy.

The JCCC does not advocate or support searches for British missing however; in the Netherlands the JCCC works closely with the Dutch Army Recovery and Identification Unit regarding wrecks found in the Netherlands.

Appendix A

Casualties to RAF Dominion and Allied Personnel at RAF Posting Disposal

CASUALTIES TO R.A.F. DOMINION AND ALLIED PERSONNEL AT R.A.F. POSTING DISPOSAL
3rd SEPTEMBER 1939 — 14th AUGUST 1945   AMENDED AS AT 31·5·47.

	FLYING BATTLE				FLYING ACCIDENT				GROUND BATTLE				GROUND			ALL CAUSES				
	KILLED	MISSING	P.O.W.	WOUNDED OR INJURED	KILLED	MISSING	POW	WOUNDED OR INJURED	KILLED	MISSING	P.O.W.	WOUNDED OR INJURED	KILLED	DIED OF NATURAL CAUSES	WOUNDED OR INJURED	KILLED	MISSING	P.O.W.	DIED OF NATURAL CAUSES	WOUNDED OR INJURED
OFFICERS																				
R.A.F. / W.A.A.F.	13266	(1150) 12	(2204) 1	2084	4343	(22) 8	(31)	2773	344	(70) 1	(390)	220	369	432	352	18322	(1242) 17	(2625)	432	5429
R.C.A.F.	5962	(630) 10	(1242) 1	533	1240	(8) 12	(9)	549	15	(6)	(8)	30	44	13	56	7261	(644) 22	(1259)	13	1168
R.N.Z.A.F.	846	(90)(184)	(144)	123	275	(1)	(2)	116	8		(19)	6	5	1	6	1134	(91)(190)	(165)	1	251
R.A.A.F.	2066	4	(346)	259	428	(2)	(1)	230	22	(4) 1	(6)	19	11	7	20	2527	5	(353)	7	5
S.A.A.F.	912	(157)	(191)	286	322	(8)	(4)	177	2		(1)	4	8	3	11	1244	(165)	(196)	3	478
OTHER DOM.	32	(6)	(4)	3	47			18	1		(1)					80	(6)	(5)		21
POLISH	460	(58)(77)	(110)	135	244		(3)	156		(1)		8	10	9	10	718	(58)(78)	(113)	9	309
ALLIES	582	1	(99)	145	287		(1)	195	8		(2)	5	12	2	10	889	2	(102)	2	355
TOTAL	24126	(2352) 27	(4340)	3568	7194	(42) 17	(51)	4216	405	(80) 2	(427)	295	465	476	476	32190	(2474) 46	(4818)	2	8555
AIRCREW AIRMEN																				
R.A.F. / W.A.A.F.	34793	(2417) 18	(5664) 3	4579	11526	(113) 12	(54)	7056	4937	(520) 23	(4152) 6	2993	3216	3738	2867	54472	(3050) 42	(9870)	9373	17495
R.C.A.F.	5099	(402) 11	(987) 1	742	1802	(6) 4	(7)	939	54	(14) 2	(8)	104	88	55	117	7043	(422) 17	(1002)	55	1902
R.N.Z.A.F.	1280	(63)(257)	(265)	197	393	(1)	(4)	248	10	(10)(7)	(12)	12	13	10	7	1696	(269)	(286)	10	464
R.A.A.F.	3261	(36) 7	(501)	489	1057	(5)	(3)	568	36	(7) 1	(48)	35	26	25	40	4380	(552) 8	(269)(57)	25	1132
S.A.A.F.	270	(23)	1	75	109	(4)		51	4	(14)	(21)	32	47	27	33	430	(41) 1		27	191
OTHER DOM.	31	(9)	(2)	6	14	(1)		6	3	(1)			7	22	2	55	(10)(60)	(3)	22	14
POLISH	711	(59) 2	(170)	129	365		(7)	237	1		2	31	40	25	53	1133	(59)(60) 2	(179)	25	450
ALLIES	616	(57) 1	(98)	153	343	(2)		189	16		(2)	17	41	41	45	1016	(59) 1	(100)	41	404
TOTAL	46062	(3287) 39	(7723)	4637	15621	(131) 5	(76)	9303	5127	(567) 23	(4250)	3400	3592	4207	3382	70402	(3985) 71	(12049)	10	22456
ALL RANKS																				
R.A.F. / W.A.A.F.	48059	(3567) 30	(7868) 4	6663	15869	(135) 5	(85)	9829	5281	(590) 24	(4542) 6	3213	3585	4170	3219	72794	(4292) 59	(12495)	192	22924
R.C.A.F.	11061	(1032) 21	(2229) 1	1275	3042	(14) 16	(16)	1488	69	(20) 2	(16)	134	132	68	173	14304	(1066) 39	(2261)	68	3070
R.N.Z.A.F.	2126	(153)(441)	(409)	320	668	(2)	(6)	364	18	(10)(3)	(18)	13	18	11	13	2830	(165)	(451)	11	715
R.A.A.F.	5327	11	(847)(227)	748	1485	(7)	(4)	798	58	(1) 2	(54)	54	37	32	60	6907	(459) 13	(905)(253)	32	1660
S.A.A.F.	1182	(180)	1	361	431	(12)	(4)	228	6	(14)	(22)	36	55	30	44	1674	(206)		30	669
OTHER DOM.	63	(15)	(6)	9	61		(1)	24	4	(1)	(1)		7	23	2	135	(16)	(8)	23	35
POLISH	1171	(134)	(280)	264	609	(3)	(10)	393	21	(1)	(2)	39	50	34	63	1851	(137)	(292)	34	759
ALLIES	1198	2	(197)	298	630	(1)	(1)	384	24		(4)	22	53	43	55	1905	3	(202)	43	759
TOTAL	70188	(5639) 66	(12063)	9939	22815	(173) 22	(127)	13519	5532	(647) 29	(4677)	3699	4057	4683	3858	102592	(6459) 117	(16867)	12	31011

NOTE. THE FIGURES IN BRACKETS REPRESENT PERSONNEL WHO WERE CASUALTIES UNDER THE HEADING SHOWN BUT HAVE NOW BEEN REPORTED SAFE.

DATA FROM A.D.M. STATS.

Appendix B

The Joint Casualty and Compassionate Centre

The Joint Casualty and Compassionate Centre (JCCC) based at Innsworth in Gloucester is part of the Ministry of Defence, Defence Business Services. In addition to handling current casualty and compassionate cases amongst the British armed forces there is also a small section handling historic cases from campaigns going back to the First World War and, very occasionally, beyond that. It is the Authority which makes the decision regarding the identification of historic remains.

Historic Remains

When remains believed to be those of RAF, Commonwealth or Allied Air Forces personnel are discovered, the JCCC is notified and the Commemorations Section coordinates the effort made to identify the remains in conjunction with the MOD Air Historical Branch (AHB), the Commonwealth War Graves Commission (CWGC), and, where appropriate, the authorities of the country where the remains were discovered. If the remains are identified as being those of a member of a Commonwealth Air Force such as the Royal Canadian Air Force or the Royal Australian Air Force then that country takes over responsibilities for the remains. Where the remains are identified as being those of a member of the Royal Air Force (including citizens of Commonwealth countries who joined the RAF) JCCC is the authority which confirms the identification and is responsible for tracing the next of kin or descendants, arranging the military funeral and burial (in close liaison with the CWGC) and funding two entitled relatives to attend. Other relatives are obviously welcome but pay their own way. The JCCC also funds a small reception after the funeral and burial.

The JCCC works in conjunction with the Air Historical Branch (AHB) (who may also consult the CWGC records) to establish the identity of historic Air Force remains. When the remains are identified as RAF the final decision as to their identification lies with JCCC with input from AHB. When the remains are found to be those of a Commonwealth Air Force individual, the acceptance of identity decision is made by the appropriate Commonwealth Ministry.

Identification of Unknowns

Sadly, despite efforts to identify them, many Air Force casualties were buried as 'Unknown'. Today there are numbers of researchers, both at home and overseas, who submit cases regarding the possible identity of individuals buried as 'Unknown'. JCCC is the **deciding Authority** in all cases of RAF personnel previously buried as Unknown. Any case is presented through the CWGC who forward the submission to the AHB for analysis. After a thorough investigation, the AHB will make their recommendations to JCCC. It is for the JCCC to decide whether the recommendations are accepted or not.

When a case for an identity is accepted by the JCCC the Commemorations Section takes on the responsibility for tracing next of kin or descendants, arranging a rededication ceremony for the new headstone (which the CWGC provides), funding the attendance of two entitled relatives at the rededication service and a small reception.

Immediately post-war the RAF burial policy required unidentified members of aircraft crews in cases where the aircraft was identified but all the crew were not recovered to be buried as 'Unknown'. In 2014 it was decided by the RAF that, where an investigation could not confirm an individual identity for a crew member (or crew members) but did establish the identity of the aircraft the crew were flying, the headstone would record the aircraft type and serial number. Instead of 'An Unknown Airman' the inscription would read 'A Member (or Members) of the Crew of [Type/Serial Number]' eg Wellington ZR652. In these cases JCCC arranges for a new headstone or inscription to be provided by the Commonwealth War Graves Commission.

Appendix C

The Commonwealth War Graves Commission

As the note on the work of the Joint Casualty and Compassionate Centre (JCCC) of the Ministry of Defence explains, JCCC is the authority which makes all the decisions regarding the identity of British casualties; this is not in the remit of the Commonwealth War Graves Commission. However, the Ministry of Defence look to the Commonwealth War Graves Commission to commemorate casualties either through the provision of a grave and headstone or an appropriate memorial and to care for that grave or memorial in perpetuity.

The CWGC was founded as the Imperial War Graves Commission in 1917 by Royal Charter. The six member countries are Australia, Canada, India, New Zealand, South Africa and the United Kingdom, each of whom contributes financially towards its work. The amount each contributes is in ratio to the number of dead from that country. The UK is the largest contributor, giving some £45 million annually. Policies adopted by the CWGC or changes made to them must be agreed by all the member countries. At its foundation the Commission was tasked with caring for the graves of all members of the Imperial forces who died of wounds, illness or by accident while on active service. It was to provide for burials and maintain records of grave sites, erect and care for memorials, and build and maintain cemeteries. Today it cares for 23,000 grave and memorial sites from the two world wars in over 150 countries and territories.

All service personnel of the Imperial forces who died between 4 August 1914 and 31 August 1921 for the First World War and 3 September 1939 to 31 December 1947 for the Second World War are entitled to be commemorated by the CWGC. The extended dates allow for persons dying of wounds or other causes attributable to their service to be included. The vast number of dead from the First World War could not be catered for by existing cemeteries and so the War Graves Commission built their own cemeteries in keeping with their locations around the world. More cemeteries were added after the Second World War, such as those in Germany built to accommodate the graves of air crew lost over Germany and members of the armed forces killed in the battle for Germany.

CWGC Grave Markers

There are different types of headstones at CWGC sites depending on what is most suitable for the location. Once the form of grave marker is chosen all CWGC graves at that site will normally have the same marker. The wording of the commemoration is standardised but the IWGC contacted next of kin in case they wished to add a personal inscription at the foot of the headstone. The message was limited to 66 letters and the IWGC retained the right to reject the submitted inscription or ask for it to be amended. Special memorials were used where the exact site of burial was not known and bear one of the following inscriptions:

'Buried elsewhere in this cemetery'
'Believed to be buried in this cemetery'
'Known to be buried in this cemetery'
'Buried near this spot'
'Buried in ……..cemetery (or churchyard)'

Private Graves

Where the next of kin chose to have a private funeral/burial and headstone the CWGC is **not** responsible for the maintenance of such graves or headstones but may choose to provide a new headstone where one is damaged.

The CWGC address is:

The Commonwealth War Graves Commission
2 Marlow Road
Maidenhead
Berkshire
SL6 7DX

Appendix D

DNA Testing of Remains

It is a basic principle of the CWGC that the remains of war casualties should not be exhumed or disturbed unless the grave cannot be maintained, or is at risk of disturbance, or for any reasons of overriding public necessity. Although burials were exhumed immediately after the two world wars as efforts were made to establish the identities of the dead and they were concentrated into war cemeteries, once the cemeteries were established, exhumations ceased and it was agreed that further exhumations for identification purposes would not be permitted. The DNA testing of buried remains or other means of establishing an identity which requires a grave to be disturbed is therefore not permitted.

DNA tests are possible in some circumstances. When confirmed Commonwealth remains are found at crash sites etc, and the nationality established, it is a matter for the appropriate member government/s to try to establish the identity of the dead. Objects found with the remains, such as badges of rank, flying brevets, clothing, equipment or personal effects, can help with identification. Study of casualty files and other documentation are also an essential element. When there is evidence which indicates a specific individual for a British casualty, the Ministry of Defence JCCC may opt to use DNA testing, using a sample from an appropriate relative, to confirm the identity. The cost of the DNA testing of British casualties is met by JCCC and by the appropriate government of the other member states for other Commonwealth casualties.

The member states of the CWGC agreed that war casualties from the First and Second World Wars would not be repatriated but lie in an appropriate cemetery in the country in which they died or where their remains were found. In keeping with this agreement, remains are removed from crash sites or battlefield graves but do not leave the country in which they are found unless there is no maintainable burial site. This has implications on the removal of remains for DNA testing. Where the appropriate laboratory for the DNA testing lies outside the country in which the remains were found, small samples of the remains may be sent to the laboratory for testing, but the removal of all the remains to the laboratory is not permitted. Any remains forming the small samples must be returned on completion of the DNA testing to be buried with the rest of the remains.

Appendix E

Next of Kin (Precedence)

The Air Ministry and later the Ministry of Defence, to determine the closest next of kin, use the order of priority for next of kin established for cases of intestacy under the Administration of Estates Act 1923. When making decisions about the deceased it is the closest next of kin whose wishes are followed. The order of priority is as follows:

1. Spouse
2. Issue (children, grandchildren, great grandchildren etc)
3. Parents
4. Brothers and sisters of the whole blood
5. Issue of brothers and sisters of the whole blood
6. Brothers and sisters of the half blood
7. Issue of brothers and sisters of the half blood
8. Grandparents
9. Uncles and aunts of the whole blood
10. Issue of uncles and aunts of the whole blood
11. Issue of uncles and aunts of the half blood
12. Issue of uncles and aunts of the half blood

Fiancées were **not** regarded as next of kin and were usually included by the serviceman as an additional person to be informed.

The Air Ministry and latterly the Ministry of Defence only in very exceptional circumstances reversed decisions made by the closest official next of kin. One case where they have is that of Sergeant Ernest Scott of 222 Squadron who went missing on the afternoon of 27 September 1940. In 1975 a group of aviation archaeologists requested permission to excavate the site of his aircraft crash. Permission to do so was refused by the MOD as his parent had said they wished his remains to stay with his aircraft. In 1990, by which time Sergeant Scott's parents had died, his sister requested his remains be excavated for burial. She wrote to the Prince of Wales asking for his support. The MOD agreed that an excavation could take place and the RAF's Aircraft Recovery and Transportation Unit undertook the work. The remains of Sergeant Scott were found still in the cockpit of his Spitfire and were buried with full military honours in February 1991 at Margate Cemetery, Kent.

Appendix F

Missing Research and Enquiry Service Areas of Operation

HQ RAF Missing and Enquiry Service Northwest Europe Missing Research and Enquiry Units HQ and Search Sections locations.

INITIAL SEARCH SECTIONS 1944-1945 – Areas of Operation

No 1 Section	December 1944	France (based Paris)
No 2 Section	May 1945	Belgium (based Brussels)
No 3 (Mobile) Section	June 1945	Conducted area sweeps in France
No 4 (Mobile) Section	June 1945	Conducted area sweeps in France
No 5 Section	July 1945	Holland (based The Hague)
No 6 Section	July 1945	Norway (based Oslo)
No 7 Section	August 1945	Denmark (based Esbjerg)
No 8 Section	August 1945	Germany (based Bunde)

In July 1945 there was a reorganisation and enlargement of the Missing Service and search units were restructured, renamed and placed under 28 Group Technical Training Command. HQ Missing Research Enquiry Service North West Europe (HQ MRES(NWE)) was formed within HQ British Air Force of Occupation (HQ BAFO). The Search Sections became Missing Research and Enquiry Units with larger areas of operations. These are given in MRES Missing Research Memorandum No 19 and 19A.

1 MREU   August 1945 to 31 July 1947   France and Luxembourg. HQs Le Mans then Chantilly.

On disbandment at the end of July 1947 a detachment remained in Paris and liaised with the Imperial War Graves Commission.

2 MREU	August 1945 to 14 October 1947	Belgium, Holland, French Zone of Germany, Czechoslovakia. HQ Brussels then Schloss Schaumberg, Diez, Germany.
3 MREU	August 1945 to 29 February 1948	Norway, Denmark, American Zone, Germany. HQ Esbjerg then Karlsruhe, Germany (co-located with HQ US Army Grave Service)
4 MREU	August 1945 to 30 September 1949	British & Russian Zones, Germany, Poland. HQ Hamburg, then Wesendorf & Sudern. HQ for Russian Zone searches was in Berlin.

Mediterranean and North Africa

The RAF (Mediterranean/Middle East) Missing Research and Enquiry Unit was established in August 1945 and was originally under the direct control of P4(Cas). Casualty enquiries sent to them from the Missing Section of P4 Cas had a prefix of M (e.g. Casualty Enquiry M64. Those sent by the Missing Research Section had an additional S (eg M90 S).

| Mediterranean | 27 July 1945 to 10 August 1948 | Italy, Sicily, Balkans, Hungary, Greece, Crete & Aegean islands, North Africa. |

Appendix G

Locations of Aircraft Engine Numbers

The Aeronautical Inspection Directorate Headquarters, Leatherhead, supplied the Air Ministry Casualty Branch with information about the locations of numbers on Rolls Royce engines to help with the identification of crash aircraft. This contemporary information gave the location of numbers on Rolls Royce engines as follows:

Cylinder Blocks
Engine number and rest piece number stamped at propeller end. Engine number stamped on No 7 camshaft bracket, also on cylinder block adjacent to inclined camshaft drive bevel gear.

Reduction Gears
Engine number stamped on reduction gear casing. The reduction gears are always in pairs and given a serial number from which it is possible to trace engine numbers.

Crankcase
The crankcase is stamped front foot port side.
The lower half crankcase is stamped at front end. Oil pump inlet (lower half of crankcase) engine numbers are stamped with very small sized letters.

Wheelcase
Engine numbers stamped near to coolant pump drive.

Supercharger Casings
Engine numbers stamped at centre of rear casing on boss provided.

Dual Drive Unit
A serial number is stamped from which the engine number can be traced.

Crankshaft

Engine number is etched on No 6 crank web and stamped or etched on the spring drive shaft adaptor.

Supercharger Gear Train

All gear trains are given a serial number, e.g. main drive gear, supercharger layshaft gears and clutch gears would be marked 96 A 96 B96.

Appendix H

RCAF, RAAF, and RNZAF Casualty Sections Wartime Locations in London

Canadian Casualties

Canadian Casualty Branch
Air Ministry (P4 Cas (Can))
77 Oxford Street
London W1

Australian Casualties

Royal Australian Air Force
Overseas Headquarters
Casualty Section
Kodak House
63 Kingsway
London WC2

New Zealand Casualties

Royal New Zealand Air Force Casualty Officer
Royal New Zealand Air Force
Overseas Headquarters
Kern House
Kingsway
London WC2

Appendix I

The Status of RAF Education Officers before 1 October 1946

The RAF was alone amongst the 3 Services in not having a militarised Education Branch. It was formed soon after the 1918 as a civilian service probably because it was cheaper and successive Governments followed this policy. Thus it was that in September 1939 the RAF, in so many ways the most progressive of the Services, only the civilian education service and remained civilian until 1st October 1946.

RAF Education Officers joined under civilian conditions of service, and therefore, they did not receive Service pay or allowances. They were paid the Burnham scale, the national pay scales for teachers and lecturers, with a slight addition and did not receive the tax reliefs paid to military officers. If they received any injuries in the course of their duties they were awarded civilian compensation and not the higher rate of compensation applied to the Services. When Education Officers left the RAF at the end of the war they did not receive the War Gratuity that was normally paid to officers for war service because military benefits could only be paid for periods of war service in the Forces on full Service pay. However, they wore RAF Officer's uniform; they carried the normal Service identity cards, were subject to Air Force law and were frequently called upon by commanding officers to perform the duties of a fully mobilised officer. This was despite an Air Ministry letter of 28 May 1942 sent to all commanders-in-chief, expressly pointing out that RAF Education Service Officers were civilians and restricting how they might be used on units. The letter included the warning that if education officers sustain death or injury while taking part in defence duties they were eligible for compensation only under the Civilian Injury Warrants.

One sad instance where this was the case occurred in 1945 when a flying bomb fell on an RAF school in St. John's Wood, and blinded a young education officer. If he had been in the Army or in the Royal Navy, he would have been treated as a blinded officer and received a Service pension.

However, because he was in the RAF he only received a civilian pension which was less than half the amount he would have received if he been in either of the two other Services.[1]

On 1 October 1946 the Education Branch was fully integrated into the RAF and the officers who served in it became full serving officers and no long civilians in uniform.

---

1. This example is from a parliamentary debate of 28 Nov 1946 about the treatment of RAF Education Officers recorded in Hansard.

Appendix J

Further Sources of Information

The National Archives

The National Archives was formed in 2006 through the amalgamation of the Public Records Office, the Royal Commission on Historical Manuscripts, Her Majesty's Stationary Office and the Office of Public Sector Information, under the generic title of The National Archives.

The Public Records Act of 1958 set up a system whereby documents created by governmental departments, and some other public bodies, which were selected by the department or public body for permanent preservation, were to be transferred to the Public Records Office and made available to the public after fifty years. Documents not selected were to be destroyed. The responsibility for public records and the Public Record Office was given to the Lord Chancellor and the management of them to the Keeper of Public Records. In 1967 a further Public Records Act reduced the timescale for public release from 50 to 30 years but sensitive information would remain closed. Records from the First World War now became available to the public. The timescale for public release was reviewed again following the 2000 Freedom of Information Act and since 2013 has been was reduced to twenty years. The main repository for public documents is the National Archives at Kew, but there are some other Places of Deposit appointed by the National Archives: for example the Royal Air Force Museum at Hendon is approved by the National Archives as a Place of Deposit.

In addition to RAF Operational and Flying Accident Casualty Files the National Archives holds a large number of RAF records and publications in the AIR series. Amongst them are copies of Night Raid Reports which contain details of Bomber Command night-time attacks. There are also other RAF-related documents in the WO (War Office) series which also hold war crimes records.

The Royal Air Force Museum

In addition to the aircraft and other artefacts on display, the RAF Museum has an archive and library containing a wide range or material relating to the RAF. The collections include copies of RAF Aircraft Accident Cards and Bomber Command Loss cards. They also hold copies of RAF publications such as Air Ministry Orders. Their address is:

The Royal Air Force Museum
Grahame Park Way
Hendon NW9 5LL

Ministry of Defence

Air Historical Branch (RAF)

Information from RAF Casualty Files other than those in the National Archives can be requested from the Air Historical Branch (RAF) under the Ministry of Defence Publication Scheme. Information on how to do this can be found at *Requesting information held on the RAF Casualty Files* at www.gov.uk. The Air Historical Branch is a closed archive and does not accept visits from members of the general public but can be contacted in writing at:

Air Historical Branch
RAF Northolt
West End Road
Ruislip
Middlesex HA4 6NG

RAF Disclosures Section

The RAF Disclosures Section hold the Records of Service for RAF personnel. Information from these records can be requested under the MOD Publication Scheme. Guidance on how to do this and the relevant application forms can be found at *Request records of deceased service personnel* at www.gov.uk. They can also be contacted in writing at:

RAF Disclosures Section
Trenchard Hall

RAF Cranwell
Sleaford
Lincolnshire NG34 8HB

Prisoners of War

The National Archives
AIR20/2336 contains a list of all air crew known to have been held in Germany.

The Red Cross
The International Red Cross holds some information on Second World War prisoners of war. Immediate relatives of the prisoner can apply through the British Red Cross. All other applications for information must be made to the International Committee of the Red Cross. When making an application for information, as much information about the prisoner should be supplied. At a minimum, name, rank and service number should be given. Contact details are:

British Red Cross
UK Office
44 Moorfields
London EC2Y 9AL
Tel: 0344 871 1111

International Committee of the Red Cross
19 Avenue de la Paix
1202 Geneva
Switzerland

www.icrc.org

Disposal of Personal Effects

Information about the disposal of personnel effects can be found in the following documents available at the National Archives:

Air Ministry Order A1087/41 (covering RCAF personnel)
Air Ministry Order A555/42 (covering RAAF personnel)

Air Ministry Order A842/42 (covering RNZAF personnel)
Air Ministry Order A420/41 (covering Allied Air Forces personnel)
Air Ministry Order A531/39
Air Ministry Order A318/43
Air Ministry Order A1129/42

Air Publication 1922
Kings Regulations Paragraph 2608 – Missing & PoWs

UK General Register Office

The General Register Office holds an Index of War Deaths, Royal Air Force all ranks 1939-48. The Index can be viewed online at a number of genealogical web sites. Certified copies of the Service registration entries it contains can be obtained from:

General Register Office
Overseas Section
PO Box 2
Southport
PR8 2JD

www.gro.gov.uk

Further Reading

Below are a very few suggestions for further reading taken from amongst the many books written about the RAF in the Second World War.

General

Right of the Line by John Terraine (A history of the RAF in the European Theatre during the Second World War)
The Forgotten Air Force: The Royal Air Force in the War Against Japan 1941-1945 by Henry Probert (Brasseys)
RAF Squadrons by Wing Commander C.G. Jefford (Airlife)
The Bomber Command War Diaries: An Operational Reference Book 1939-1945 by Martin Middlebrook & Chris Everitt (Viking)
National Archives On Line Guides to RAF related records, nationalarchives.gov.uk

RAF Regiment

The RAF Regiment at War 1942-1946 by Kingsley M. Oliver (Pen & Sword)
Constant Vigilance, The RAF Regiment in the Burma Campaign by Nigel W.M. Warwick (Pen & Sword)
In Every Place, The RAF Armoured Cars in the Middle East 1921-1953 by Nigel Warwick (Pen & Sword)

Casualties

Missing Believed Killed: The Royal Air Force and the Search for the Missing 1939-1952 by Stuart Hadaway (Pen & Sword)
Royal Air Force Bomber Command Losses of the Second World War by W.R. Chorley:

RAF WWII OPERATIONAL

Volumes 1-6 covering the years 1939 to 1945

Volume 7 covering losses from Operational Training Units 1940-47

Volume 8 covering Heavy Conversion Units and Miscellaneous Units 1939-47

Volume 9 Roll of Honour 1939-47

Royal Air Force Bomber Command Losses in the Middle East and Mediterranean 1939-1942 by D. Gunby and P. Temple